Comparative Health Systems

The standard classifications of health systems do not allow for the complexity and variety that exists around the world. Federico Toth sets out a new framework for understanding the many ways in which health systems can be organized and systematically analyzes the health systems chosen by twenty-seven member countries of the Organisation for Economic Co-operation and Development (OECD). He provides a great deal of up-to-date data on financing models, healthcare spending, insurance coverage, methods of organizing providers, healthcare personnel, remuneration methods for doctors and hospitals, development trajectories and recent reforms. For each of the major components of the healthcare system, the organizational models and the possible variants from which individual countries can ideally select are defined. Then, based on the organizational solutions actually adopted, the various national systems are grouped into homogeneous families. With its clear, jargon-free language and concrete examples, this is the most accessible comparative study of international healthcare arrangements available.

FEDERICO TOTH is Full Professor of Political Science at the University of Bologna, Italy, where he teaches Organization Theory and Health Systems.

Comparative Health Systems
A New Framework

FEDERICO TOTH
University of Bologna

CAMBRIDGE
UNIVERSITY PRESS

University Printing House, Cambridge CB2 8BS, United Kingdom

One Liberty Plaza, 20th Floor, New York, NY 10006, USA

477 Williamstown Road, Port Melbourne, VIC 3207, Australia

314–321, 3rd Floor, Plot 3, Splendor Forum, Jasola District Centre,
New Delhi – 110025, India

103 Penang Road, #05–06/07, Visioncrest Commercial, Singapore 238467

Cambridge University Press is part of the University of Cambridge.

It furthers the University's mission by disseminating knowledge in the pursuit of
education, learning, and research at the highest international levels of excellence.

www.cambridge.org
Information on this title: www.cambridge.org/9781108477963
DOI: 10.1017/9781108775397

© Federico Toth 2021

This publication is in copyright. Subject to statutory exception
and to the provisions of relevant collective licensing agreements,
no reproduction of any part may take place without the written
permission of Cambridge University Press.

First published 2021

A catalogue record for this publication is available from the British Library.

Library of Congress Cataloging-in-Publication Data
Names: Toth, Federico, author.
Title: Comparative health systems : a new framework / Federico Toth.
Description: Cambridge, United Kingdom ; New York, NY : Cambridge University
    Press, 2021. | Includes bibliographical references and index.
Identifiers: LCCN 2021019744 | ISBN 9781108477963 (hardback) |
    ISBN 9781108745314 (paperback) | ISBN 9781108775397 (epub)
Subjects: MESH: Delivery of Health Care–economics | Healthcare Financing |
    Health Care Reform | Cross–Cultural Comparison
Classification: LCC RA971.3 | NLM W 84.1 | DDC 362.1068/1–dc23
LC record available at https://lccn.loc.gov/2021019744

ISBN 978-1-108-47796-3 Hardback
ISBN 978-1-108-74531-4 Paperback

Cambridge University Press has no responsibility for the persistence or accuracy
of URLs for external or third-party internet websites referred to in this publication
and does not guarantee that any content on such websites is, or will remain,
accurate or appropriate.

To Paolo

Contents

List of Figures	*page*	viii
List of Tables		ix
Acknowledgments		x
List of Acronyms		xii
Introduction		1
1	Seven Financing Models	6
2	Funding Healthcare: Variants and Hybrid Systems	37
3	Healthcare Expenditure and Insurance Coverage	66
4	Healthcare Provision: Integrated versus Separated Systems	88
5	Financing and Provision: Four Families and a Few Outliers	111
6	Hospitals, Doctors and Nurses	145
7	Healthcare Reforms over the Last Thirty Years	179
8	Health Politics	208
	Conclusions	240
	References	247
	Index	273

Figures

3.1	Health expenditure per capita	*page* 70
3.2	Percentage of population with healthcare insurance coverage	78
3.3	The uninsured in the OECD countries (2000–2019)	86
3.4	The uninsured in European Union countries (2000–2019)	86
4.1	The Integration Index: twenty-seven countries compared	108

Tables

1.1	Comparison of financing models	*page* 30
2.1	Funding of health services in twenty-seven OECD countries	39
3.1	Current expenditure on health, as a share of GDP	67
3.2	Healthcare expenditure, as a share of GDP (1975–2015)	72
3.3	Health expenditure by type of financing	74
3.4	Percentage of population with healthcare insurance (1975–2015)	81
4.1	Integrated model versus separated model	92
4.2	Integration versus separation: national cases compared	105
5.1	Financing and provision	112
6.1	Hospital beds	146
6.2	Hospital payment methods	151
6.3	Number of practicing physicians (2000–2019)	153
6.4	Foreign-trained doctors and nurses	158
6.5	Female practicing physicians (2000–2019)	161
6.6	Number of practicing generalist and specialist doctors	163
6.7	Remuneration methods for doctors	166
6.8	Practicing nurses (2000–2019)	174
6.9	The nurse-to-doctor ratio	176
8.1	Introduction of major healthcare compulsory programs	214
8.2	First laws introducing social health insurance	225
8.3	Laws introducing a universalist scheme	227

Acknowledgments

I started dealing with healthcare systems and health policies more than twenty years ago. Initially, Giovan Francesco Lanzara led me on this fascinating research path, to whom I am – and always will be – very grateful, for this and for many other reasons. Without the guidance and example of Giovan Francesco Lanzara, I probably would not have chosen this profession, and I certainly would not have done it in the same way.

Over the years, I have been able to take advantage of the advice and encouragement of an undisputed authority in the field of healthcare organization, Professor Giorgio Freddi. As Professor Freddi is aware, the professional esteem I have for him is great; however, my personal respect is – if possible – even greater.

I am indebted to many of my colleagues in the Department of Political and Social Sciences of the University of Bologna. Special thanks go to Giliberto Capano, Elisabetta Gualmini, Salvatore Vassallo, Filippo Tronconi, Roberto Cartocci, Stefania Profeti, Renata Lizzi, Marco Albertini, Gianfranco Baldini, Michele Sapignoli and Valerio Vanelli. I turned to each of them for help, although they may not recall this, in order to overcome some blind alleys in which I was stranded, and they suggested solutions that I appreciated and tried to put into practice, as far as was within my capacity.

Also in other departments of the University of Bologna, I was able to interact with colleagues who have exceptional knowledge in the field of healthcare, from whom I have learned a great deal. Among these are, certainly, Maria Pia Fantini and Daniele Fabbri, for whom I have great esteem and affection.

The theoretical framework presented in this book is the result of a long process of speculation – which is still in progress – and is marked by rethinking, adjustments and various intermediate versions. During this journey in search of a classification scheme that would fully convince me, interaction with colleagues at the conferences and workshops organized by the International Political Science Association and the International Public Policy Association has been most useful. I would like to thank those who, more than others, had to put up with the subsequent provisional versions of my work: Kieke Okma, Ted Marmor, Jim Bjorkman, Howard Palley, Tony Zito, Jeremy Rayner, Ryozo Matsuda, Lenaura Lobato, Tatiana Chubarova, Natalia Grigorieva, Amardeep Thind and Michele Castelli.

My sincere thanks go to Philip Good, my contact person – my Virgil, to use a Dantesque description – at Cambridge University Press. I thank Philip for the support he provided and for believing in this book immediately. It is a great honor for me to have this volume published by Cambridge University Press, even though, frankly, I still do not fully understand how they could have accepted my editorial proposal.

Finally, I wish to thank the one who, most of all, has shared in the adventure of writing this book with me: my wife Carlotta. I do not wish to be overly rhetorical: Probably, even without my wife's support, the book – in one way or another – would have been completed. But doing this without her would have been much more difficult and a great deal less pleasant.

During the months in which I wrote this book, the most beautiful thing that could ever occur, happened to me: My son Paolo was born. Although he may never read it, this book is dedicated to my son.

Acronyms

AARP	American Association of Retired Persons (US)
AFL-CIO	American Federation of Labor and Congress of Industrial Organizations (US)
AHIP	America's Health Insurance Plans (US)
AMA	American Medical Association
ARS	*Agences régionales de la santé* (France)
AWBZ	Dutch Exceptional Medical Expenses Act, *Algemene Wet Bijzondere Ziektekosten*
BMA	British Medical Association
CHIP	Children's Health Insurance Program (US)
CMU	*Couverture maladie universelle* (France)
CNAM	*Caisse nationale de l'assurance maladie* (France)
DHA	District Health Authority (UK)
DHB	District Health Board (New Zealand)
DRG	diagnosis-related group
EOPYY	Greek National Organization for Healthcare Provision
ESY	Greek National Health Service, *Εθνικό Σύστημα Υγείας*
EU	European Union
FEHB	Federal Employees Health Benefits (US)
FFS	fee-for-service
GDP	gross domestic product
GHIS	General Health Insurance Scheme (Turkey)
GKV	German Social Health Insurance Scheme, *Gesetzliche Krankenversicherung*
GP	general practitioner
HFA	Health Funding Authority (New Zealand)
HMO	Health Maintenance Organization
HSE	Health Service Executive (Ireland)
ISFAS	*Instituto Social de las Fuerzas Armadas* (Spain)

LHN	Local Hospital Network (Australia)
MSA	medical savings account
MUFACE	*Mutualidad General de Funcionarios Civiles del Estado* (Spain)
MUGEJU	*Mutualidad General Judicial* (Spain)
NFZ	Polish National Health Fund, *Narodowy Fundusz Zdrowia*
NHS	National Health Service
OECD	Organisation for Economic Co-operation and Development
PHN	Primary Health Network (Australia)
PhRMA	Pharmaceutical Research and Manufacturers of America (US)
PKV	German Private Health Insurance Scheme, *Private Krankenversicherung*
RHA	Regional Health Authority (Canada)
SHI	social health insurance
THE	total health expenditure
UK	United Kingdom
VHA	Veterans Health Administration (US)
VHI	voluntary health insurance
WLZ	Dutch Long-Term Care Act, *Wet langdurige zorg*
ZVW	Dutch Health Insurance Act, *Zorgverzekeringswet*

Introduction

In the months I was writing this book, the COVID-19 epidemic broke out. The measures taken in various countries to tackle the spread of the coronavirus have brought health systems, and the professionals who are part of them, back into the spotlight. The pandemic has confirmed what we are all aware of, but which we often tend to take for granted, and that is how very important the organization of healthcare services is.

Healthcare is a crucial sector from many points of view; from a personal point of view, first of all. We always hope to have to use it as little as possible, but when we need it, we would like to be able to count on high quality health services; to know whether we do or do not have the financial backing of an insurance scheme; to have, or not have, the right to freely choose which provider to be treated by. This makes all the difference in the world. The ways in which healthcare services are governed should interest us not only as potential users but also from a social, economic and political point of view. Suffice it to say that the most economically developed countries devote, on average, around 10 percent of their gross domestic product to healthcare, and this percentage is continuously increasing over the years.

In an era of globalization, of a push toward institutional isomorphism and policy convergence, it would be easy to expect that countries with advanced economies govern health services in a similar way. It is not so. As will be seen in the following chapters, in terms of the financing and organization of healthcare, the differences between member countries of the Organisation for Economic Co-operation and Development (OECD) are marked. In some countries,

2 INTRODUCTION

all residents enjoy generous coverage against the risk of becoming ill; in others, there are millions of uninsured (and underinsured) people. There are systems in which the choice of a specialist doctor or of the hospital facility where one may be treated is severely limited. In other systems, on the contrary, patients – without any additional economic burden – can freely choose from all the providers in the country. There are countries where the public health service – think of the National Health Service (NHS) in the United Kingdom – manages the vast majority of inpatient and outpatient facilities themselves, and has hundreds of thousands of employees, making it the largest employer and the largest company in the country. In other countries, the State does not manage a single hospital and has no healthcare personnel on the payroll. In some systems, a referral from your family doctor is required to access specialist care; in other systems, patients have direct access to specialist visits and diagnostic tests. And the list of differences between the different national systems could continue, but it is better to stop here in order to not spoil the content of the following chapters. For the moment it is sufficient to make it clear that the healthcare systems of the OECD countries are by no means similar to each other.

I would like to make explicit the logic with which this volume is designed; it is a logic that has several similarities to the software used for creating the identikits of people sought by the police. These programs allow you to choose from a wide range of different face shapes, various hair lines, differently shaped and sized noses, multiple types of eyebrows, different eye shapes and so on. The identikit is composed of the somatic characteristics, selected from those available in the catalog, which are closest to those of the face to be reconstructed. A very similar *modus operandi* can also be applied to the study of health systems. Each health system is made up of different components. In this book, the logic followed for each of these components will be to first present the different, possible options on a theoretical and organizational level; then show which countries have adopted one solution and which another.

The theoretical framework will be tested on a large number of cases, that is, the health systems of twenty-seven OECD countries.[1] Following the "logic of the identikit," the individual national systems will all end up being described as *mestizo* creatures, which mix together – in not always a congruent and a harmonious way – elements attributable to ideally opposed models. Commenting on some of my previous works, some colleagues have defined – kindly, I hope – this way of proceeding as similar to a "Lego-like" (like building blocks) construction. Moreover, in the following chapters, the analogy of the cocktail will be evoked. Beginning with the same ingredients very different drinks can be made, depending on how they are combined.

To better focus on the content in the following chapters, it may be useful to introduce at this point the image of the "health triangle." Several authors (Mossialos and Dixon, 2002; OECD, 2002; Rothgang et al., 2005) agree in considering the healthcare system as the intertwining of interactions established among three categories of actors: users, providers and insurers. By providers we mean all entities that provide healthcare services directly, therefore, these include hospitals, outpatient clinics, healthcare labs, doctors, nurses and, in general, all healthcare professions. Insurers are either for-profit or not-for-profit entities that collect financial resources to be allocated for coverage of medical expenses of third parties. All individuals – regardless of their health conditions – are potential users of the healthcare system. Each of us can, indeed, face health problems and consequently need healthcare services. Providers, insurers and users are the vertices of the healthcare triangle.

---

[1] There are currently thirty-seven members of the OECD. Of these thirty-seven member states, ten are not analyzed in this book. The choice is justified by the fact that, particularly for recently joining countries, the OECD Health Statistics database does not provide the complete time series of data. Moreover, many of the excluded countries are small in size (with a population of fewer than three million inhabitants), and there is a lack of adequate scientific publications in English on the organization of the respective healthcare systems. The twenty-seven countries considered in this study are those for which the OECD Health Statistics provides a complete dataset, and for which an abundant literature in English is available.

4 INTRODUCTION

In addition to the vertices, it is also possible to dwell on the sides of the triangle, that is, on the relationships among users, providers and insurers. When focusing on the relationship between users and insurers, we are talking about the funding of the system. When considering the relationship between providers and users, we are dealing with healthcare service provision. The third side of the triangle pertains to the relationships established between insurers and providers and, in particular, the ways in which providers are remunerated. The State has the important task of regulating the sides of the triangle. Depending on the country, in addition to regulation, the public actor can take on the role of financier of the system, and in some cases, also that of direct provider.

The book is structured as follows. The first three chapters focus on the funding side of healthcare services. Chapter 1 presents seven "primary" models through which it is possible to finance healthcare services and protect oneself from the risks of disease. In Chapter 2, many variants of the primary models are reviewed, and it will be understood how all national systems are hybrid and segmented internally. In Chapter 3, some data are provided to explain the effects produced by the individual national financing systems, in terms of overall expenditure and insurance coverage of the population.

With Chapter 4, we will move from the funding side to the provision of care. First, two rival ideal types (separated versus integrated models) and the different elements that characterize them are presented, and then we go on to see which of these organizational elements are actually applied in the individual countries. In Chapter 5, the financing methods are cross-referenced with healthcare provision arrangements. In this way, four "health families" and some outliers are identified. Chapter 6 completes the description of the delivery system, focusing on some fundamental categories of providers – hospitals, doctors and nurses – and the ways in which they are remunerated.

Health systems are in constant evolution. Chapter 7 is, therefore, dedicated to the health reforms adopted over the last few decades. The innumerable initiatives undertaken in the various countries are condensed into some major reform themes.

Finally, Chapter 8 will try to answer the "why" question: Why do OECD countries adopt different healthcare organization models? In an attempt to answer this question, some explanations that have already been advanced in the literature will be reported, adopting, in particular, the perspective of "health politics."

*

I Seven Financing Models

In this chapter, we shall focus on how financial resources that are destined to the payment of healthcare costs are collected and utilized. To this purpose, we shall present seven different models based on how healthcare services can be financed. For each model discussed in the following sections, it is essential to pay attention to the dimensions listed:

(1) who pays and who benefits from the system;
(2) the number and legal status of the insurers;
(3) the methods by which users contribute financially;
(4) the freedom of choice granted to citizens;
(5) the relationships between insurers and providers;
(6) the level of public intervention (i.e., the role played by the State).

I.I THE DIRECT MARKET MODEL

The "direct market" system (which can also be referred to as the "simple market") differs from other models in that it does not envisage the figure of insurers. The "healthcare triangle" is therefore left with only two vertices: providers and users.

In this model, providers and users of healthcare services interact with each other directly, without the intermediation of third parties. Providers set the price of their services without restrictions; users are free to select their provider of preference, and each time they avail themselves of a service, they pay the provider directly, out of their own pocket.

In such a system, the role of the State is limited to regulating the providers. Public authorities, for instance, must verify compliance with given quality standards by hospitals and outpatient facilities as well as the possession of adequate qualifications to practice healthcare professions.

The market system – at least in theory – offers some advantages. First, it should grant citizens a broad choice: Users have no insurance or contribution obligations and they are free to choose any provider. Under conditions of free competition, providers should strive not only to organize themselves efficiently but also to achieve high levels of service quality while offering competitive prices. Second, patients pay for only the services they actually use. In this model, there are no incentives to request unnecessary procedures.

One of the major limitations of the simple market lies in the fact that unhealthy individuals end up paying more than those who are healthy since one pays depending on the actual use of healthcare services. Indeed, the risk of illness involves the individual (or the household) and is not shared with others. Patients with fewer economic means may also be unable to afford certain healthcare professionals or treatments because they are too expensive. Therefore, the greatest flaw attributed to the market system is that it is not equitable.

In the direct market system, there is a perfect correspondence between those who pay and those who benefit from healthcare. The individual who avails himself of a healthcare service is required to bear the relative costs. One only pays for the services received. If no healthcare services are used, there are no charges.

1.1.1 Dental Care in Italy and Spain

The direct market system is very widespread. As we shall see in Chapter 2, in almost all countries some healthcare services are purchased under market conditions. It is, however, difficult to find countries that finance healthcare by depending solely on the market model. At least in OECD countries, the simple market usually plays an ancillary role in the overall architecture of the healthcare system, focusing on forms of care that are either excluded or not adequately covered by the prevailing insurance schemes.

8 SEVEN FINANCING MODELS

Two concrete examples of this are found in the countries of Italy and Spain, where the highest percentage of adult dental care is funded and provided within a market system in which patients can freely choose their dentist from all practicing dentists based on reputation, treatment prices and location, paying out of their own pocket for the dental work and procedures. Those who are not satisfied with the care they have received may contact another professional for future treatments. Of course, it may occur that some citizens give up certain dental treatments or get treated by specific professionals because others are too expensive. The State limits itself to setting quality standards that providers must respect.

I.2 VOLUNTARY HEALTH INSURANCE

Falling ill and having to undergo medical treatment has always been an unforeseeable event capable of giving rise to very unpleasant circumstances – also in terms of economic impact (Blomqvist, 2011). But, as with other types of risk (consider life or theft insurance), one can take out a policy against the financial risks of illness. Hence, in the second financing model, namely voluntary insurance, insurers come into play, in addition to users and providers.

The voluntary insurance model does not envisage the obligation to obtain insurance coverage against health risks. Tax or cash incentives may be provided to those who opt for insurance, whereas penalties may be imposed on those who, despite having the economic means, decide against insurance. In any event, citizens are basically free to choose whether or not to sign up for insurance (OECD, 2004).

Those who decide against health insurance, and those who cannot afford it, fall under the foregoing direct market system: They directly bear the costs of the medical treatments that they have undergone. Conversely, those wishing to take out a health insurance policy can choose from a number of private insurers, who are in competition with each other.

Insurers may be for-profit insurance companies or nonprofit institutions (Mossialos and Thomson, 2004). In the former case, the premium will probably be risk-rated, that is, calculated on the basis of the individual risk of each subscriber (Mossialos and Dixon, 2002; OECD, 2004; Rothgang et al., 2005): elderly people, individuals suffering from severe or chronic disease and those with lifestyle risks face higher premiums. Nothing prevents nonprofit insurance entities from calculating premiums based on individual risk, but they often prefer community-rated or group-rated insurance premiums. Premiums (or contribution rates) are defined as "group rated" when they are uniform for all workers belonging to the same company or occupational category. They are "community rated" when they are the same for all residents within a given geographical area (Mossialos and Dixon, 2002).

Regardless of the methods used for calculating the premium, the insurance model relies on the principle of "risk pooling" to spread the financial risk among policyholders (Kutzin, 2001; Hussey and Anderson, 2003). The expenses incurred by those who become ill are also paid with the premiums of insurance holders who stay healthy.

Compared with the simple market system, the insurance model should offer the additional advantage of providing the economic coverage that results from holding a policy, so that after paying the premium, the policyholder knows that any incurred medical expenses will be covered by the insurance. In practice, however, insurance reimbursement of all medical expenses actually paid by the policyholder is not a given; it depends on the policy. Individual insurance packages may certainly include various types of restrictions, such as deductibles, maximum coverage and co-payments. Insurance companies may deny coverage for some services and may impose limitations on the choice of providers. Theoretically, the voluntary insurance model allows for "tailored" policies negotiated between insurer and subscriber depending on the latter's economic means, health condition, risk propensity, age and lifestyle risks.

Similar to the direct market model, the problem of the poorer segments of the population is also tangible in the voluntary insurance model since those who cannot afford the cost of a private insurance policy are obviously subject to discrimination. Another problem that may arise because of insurance logics, which should be discouraged by the direct market, is the typical behavior that economists refer to as "moral hazard" (Arrow, 1963; Pauly, 1968; Zweifel and Manning, 2000); as such, the lack of a direct correspondence between the amount of medical services used and the premium paid may lead policyholders to request treatment and procedures that are either unnecessary or that they would do without if they had to pay the full price. It is similar to what happens to many of us when at a buffet or in restaurants with offers for "all you can eat." Knowing that we will not pay for every single dish we consume, we are tempted to taste many dishes, with the result that we eat too much.

Regarding healthcare provision, services are usually offered by providers outside the insurance companies, and the role of the insurer is limited to reimbursing the costs. In other cases, insurance companies may negotiate terms with some providers and enter into specific healthcare service agreements. Insurers who apply this strategy maintain a "preferred providers" network and encourage their subscribers to choose a provider within their network, usually offering a reduction in the insurance costs.

In a voluntary insurance system, the State must regulate and supervise both the providers and the insurance companies in order to prevent the latter from taking opportunistic actions to the detriment of the policyholders. Legislation may also provide for tax or monetary incentives in favor of those who subscribe to an insurance policy, or – conversely – penalties for those who decide against one.

In such a system, ultimately, who pays? Only those who voluntarily enter into an insurance contract for themselves and their household pay. Those who cannot afford it or who decide against it do not contribute to risk pooling. Who benefits from this system? Only those who hold an insurance policy and their dependants, if coverage is extended to them.

1.2.1 Voluntary Insurance in the United States

For a broader insight into the actual functioning of a voluntary health insurance system, we can examine what is available in the United States. In the United States, there are some public schemes against the risk of illness, but these are limited to the minority of the population. The majority of Americans fall within a private health insurance system. As will be argued later, in the United States, private insurance is financially incentivized, but it is not formally mandatory, at least in most states.

Hence, in the United States, there is a plethora of competing private insurers offering different types of healthcare insurance plans. The insurance companies that operate in the American market can be for-profit or nonprofit. Insurance premiums vary considerably depending on the services included in the policy: deductibles, the forms of co-payment charged to the subscriber and the freedom of choice of healthcare providers. Few insurance policies leave the subscriber free to choose any specialist or healthcare facility. Most insurance companies have their own network of "contracted" providers, and policyholders have to bear additional costs if they opt for out-of-network care.

US residents can enter into a health insurance contract in two ways: through their employer or by directly subscribing to an insurance plan. Employer-based policies are usually less costly and apply the group-rating principle. Employers negotiate with the insurance companies and choose the type of insurance policy to offer to their employees. Policies taken out individually are generally more expensive, but the subscriber can enjoy greater freedom of choice and premiums can be calculated based on individual risk (Rice et al., 2013). In 2019, 56 percent of Americans had private employer-based health insurance, while 10.2 percent had insurance policies that were purchased individually (US Census Bureau, 2020).

There are two reasons why, in the vast majority of cases, private insurance is provided by the employer: one of a fiscal nature and the other of a historical nature. The fiscal reason simply stems from the fact that for companies, the contributions paid for employee health insurance are tax-free (Mossialos et al., 2017). For the historical reason, we must instead go back to the Second World War. During wartime, in order to contain inflation, the American government had placed strict controls on wage increases. Not being able to directly increase wages, companies decided to attract workers by offering them various benefits, one of which was, precisely, health insurance, which is a practice that continues to date (Blumenthal, 2006).

In the American system, due to the voluntary nature of insurance coverage, there is an inevitable result in that part of the population may not have health insurance, either because they do not want to subscribe to an insurance policy or because they cannot afford the related costs. In 2019, about twenty-six million Americans (8 percent of the population) did not have any type of health insurance (US Census Bureau, 2020).

With the aim of progressively reducing the number of uninsured, Obama's reform, which was approved in 2010, introduced some substantial novelties in the health insurance market (Jacobs and Skocpol, 2010; Jones et al., 2014). From 2014, each state was to have set up its own "health insurance marketplace," that is, a sort of online health insurance stock market that would make it easy for citizens to compare the policies and costs of different insurance companies. For some years now, economic aid is being provided to help medium- and low-income households pay for an insurance policy. However, for a period of time (later this measure was revoked), those who had a sufficiently high income but did not subscribe to a healthcare insurance policy incurred a fine. A tax penalty was also foreseen for companies with more than fifty employees, which do not offer any insurance coverage to their employees.

It is important to clarify that the presence of financial incentives (or disincentives) aimed at encouraging the purchase of an insurance policy does not indicate that the United States had introduced a mandatory insurance system in that those who do not want an

1.3 SOCIAL HEALTH INSURANCE

insurance plan can decide against it. All in all, the American system is still one of voluntary insurance, despite Obama's reform.

1.3 SOCIAL HEALTH INSURANCE

The basic principle behind the social health insurance (SHI) model is that the government requires certain categories of workers to pay contributions from their salary in order to have coverage for the risk of illness. In this model, the role of the insurer is played not directly by the national government but by sickness funds, which are quasi-public, nonprofit organizations that are subject to strict governmental regulations (Saltman, 2004) and are appointed to collect contributions based on occupational or territorial criteria. Hence, there may be a fund for industry workers, one for state employees, another for the employees of a given region and so on. The sickness funds undertake to reimburse medical expenses incurred by members and their dependants in exchange for the contributions paid.

The SHI model therefore divides the population into two groups. On the one hand, there are those who, as members of certain working groups, must pay mandatory contributions. They cannot choose whether or not to sign up for the health insurance scheme since they are forced to do so. On the other hand, there are those who are not subject to any obligations, who may, if they wish, take out a voluntary insurance policy or resort to out-of-pocket spending for their healthcare.

The first country to introduce a form of mandatory health insurance was Germany, under Chancellor Bismarck, from the end of the nineteenth century. For this reason, SHI is also referred to as the Bismarck Model. We can take a look at the German case to gain insight into how this system was conceived, and how it has evolved over time. According to the Bismarckian legislation of 1883, the obligation to make payments to a sickness fund was initially limited to industry workers who had incomes below a given threshold. However, coverage for the risks of illness was soon extended to family members of the workers who were insured. Likewise, the principle was affirmed that sickness funds should cover not only active workers but also those who had retired, who during their working lives had made regular contributions. In the following decades, even the number of occupational categories subject to the obligation of insurance coverage had also progressively increased, and so this explains why SHI schemes, originally designed to offer protection to certain categories that were considered particularly vulnerable, over time, have come to embrace the majority of the population (Alber, 1982).

The classic SHI model provides for different sickness funds that are not in competition with each other to be operative within the same country; and workers are assigned to a certain fund by law, depending on their occupation.

Let us try to elucidate, at least in principle, the strengths and weaknesses of this financing model. Compared to the previous two models, SHI certainly grants less freedom of choice but promises to reduce inequalities among subscribers. As far as users' freedom of choice is concerned, SHI systems do not give all citizens the possibility to choose whether or not to get insurance (if they belong to given categories, they are obliged to be insured). Moreover, at least with the classic version of SHI, citizens do not even have freedom to choose a sickness fund to subscribe to. Despite the drawback in terms of lack of freedom of choice on the part of the user, SHI seems to take a few steps toward fairness of treatment. While the voluntary insurance model indeed provides for premiums to be calculated on the basis of individual risk, with SHI, contributions are the same for all subscribers to the same sickness fund. Contributions are usually calculated as a fixed percentage withheld from gross salary, and, in most countries, they are shared between employee and employer (Normand and Busse, 2002). However, we should not neglect the fact that some categories are excluded from health insurance coverage and that, lacking a mechanism for compensation among funds, the sickness funds for higher-income professions may offer higher levels of treatment.

We should recall that an essential feature of SHI is that it is a typical occupational system. Therefore, the obligation to pay health contributions is not prompted by nationality or residency but rather by one's occupation. By following a rigorously occupational logic, the SHI system inevitably excludes those who do not fall within one of the occupational categories subject to the insurance obligation. The SHI systems, therefore, have a considerable limitation; that is, unless they are complemented by some "targeted" programs (which we will discuss shortly), they generally do not guarantee coverage for the entire population.

Another feature of SHI – considered to be an essential strength of this model in many countries – is that the insurers are nonprofits although they are private companies (Saltman, 2004). The sickness funds are neither for-profit insurance companies (easily accused of achieving maximum profit, even contrary to the interests of the insured) nor government agencies (characterized by the inefficiency and rigidity that is typical of public bureaucracies).

As far as the relationship with healthcare providers is concerned, differences from the previous model are not significant in that even in SHI systems, subscribers can freely choose healthcare providers and facilities, and in most cases, healthcare providers are autonomous with respect to the sickness funds.

Therefore, we can state that the SHI system is usually based on a plurality of sickness funds and that subscription to these funds is mandatory for only a part of the population. Who are the payers and who are the beneficiaries? The beneficiaries of the system are all those who pay the relative contributions along with their dependent family members. All the occupational categories that are subject to the obligation to subscribe to a sickness fund must pay for coverage. The State decides what benefits the sickness funds are required to reimburse and which categories have an obligation to pay contributions as well as those which are not. The State must also monitor the correct management of the sickness funds, and in many cases, it also determines the amount of contribution that workers must pay to the respective fund.

1.3.1 Social Health Insurance in Austria

In Austria, there is a rather typical social health insurance system, the origins of which date as far back as 1888. Everyone working in Austria, with the exception of a small group of self-employed workers (Österle, 2013; Bachner et al., 2018), is required to contribute a part of his/her salary to a sickness fund. For most categories, healthcare contributions currently account for 7.65 percent of income. This rate is established by parliament at the federal level. SHI contributions are capped. Individuals who exceed a given income threshold do not have to pay contributions for the amount that is above the threshold (Bachner et al., 2018). Contributions are paid in equal shares by the employer and the employees.

Unlike what happens, for example, in Germany, the Austrian SHI system does not allow choice of the sickness fund. Allocation to the fund is made *ex officio*, depending on residence and occupation. The sickness funds are not in competition. In Austria, there is a total of eighteen health insurance funds. They can be territorial, occupational or corporate. These include four occupational funds for farmers, self-employed workers, civil servants, railway workers and miners. Those who do not fall within the foregoing occupational categories are required to subscribe to a territorial sickness fund. There are nine territorial funds, one for each of the Austrian constituent lands. Most of the Austrian population is registered with regional funds. Finally, there are five corporate funds including some large Austrian companies that have their own sickness funds; the employees of these companies do not pay contributions to occupational or territorial funds, but instead, they contribute to the company fund.

Sickness funds are self-governing bodies, which are financed mainly through mandatory contributions by subscribers. Through tax revenue the State also contributes to the financing of healthcare, especially as far as hospital care is concerned (Gönenç et al., 2011).

All subscribers to sickness funds are entitled to a number of benefits, either in kind or in cash. The service package guaranteed by

SHI is generous and includes hospital care; outpatient primary and specialist care; physiotherapy; medication; home care; and preventive care. Upon the provision of services, users are often requested to share in the expenses. Subscribing to a sickness fund benefits not only the workers who pay contributions but also their dependants. Pensioners are also required to contribute a part of their pension to a sickness fund. Some categories at risk (including low-income citizens, recipients of unemployment benefits and asylum seekers) are covered under statutory health insurance with contributions being paid either by federal funds or the responsible Land. The overall effect is that 99.9 percent of the Austrian population is covered by one of the eighteen sickness funds operative in the country. Who makes up the remaining 0.1 percent that is excluded from social health insurance? Some categories of individuals are more likely than others to have no insurance (Österle, 2013; Bachner et al., 2018): (1) the unemployed who are not entitled to unemployment benefits; (2) part-time employees earning less than a set limit; (3) students, who have not found a regular job at the end of their studies; and (4) people who do not have stable employment following a divorce (if they were coinsured with their spouse before the divorce).

Finally, let us consider the relationship between insurers and healthcare providers. Sickness funds – with the exception of one that operates in Vienna – do not have their own hospitals, while some of them may have their own outpatient clinics (Österle, 2013). In most cases, however, healthcare providers are autonomous and are reimbursed by sickness funds on the basis of a common price list.

1.4 TARGETED PROGRAMS

In countries where either voluntary or social health insurance prevails, there are often programs that can be defined as "targeted." In the literature of the Welfare State, these are also called "residual" programs (Wilensky and Lebeaux, 1958; Titmuss, 1974). The programs that we define as "targeted" (or "residual") for the purposes of this book are those that are financed by the public budget and are intended for particular target populations. The beneficiaries of these programs are generally the most vulnerable categories, those that are most exposed to health risks, such as low-income individuals; the elderly and minors; those suffering from serious illnesses; prisoners; and refugees. Various countries have targeted programs not only for the "weaker groups" but also for certain occupational categories considered particularly worthy of protection by the government, such as the military or civil servants.

Targeted programs are, therefore, funded by the entire community. They are financed through general taxation or by earmarked taxes. There may be a number of targeted programs within the same country. Each single category of beneficiaries often has its own dedicated program, administered separately from other residual programs and with its own processes in terms of affiliation and provision of services.

A key difference between targeted programs and other financing models is that, in the latter, those who pay earn the right to benefit from the program being financed. In the case of targeted programs, this is not necessarily true since beneficiaries coincide only in part (or not at all) with those who finance such programs. A healthcare program for the unemployed, for example, is financed by taxpayers who do have a job. Healthcare for prisoners is paid by those who are not in prison. A program designed for minors is financed by adults who pay taxes, and so on. Targeted programs are, in short, programs financed by the community, but they are only available to particular categories.

Let us examine the advantages and disadvantages of such a model, at least on a theoretical basis. A favorable aspect lies in the fact that some categories of "weak" subjects, who under other systems would have no insurance coverage, are directly protected by the State. Targeted programs are based on the principle that public resources, which are limited by definition, should not be spread out over the entire population but rather used for the benefit of those who are more needy. The rest of the population, namely those who do not belong to disadvantaged classes, are expected to obtain healthcare by their own means. The main disadvantage of this model is that only a part (usually a minority) of the population is covered by public programs.

As far as relationships with healthcare providers are concerned, targeted programs can be of two types. In most cases, the State only plays the role of insurer, hence financing external providers. There is a second, albeit less frequent, type of targeted program, which envisages a public program with its own medical staff and healthcare facilities where it can provide its users with the care they need.

Finally, let us consider the role played by the public actor. In this model, the State is responsible for identifying the categories that require special protection, financing the targeted programs and, in some cases, providing healthcare directly.

1.4.1 Public Programs in the United States

We find typical examples of targeted programs in the United States. Most of the resources that the US government allocates to healthcare are indeed used to finance a plurality of typically residual programs. The major ones are Medicare and Medicaid, both established in the mid-1960s under Lyndon Johnson's presidency. Medicare's objective is to provide healthcare coverage to citizens who are more than sixty-five years of age, as well as patients with amyotrophic lateral sclerosis (ALS) and people affected by chronic kidney disease. Medicare is financed through a combination of general federal taxes, a mandatory payroll tax (shared by employees and employers) and individual premiums (Tikkanen et al., 2020). The program is divided into different parts, covering inpatient, outpatient and medication expenses.[1] In 2019, Medicare had more than fifty-eight million

---

[1] Part A (hospital insurance) covers inpatient care, which includes hospice and short-term skilled nursing facility care. Part B (medical insurance) covers certain doctors' visits, outpatient care, medical supplies and preventive services. Introduced in 2003, Medicare Part D is an optional outpatient prescription drug coverage. Medicare Advantage, also called "Part C" or "Managed Medicare," is the private health insurance alternative to the federally run original Medicare. Medicare Advantage plans are offered by private managed care organizations (Tikkanen et al., 2020). The

enrollees, which is nearly all citizens more than sixty-five years (US Census Bureau, 2020).

Medicaid is largely tax-funded, with federal tax revenues representing two-thirds of costs, and state and local revenues the remainder (Tikkanen et al., 2020). Medicaid provides healthcare to the poorer segments of the population and people with disabilities. Since each state provides different forms of protection and applies different criteria for enrolment into the programs, not all those who are disabled or in low-income brackets qualify for Medicaid, which in 2019 provided healthcare to almost fifty-six million Americans (US Census Bureau, 2020).

In addition to Medicare and Medicaid, the US government finances many other targeted programs, including the Children's Health Insurance Program (CHIP), which is addressed to minors in low-income families. Other targeted programs are designed for the armed forces, war veterans, federal employees, Native Americans, prisoners and people affected by HIV/AIDS. Overall, the targeted public programs cover a little more than a third of the US population (US Census Bureau, 2020).

1.5 MANDATORY RESIDENCE INSURANCE

The mandatory residence insurance model is based on the principle in which the government requires all residents to take out a private health insurance policy covering essential healthcare services, using individual resources. Since there is no single public scheme into which contributions can be paid, the policy has to be taken out with different, for-profit or nonprofit insurers who are in competition with each other. The mandatory residence insurance system is, therefore, a multi-payer system, in which citizens are obligated to acquire insurance and can choose their insurers.

federal government requires these Medicare Advantage plans to cover everything that original Medicare covers, and some plans include services that the original Medicare does not.

Once all residents have been obliged to get insurance coverage, the government may provide subsidies for low-income citizens (who might otherwise find it difficult to pay the insurance premiums regularly), and may impose even very strict regulatory measures on the insurance market.

Ultimately, in a mandatory national insurance system, who pays? All residents are required to take out a health insurance policy, and each one pays their own insurance premium. Who are the beneficiaries? All citizens must have health insurance, hence the entire population should by definition be covered against the risks of illness. The insurance packages usually differ from one another, as they may provide coverage that is supplemental to the minimum required by law. We must therefore bear in mind that there may be differences between the services provided to individual healthcare users.

Compared with the models discussed earlier, the main benefit guaranteed by a mandatory residence insurance system is the coverage of the entire population: If all residents comply with the insurance obligation, there should not be any uninsured individuals. Additionally, citizens are obliged to pay for a health insurance contract, but they are free to choose the insurance company they prefer.

The limits of this model are similar to those already reported for voluntary insurance. If insurance premiums are risk-rated, the most vulnerable (such as the elderly and those affected by chronic diseases) end up paying far higher premiums than the average. And if low-income individuals do not receive financial support from the State, they face the risk of not being able to regularly pay their insurance premiums.

Finally, we come to the relationship between insurers and healthcare providers. As for the other models analyzed previously, even in mandatory residence insurance schemes the providers are usually independent from insurance companies, and are reimbursed by the latter. Insurance companies may, however, also have their own healthcare facilities and staff who provide in-kind services to their subscribers, or they may enter into specific contracts with given providers.

1.5.1 *Mandatory Insurance in Switzerland*

As from 1996, Switzerland has adopted the model of mandatory residence insurance. All Swiss residents (and not just workers) are required to purchase a basic health insurance. Subscribers are required to cover the cost of the premium with their own means, and can choose from among about fifty competing insurance companies (Schmid and Beck, 2016).

Insurers need to abide by strict public regulations: They cannot make profits on the basic insurance package, nor can they apply enrolment criteria (they must accept everyone in compliance with the rule of open enrolment), and they have to calculate premiums according to the community-rating principle.[2] Lower-income families are aided by cantonal governments: About one-third of Switzerland's population is granted public subsidies to purchase health insurance (Biller-Andorno and Zeltner, 2015; De Pietro et al., 2015).

This regulatory framework pertains to the package of essential care, namely healthcare subject to the insurance obligation. Although the basic package is generous, some services, including most dental care, are excluded. To cover nonessential services, the Swiss can request complementary insurance. Each insurance company usually offers different insurance packages to choose from: The premium may vary depending on the deductible, the freedom of choice in terms of provider and the inclusion of services other than the essential ones. We ought to point out that many of these insurance packages apply the "managed care" formula: This means that insurance companies set up their own network of preferred providers; policyholders who accept to select only preferred providers pay lower insurance premiums. Forms of this kind are increasingly widespread, and more

---

[2] Premiums are allowed to vary only by three age categories, with different prizes for children (0–18 years), young adults (19–25 years), and adults (26 years or older). In addition to this, basic package premiums may vary depending on the extent of the deductible and for managed care insurance policies.

than half of today's insurance plans are estimated to be of the managed care type (De Pietro et al., 2015).

1.6 THE UNIVERSALIST MODEL

A universalist system is defined as a single-payer insurance scheme (therefore, one for the entire nation) covering all residents and financed through taxation. Similar to the mandatory residence insurance model, the universalist model guarantees healthcare coverage to the entire population. Compared with other insurance schemes, the universalist system is marked out by the fact that the right to healthcare is not linked with payment of a premium or a contribution, but to residing in a given country. Healthcare is therefore a right of the citizens of that country. Care may be provided free of charge or with co-payment (usually a small fee) covered by the patient.

From the point of view of those who have to contribute financially, the universalist system does not grant freedom of choice. Unless a form of opting out is provided, residents cannot choose whether or not to finance the universalist scheme; instead, they are required to pay taxes in order to finance the program. And, given that (direct) taxes are usually paid more than proportionally with respect to income, the universalist scheme turns out to be a typically progressive financing system (Mossialos and Dixon, 2002; Hussey and Anderson, 2003).

It is important to underscore that, unlike the social health insurance model, the universalist system envisions taxation not only on work income, but on all forms of income. Financing of the universalist scheme, therefore, has a clear redistributive intent in that the richest end up paying for the healthcare services provided to the poorer citizens, at least in part.

A further difference from the models examined earlier is that, while the former tolerate disparities in treatment between citizens, however, in the universalist system all citizens should be entitled – at least in theory – to the same package of services.

As discussed in the following chapters, there are two types of universalist models: one that is "separated" and another that is "integrated." The key difference between the two lies in the relationships between the insurer and the providers. In the separated model, the State is only committed to financing healthcare, which is provided by autonomous providers. In the integrated type – corresponding specifically to the National Health Service – the State not only finances healthcare but also provides it directly through its own facilities and staff.

In universalist systems – both separated and integrated – the State ends up playing a pivotal role by acting as the insurer for the entire population. It is indeed the State that collects the financial resources that are to be allocated to healthcare, and that decides how providers are remunerated. In integrated universal system, the State is also the actual healthcare provider.

Therefore, who benefits from a universalist program? The entire resident population is entitled to essential healthcare. Who finances the program? All taxpayers.

1.6.1 *Medicare in Canada*

Canada is an example of a separated universalist system. The Canadian healthcare system is structured around a single public scheme, known as Medicare, which acts as the insurer for the entire population. The Medicare scheme is financed through tax revenue and does not involve co-payment by users (Marchildon, 2019). Although the federal government imposes a regulatory framework that is common throughout the country, Medicare is managed at a provincial level. Therefore, there may be differences in organization and management of services between one province and another. The provision of healthcare services is not guaranteed by facilities and staff that operate directly under the Medicare scheme, but by independent providers (Marchildon, 2013).

Medicare undertakes to cover primary, specialist outpatient and hospital care. The reimbursement of services pertaining to physiotherapy, long-term care, eye and dental care is partial, and varies according to the province of residence. For services that are not included in the Medicare package, two-thirds of Canadians subscribe to private complementary insurance (Martin et al., 2018). Most private insurance policies are paid through employers, unions or professional associations under a group contract (Marchildon, 2013; Mossialos et al., 2017).

1.6.2 *The National Health Service in the United Kingdom*

The British NHS embodies the prototype of the integrated universalist system. The United Kingdom was, in fact, the first large country (and the first European country) to adopt the national health service model, established in 1946.

Despite the devolution (the NHS is now subdivided into four distinct administrations, for Northern Ireland, Scotland, Wales and England), and other radical reforms introduced over the years, the NHS has always retained some distinctive features: It continues to be financed through tax revenue and provides care to all legal residents of the United Kingdom. The British NHS owns and operates its own hospitals and outpatient clinics, covering the entire national territory. Most healthcare personnel are employed by the NHS.

Users mostly benefit from NHS services free of charge. In the United Kingdom, the only forms of co-payment involve medication and dental care. However, many categories of patients (children, the elderly, the chronically ill, low-income households, the disabled, pregnant women, etc.) are exempt from co-payment (Cylus et al., 2015).

1.7 MEDICAL SAVINGS ACCOUNTS

An additional financing model for medical care – still not widespread, but the object of great interest in recent years, even at theoretical level (Wouters et al., 2016) – involves the so-called medical savings accounts (MSAS). These are individual deposit accounts whose holders periodically pay an agreed amount or a percentage of their salary. The MSAs allow for tax deductions and may be combined with high-deductible catastrophic health insurance (Mossialos and Dixon, 2002; Wouters et al., 2016).

Reserves accrued on these deposit accounts can only be used to reimburse healthcare expenses. An account holder can withdraw from the account only to pay for healthcare services received personally or by a dependant family member. Interest is paid on the account balance at the end of the year. Unused amounts are accumulated for the future.

Compared to the traditional insurance scheme, the main advantage of MSAs is that they do not incentivize moral hazard (Hsiao, 1995; Barr, 2001; Mossialos and Dixon, 2002).

The MSA system can be broken into two types: a "mandatory" type whereby workers (or residents of a particular country) are legally required to open their own account and deposit contributions on a regular basis; and a "voluntary" type, which gives individual enrollees the freedom to open an account (which often supplements another type of insurance coverage). In both versions, healthcare providers have no relationship with the institution where deposit accounts are held (whether they are social security agencies, credit institutions or insurance companies). Hence, account holders can choose the providers they prefer by using a market-based approach.

Especially in the mandatory MSA model, the State performs important regulatory functions. Public authorities are indeed responsible for: (1) deciding which categories must mandatorily open individual medical savings accounts; (2) determining the amount of contributions to be deposited into the accounts and the criteria for using the deposited resources; (3) supervising the institutions where the deposit accounts are held.

According to some commentators, medical savings accounts can be regarded as a variant of the insurance principle. If this were the case, mandatory deposit accounts would then be a variant of social health insurance or of mandatory residence insurance, while voluntary MSAs would be a variation of voluntary insurance. This is true only to a certain extent, and we need to point out the essential element that differentiates MSAs from the insurance models discussed earlier, that is, medical savings accounts are individual deposit accounts, whose purpose is to guarantee coverage to the individual deposit holder from the risks of illness, especially in anticipation of old age. Unlike voluntary insurance or mandatory social insurance, MSAs do not imply any solidarity among deposit holders, nor do they provide for any form of risk pooling with others (Hsiao, 1995; Mossialos and Dixon, 2002; Hussey and Anderson, 2003). Medical savings accounts bear a strong individualistic imprint (Barr, 2001; Robinson, 2005). Each deposit holder accrues resources for themselves, and the solidarity element is confined to the narrow family circle.

1.7.1 *Medisave in Singapore*

Medical savings accounts are used in some countries, such as, China, Singapore, South Africa and the United States (Wouters et al., 2016). In the United States, as well as in South Africa, it is possible to open voluntary healthcare accounts alternatively or in addition to other forms of insurance. In China, MSAs are utilized in combination with compulsory insurance that covers catastrophic medical expenses. None of the twenty-seven OECD countries contemplated in this study adopt a mandatory MSA system. To get an idea of how a mandatory MSA system operates, one can review the system implemented in Singapore. In this country, workers are required to contribute to the mandatory savings scheme called Medisave, which was introduced in 1984 and managed by Singapore's pension institution.

Within this scheme, workers hold individual deposit accounts into which they must deposit from 8 percent to 10.5 percent of their salary on a monthly basis (Yin and He, 2018). All contributions placed into Medisave accounts are tax-exempt, accrue interest and may be used by the account holder only to pay for certain healthcare expenses, such as hospital care, day surgery, some outpatient procedures, rehabilitative care and long-term care (Barr, 2001).

The funds accrued in these deposit accounts do not participate in any form of risk pooling (Hsiao, 1995), rather it is at the disposal of the account holder, who can transfer it to only family members such as a spouse, children, parents and grandparents. Resources left unused at the end of the year are kept in the account to cover healthcare expenses incurred in the future. The underlying principle of the Medisave program is to compel all Singapore residents to set aside part of their salary during their working lives in anticipation of unforeseeable medical expenses and, more importantly, old age.

Healthcare providers are not connected with Medisave. In Singapore, patients can freely choose their healthcare provider or the facility they prefer and can decide whether to pay for any service received out of their pocket or from their Medisave account.

For the sake of completeness, we ought to point out that Medisave is not the only public health insurance scheme in Singapore. In addition to Medisave, there are two other government programs. One is called MediShield Life and consists of mandatory health insurance, which is the same for the entire population, and covers "catastrophic" healthcare costs such as very expensive inpatient procedures or costs arising from ongoing treatments such as dialysis and chemotherapy. The MediShield program covers all Singapore residents and those who have the economic resources are requested to contribute to the program by paying an annual premium. Those who can document a lack of resources to pay the premium receive a special government subsidy (Yin and He, 2018). Medisave and MediShield are complemented by a third national program called Medifund, which is a targeted program financed by the government and designed to reimburse all healthcare costs – not only the exceptional expenses – incurred by the poor.

1.8 COMPARING THE SEVEN MODELS

To synthesize the topics discussed in the previous sections, it seems opportune to recapitulate the major similarities and differences between the seven financing models. To do this, it is advisable to recall the six dimensions identified earlier in this chapter.

1.8 COMPARING THE SEVEN MODELS   29

The main characteristics of the different financing models are summarized in Table 1.1. Since there are two types of medical savings accounts, it was preferable to keep the compulsory version of MSAs separate from those that are voluntary, within the table.

1.8.1   Payers and Beneficiaries

In two models (i.e., direct market and medical savings accounts), those who receive healthcare services are required to pay the full cost. Everyone pays for only the medical care received. Hence, there is a perfect correspondence between those who benefit from the services and those who finance them. Conversely, in targeted programs, those who finance the program coincide only partially (or may not coincide at all) with those who benefit from the services. In the other four models, the insurance approach prevails. Many subscribers contribute financially to the risk pooling scheme, acquiring the right – in case of illness – to receive reimbursement for incurred medical expenses. Whoever takes out an insurance policy, even if healthcare services are not utilized, contributes to financing the system. Thus, the healthy part of the population ends up paying for the care of the sick.

Focusing once again on the recipients of the different insurance coverage schemes, we can state that in the universalist model the beneficiaries are all residents of a given country, regardless of whether they contribute or not to financing the scheme. The beneficiaries of voluntary insurance systems, SHI, mandatory residence insurance and medical savings accounts are those who regularly pay premiums or contributions. In targeted programs, beneficiaries are specific "privileged" or "vulnerable" categories (Frenk and Donabedian, 1987; Lee et al., 2008).

It is important to specify how risk pooling takes place on a different scale depending on the model (Mossialos and Dixon, 2002; Hussey and Anderson, 2003). As seen in voluntary insurance and mandatory residence insurance, risk sharing occurs only among subscribers of the same insurance company; while in SHI, fund pooling takes place among all members of the same sickness fund (which

Table 1.1 *Comparison of financing models*

	Who pays?	Who benefits?	Multi- versus single- payer	Private versus public insurers	Payment methods	Mandatory versus voluntary	The role of the State
Direct market	All those who benefit from the services	All those who pay for the services	No insurers	No insurers	Prices	Voluntary	Regulates only providers
Voluntary insurance	All those who purchase an insurance policy	Only those who are covered by an insurance policy	Multi- payer	Private	Risk-rated premiums	Voluntary	Regulates the insurance- market
Social health insurance	Categories of workers subject to obligation	Registered workers and dependant family members	Multi- payer	Private not for profit	Group-rated contributions	Mandatory (for certain occupational groups)	Imposes an obligation and regulates sickness funds
Targeted programs	All those who pay taxes	Specific privileged or vulnerable categories	Single- payer (multiple programs possible)	Public	Taxation	Mandatory (for those forced to finance programs)	Acts as the insurer

Mandatory residence insurance	All residents	All the insured (which should coincide with all residents)	Multi-payer	Private	Premiums	Mandatory (freedom to choose the insurer)	Imposes obligation and regulates the insurance-market
Universalist model	All those who pay taxes	All residents	Single-payer	Public	Taxation	Mandatory	Acts as the insurer
Mandatory MSAs	Categories of workers/residents subject to obligation	Only the MSA holder (and dependant family members)	Single-payer	Public	Mandatory contributions	Mandatory	Imposes obligation and can maintain MSAs
Voluntary MSAs	Those who voluntarily open an account	Only the MSA holder (and dependant family members)	Multi-payer	Private	Voluntary contributions	Voluntary	Can regulate MSAs

32 SEVEN FINANCING MODELS

could also coincide with the occupational category). In the universalist model, the risks of sickness are spread over the entire population, while in direct market models and medical savings accounts there is no form of risk sharing with other individuals.

1.8.2 Number and Legal Status of Insurers

In the literature (Kutzin, 2001; Hussey and Anderson, 2003), a distinction is usually made between single-payer systems, where there is one single insurer for the entire population, and multi-payer systems in which a plurality of insurers operates in the same country. The universalist model is, therefore, a single-payer system. Voluntary insurance, SHI and mandatory residence insurance are, on the contrary, multi-payer models. MSA and targeted programs can be single-payer or multi-payer, depending on how the system is designed.

In multi-payer systems, the legal status of insurers is significant. In SHI, sickness funds by definition are necessarily nonprofit; they cannot be for-profit entities. In voluntary insurance and mandatory residence insurance, insurers can be either nonprofit or for-profit organizations. Within the multi-payer models, we can further distinguish between systems in which insurers compete among themselves, (this is the case in voluntary insurance and mandatory residence insurance), and from those where allocation to the fund is made *ex officio*, depending on residence or occupation (as seen in the classic SHI model).

1.8.3 Contribution Methods

Depending on the model, citizens' financial contribution can take on different forms (Evans, 1987; Thomson et al., 2009). In the direct market and the medical savings account models, users pay the full price for the services they make use of and so the total expense is, therefore, commensurate with the care received. In voluntary insurance and mandatory residence insurance systems, each user pays an insurance premium regardless of the care they will receive, and the premium may be risk-rated or group/community rated. In the SHI model, subscribers regularly pay sickness contributions, drawn from their work income. In the universalist model and targeted programs, insurance schemes are financed through taxes.

The choice of contribution method determines the degree to which the funding schemes end up being "progressive" or "regressive" (Wagstaff and van Doorslaer, 1992). Progressive systems are those in which the proportion of income contributed rises with income levels so that the wealthy contribute a greater share of their income than do the poor (Hussey and Anderson, 2003). Regressive financing arrangements, on the contrary, are those in which higher-income households contribute a lower proportion of their income than do lower-income households.

Health systems financed through general taxation are typically the most progressive while those based on insurance premiums (and out-of-pocket payments) represent the most regressive options since each individual pays the same amount, regardless of income (Wagstaff and van Doorslaer, 1992; Hussey and Anderson, 2003; Wagstaff, 2010). The typical SHI systems, based on payroll contributions and an equal rate for all workers, tend to be "proportional" in that they are neither progressive nor regressive.[3]

To grasp the differences between the financing models, in terms of how progressive or regressive they are, here is a fictitious example. Imagine two individuals, who are in the same profession, who reside in the same locality and who have roughly the same health risk profile. The first – who we will call Scrooge McDuck – receives an annual earned income of $100,000, the second – who we will call Donald Duck – has an income of $10,000.

If we are in a voluntary insurance system or mandatory residence insurance, the two parties contribute to the financing of the system by paying insurance premiums. Let us suppose that the State

---

[3] The SHI systems are basically proportional, unless: (1) there are upper limits on the overall amount that must be paid in contributions (in this case the system ends up being regressive); (2) part of the financing to the sickness funds comes from general revenues (in this case the system becomes more progressive).

does not provide any financial support for the purchase of a healthcare policy. Whether the rewards are risk-rated or community rated, Scrooge McDuck and Donald Duck – since they have the same risk profile – will pay the same premium: $5,000 a year. Although the outlay is the same, for Scrooge the premium corresponds to 5 percent of his income, while for Donald the premium absorbs a full 50 percent of his income.

For a second scenario, let us assume that the two individuals live in a country where there is an SHI system and that health contributions are calculated at a rate of 10 percent for all workers. Scrooge McDuck will pay $10,000 to the health insurance fund, while Donald Duck will pay $1,000 to the same health insurance fund. Regardless of how much they have actually paid (Scrooge pays a contribution that is ten times higher than Donald's), the two individuals will be entitled to the same healthcare services from the sickness fund.

Finally, imagine that we are in a country where the health system is financed by general taxation and that public health schemes absorb around 20 percent of the government budget. In most Western countries the tax system is progressive. Let us assume then, that Scrooge McDuck, having an income of $100,000, pays 40 percent of taxes, while Donald Duck, with a much lower income, has a rate of 20 percent. In this scenario, Scrooge will end up contributing $8,000 to the financing of public health services (20 percent of $40,000), while Donald Duck will contribute just $400 (20 percent of $2,000). Again, although Scrooge pays much more than Donald (twenty times as much), they will receive the same level of coverage.

The example, however simplistic, helps us understand how the seven models presented previously – if they are not "corrected" to some extent – produce very different effects in terms of income redistribution and therefore of the "solidarity" of the system.

1.8.4   User's Freedom of Choice

The level of compulsion of the scheme and, therefore, the freedom of choice granted to individual users varies considerably depending on the model under consideration (Hurst, 1991; OECD, 1994, 2004). Market and voluntary insurance systems leave total freedom of choice. In the Voluntary Health Insurance (VHI) model, the user has no insurance obligation and can freely choose whether or not to get insurance and from which insurance company to take out a policy. The user's freedom of choice is minimal in the universalist model. All residents are compelled to contribute – through taxes – to financing the system, and there is no freedom of choice with respect to the insurer. The same holds for targeted programs.

In terms of freedom of choice, the other models fall within intermediate positions. In mandatory residence insurance there is the obligation to purchase a health policy, but the user is free to choose the insurer. In both the SHI model and the MSA system, adopted in Singapore, the obligation to get insurance applies only to certain categories of workers. In many countries the latter cannot choose the insurer.

1.8.5 *The Relationship between Insurers and Providers*

In some models, insurers and providers are integrated with each other – this means that the same entity acts as both insurer and provider – while in others they are autonomous. This topic will be discussed in detail in Chapter 4. For the time being, let us just say that in "integrated" systems, insurers directly provide healthcare services to their subscribers through their own facilities and staff. Conversely, in "separated" settings, providers are autonomous with respect to insurers, who are only committed to reimbursing the expenses.

MSAs are always separated systems. Universalist systems, as well as targeted programs, can be either integrated or separated. Generally, voluntary insurance, SHI and mandatory residence insurance are separated models, although there may be – within such systems – individual insurers who prefer to directly provide healthcare through their own network.

1.8.6 The Role of the State

Finally, we come to the role played by the State in the field of healthcare (Rothgang et al., 2005; Lee et al., 2008). In all models, public agencies are responsible for regulating healthcare providers. In the direct market, the commitment of the State is limited to this aspect. In the voluntary insurance model, the State does not impose any insurance obligation, but may have an interest in regulating the insurance market, sometimes even in a rather decided manner. In SHI and mandatory residence insurance, the State requires workers or the entire population to subscribe to an insurance policy. Insurers are private entities, but public regulatory measures pertaining to insurers are, in this case, very stringent.

Public intervention is even more substantial in the universalist model and in targeted programs. In these models, the State not only plays a regulatory role, but acts as the insurer. Integrated universalist systems work under maximum public intervention, as the State not only acts as an insurer but also as a provider of services.

Finally, regarding medical savings accounts, the role of the State is more prominent in mandatory MSA systems (as in Singapore), while it is less significant in the case of voluntary MSAs (as in the United States).

2 Funding Healthcare
Variants and Hybrid Systems

In Chapter 1, seven different ways of financing healthcare were presented. These seven methods of financing must be considered as pure models, as "ideal types," which do not always find an accurate reflection in reality. When switching from the illustration of the ideal models to the descriptions of how the individual national systems actually operate, three factors must be kept in mind.

First, it is necessary that the ideal models are brought into a specific national context and consequently be translated and adapted locally. As seen in the following chapters, each individual, national system follows its own evolutionary path, collects the legacy of previous arrangements, is the result of specific political agreements, presents organizational and cultural characteristics that differentiate it from other countries (Blank et al., 2018). Therefore, we must expect that the same ideal model can be applied in different ways – at least in part – according to the country.

Second, as mentioned in Chapter 1, some of the financing models have been applied for many decades. The Bismarckian model of SHI, for example, is more than a century old. Therefore, it is natural that, over time, the original model has evolved, following physiological "policy learning" processes (Bennett and Howlett, 1992; Hall, 1993; Helderman et al., 2005). Once implemented, each system inevitably presents limits and problems. National policy makers can respond to these problems by making corrections to the original model. It should, therefore, be kept in mind that different variants and corrections may exist for each pure model.

The third factor, what has already been widely supported in literature (Roemer, 1960; Terris, 1978; Frenk and Donabedian, 1987;

OECD, 2004; Burau and Blank, 2006; Wendt et al., 2009; Böhm et al., 2013), should be reiterated, namely that all national healthcare systems are hybrid systems. Those who study healthcare systems from a comparative perspective know that there are no – or at least there no longer are – national systems that use only one of the models discussed in Chapter 1. As we will see shortly, (see Table 2.1), all countries analyzed in this book mix at least three funding models, if not more. Similarly to the theory formed regarding the welfare state in general (Esping-Andersen, 1999; Arts and Gelissen, 2002; Kasza, 2002), in the healthcare sector the principle that applies is that all national systems are hybrid and composite.

By combining the three factors illustrated earlier, it can be concluded that different national "translations" may exist for each ideal model. Over time, the models discussed in Chapter 1 have undergone modifications and hybridization processes. Each single, national system can be described as a patchwork that comprises different subsystems and inspiring principles.

The purpose of this chapter is to think about the tools and the logic through which hybrid systems are designed. In the following sections we will go into the dynamics that characterize private insurance, and we will focus on some of the variants to the original SHI and universalist systems. The fundamental concept of segmentation of healthcare systems will be introduced, according to which each national system can be broken down into subsystems, to which different models are applied. To better understand the different forms of segmentation, some examples will be given. The healthcare financing systems adopted in the Netherlands, France, Germany and the United States will be briefly outlined. These explanations will be concise and, therefore, far from exhaustive; however, what will be highlighted is the hybrid and "segmented" architecture of these four national systems. The final section compares the twenty-seven countries covered in this analysis. For each individual national system, not only will the prevailing financing model be indicated but also the "ancillary" models used. It will be clear that national

FUNDING HEALTHCARE: VARIANTS AND HYBRID SYSTEMS 39

Table 2.1 *Funding of health services in twenty-seven OECD countries*

	Prevalent model	Ancillary models
Australia	Universalist	Market, VHI
Austria	SHI	Market, TP, VHI
Belgium	SHI	Market, VHI
Canada	Universalist	Market, VHI
Czech Republic	SHI	Market, VHI
Denmark	Universalist	Market, VHI
Finland	Universalist	Market, SHI, VHI
France	SHI	Market, TP, VHI
Germany	SHI and MRI	Market, TP, VHI
Greece	Universalist and SHI	Market, VHI
Hungary	SHI	Market, MSAs, VHI
Ireland	Universalist	Market, TP, VHI
Israel	Mix of MRI, SHI, universalist	Market, VHI
Italy	Universalist	Market, VHI
Japan	SHI	Market, TP, VHI
Korea	SHI	Market, TP, VHI
Netherlands	MRI and Universalist	Market, TP, VHI
New Zealand	Universalist	Market, VHI
Norway	Universalist	Market, VHI
Poland	SHI	Market, VHI
Portugal	Universalist	Market, SHI, VHI
Spain	Universalist	Market, SHI, VHI
Sweden	Universalist	Market, VHI
Switzerland	MRI	Market, VHI
Turkey	SHI	Market, VHI
United Kingdom	Universalist	Market, VHI
United States	VHI and TP	Market, MSAs

MRI – Mandatory Residence Insurance; MSAs – Medical Savings Accounts; SHI – Social Health Insurance; TP – Targeted Programs; VHI – Voluntary Health Insurance.

health systems should not be seen as pure models (i.e., relying on a single source of funding), but rather as mixed systems that combine different funding mechanisms.

2.1 PRIVATE HEALTH INSURANCE

It has already been mentioned in Chapter 1 how the underwriting of a private insurance policy (both mandatory and voluntary) may involve problems and induce opportunistic behavior – if not downright fraud or abuse – by both the insurers and the insured.

Insurers may, for example, intentionally adopt "cream skimming" practices (Pauly, 1984; Hussey and Anderson, 2003; Zweifel, 2011), which consist in selecting members for their own benefit. Insurance companies obviously have an interest in taking care of low-risk individuals (such as young people and, in general, those who are healthy) as well as getting rid of those with a higher risk of incurring medical costs (such as the elderly, chronically ill). The selection of patients based on individual risk is also called "cherry picking" (Maarse, 2006).

The insured, for their part, can fall into moral hazard in that once insurance coverage has been obtained, users can be tempted to do nothing to keep themselves healthy or – easier yet – to have an excessive consumption of health services, also requiring care they do not really need.

2.1.1 Policy Measures to Counteract the Cream Skimming

To counter cream skimming practices, and therefore to protect potentially more at-risk users, national policy-makers can impose certain constraints on insurers (Hussey and Anderson, 2003; Paolucci, 2010).

A first measure is to impose "open enrolment," that is, a rule according to which insurers cannot select their clients, but instead they must accept all those who apply. This constraint applies, for example, to basic (mandatory) coverage in the Netherlands or in Switzerland, but also to voluntary supplementary coverage in Australia. In order for the principle of open enrolment to work fully, it is often accompanied by the obligation to calculate insurance premiums on the basis of the "community-rating" principle. Based on this principle, as mentioned in Chapter 1, insurance premiums must be uniform for all residents in a specific geographical area or – in the case of group-rating – for all members in the same occupational category. The community rating obligation applies, for example, to Australia, the Netherlands and Switzerland (in the latter two countries it applies only to the basic compulsory coverage, not to voluntary complementary coverage).

A further measure which, in addition to discouraging cream skimming practices, aims to make competition between insurers more equitable, consists in the introduction of a mandatory risk compensation mechanism (also called risk-adjustment or risk equalization). In most cases, the insurers deposit a part of the premiums paid into a mutual fund, which is then redistributed. The insurers who take on higher-risk clients (such as the elderly, the chronically ill) receive a higher transfer from the mutual fund, while insurers whose members are considered to be at lower risk receive less. Risk compensation mechanisms operate, for example, in Australia, the Netherlands, Germany and Switzerland.

2.1.2 *How to Discourage Healthcare Overconsumption*

To discourage the propensity of policyholders to moral hazard, and in particular to the excessive consumption of health services, insurance companies may provide for some countermeasures, such as the introduction in the insurance contract of co-payment or deductibles (Pauly, 1968).

The first measure is the forecast, whenever a health service is used, of a sharing of the expenses to be paid by the patients, who are consequently aware that the services they require are not free, but involve an expense that they must pay. This should dissuade policyholders from seeking redundant, overly expensive or otherwise unnecessary care. Forms of co-payment at the point of delivery – as will be seen later – can be used not only in private insurance systems, but also in universalist or SHI systems.

In addition to some form of co-payment, insurance policies may include a deductible and/or setting a ceiling. A ceiling, as is easily understood, is a maximum amount that the insurance coverage undertakes to reimburse. Any costs above this amount are paid by the insured. A "deductible" refers to the upper limit of out-of-pocket expenses borne by the insured individual, with all the costs of care over this amount borne by the insurer (Kutzin, 2001). Most of the insurance policies in Switzerland and in the United States include a deductible. An example is useful to avoid possible misunderstandings. Let us assume that I have an annual health policy and that during the year I have had medical treatment for a total of $1,500. In the event that my policy provides for a limit of $1,000, I will be required to pay the remaining $500. If the policy includes, instead, a deductible of $1,000 I will have to pay $1,000 out of my pocket, while the insurance company will reimburse the excess expenses amounting to $500.

A further measure that can be adopted to limit healthcare over-consumption regards the request for a specific medical prescription. If patients intend to request reimbursement for a certain benefit from their insurance coverage, they must first obtain the relevant prescription from a doctor. In theory, the demand for "medically unnecessary" benefits should consequently be reduced. We will discuss this mechanism called "gatekeeping" in further detail in Chapter 4.

2.1.3 Primary, Complementary and Supplementary Private Health Insurance

Private insurance policies – depending on the role they play with respect to the mandatory schemes – can be of three types: (1) substitutive, (2) complementary or (3) supplementary (Mossialos and Thomson, 2002, 2004; Hussey and Anderson, 2003).

We refer to "substitutive" insurance, also called "primary" insurance (OECD, 2004) when a private policy is taken out instead of the mandatory coverage (not in addition to it). In this case, those who subscribe to the private policy do not have any other form of basic insurance coverage.

On the other hand, "complementary" insurance is defined as a private policy that covers healthcare services not covered by or not fully reimbursed by the compulsory insurance package (Mossialos and Dixon, 2002). In many countries, there are health services (such as dental care, or physiotherapy) that are excluded from the basic insurance package. In other cases, the insurer does not reimburse the entire cost of the services incurred, providing some form of cost-sharing to be paid by the user. A private policy that reimburses expenses that are not covered by the basic insurance package is, therefore, "complementary" in that it is an integration to the basic coverage to which the insured is already entitled as a beneficiary of a mandatory scheme or a targeted program.

Finally, "supplementary" insurance is defined as coverage for benefits which are already entitled through compulsory insurance. Since this form of private insurance overlaps the compulsory scheme, it is also referred to as a "double coverage" (Mossialos and Thomson, 2002). Those who are dissatisfied with the standards guaranteed by a compulsory insurance scheme and who desire superior coverage can subscribe to a supplementary private policy of this type, thus guaranteeing greater freedom of choice of healthcare providers, shorter waiting times, higher standards of hospitalization etc.

To focus on the three types of private insurance illustrated earlier, it may be useful to give some examples. In countries such as the United States or Switzerland, private insurance is the main form of primary coverage. In the United States, private insurance as primary coverage remains to a large extent voluntary, while in Switzerland it is formally mandatory for all residents.

In countries such as Canada or France, private policies are mainly complementary, as they reimburse the services and costs that are not already covered by the compulsory basic package. In the Netherlands, insurance companies sell both primary private policies (for basic coverage) and complementary policies (for additional benefits). In countries such as Australia or Italy, as well as in most European countries (Mossialos and Thomson, 2004), private policies are partly complementary and partly supplementary. In fact, they partly reimburse services excluded from the basic package, but to a large extent they also provide "double coverage" in comparison to the services already guaranteed by the mandatory universal scheme. Additional forms of insurance are widespread especially in countries with a universalist scheme. In this respect, one of the countries analyzed in this paper is an exception: Canada. A particular characteristic in Canada has traditionally been the prohibition of taking out "supplementary" policies. Additional private policies covering the exact same services already provided by the public Medicare program (guaranteeing, for example, faster access to services, skipping waiting lists) are prohibited, or at least discouraged, by provincial laws (Flood and Haugan, 2010; Marchildon, 2013). The purchase of a private policy that is authentically complementary (which covers what is not included in the Medicare package) is not only allowed but it is also fiscally incentivized.

2.1.4 *The Regulation of the Insurance Market*

In addition to the measures already described (open enrolment, community rating, risk compensation schemes), national governments can adopt other tools to regulate the private insurance policy market. The policy tools put in place can be strictly regulatory or even financial (Doern and Phidd, 1983; Vedung, 1998; Toth, 2021). Through these tools, policy makers may wish to encourage the purchase of a private policy, but also to protect users from possible abuse and fraud by insurers. Public regulation is usually more stringent with reference to primary policies, and more permissive toward complementary or supplementary policies.

In some countries, the government places a limit on the earnings that private insurance companies can make from the sale of health insurance policies. This is the case, for example, in the United States, where the provisions contained in the Obama reform require that insurance companies use at least 80 percent of the premiums collected for reimbursements to healthcare providers and for investments to improve the quality of care. This implies that the administrative, marketing and profit costs overall cannot exceed

20 percent (15 percent for insurance companies operating in the large group market) of income from premiums. Another example of this is Switzerland, where it is prohibited to profit from the sale of mandatory basic packages; however, insurance companies can make profits through ancillary and supplemental insurance packages.

A further constraint that can be imposed by law on insurers is the obligation to renew a policy. Otherwise, the risk is that the insurance companies, at the end of the contract, dispose of the users who have in the meantime had serious health problems. This restriction to renew policies was introduced, for example, in the United States with the Obama reform. It prevents insurance companies from terminating the contract, or refusing to renew it, for clients who in the meantime have fallen ill.

National governments can encourage the spread of private healthcare policies (primary or integrative) through economic incentives or disincentives. These incentives (or disincentives) can apply to everyone, or they can be reserved for those in need. Fiscal or monetary incentives for the purchase of a policy are provided, for example, in Australia (for integrative policies), in France (for the purchase of a complementary policy), in the United States and Switzerland (for basic insurance). The financial penalty instrument (for those who, despite having high incomes, do not voluntarily sign up for a private policy) is adopted, for example, in Australia (for integrative coverage) and it has also been in the United States for a few years.

2.2 VARIANTS TO THE SHI MODEL AND THE UNIVERSALIST MODEL

2.2.1 *SHI Systems: Variants to the Original Bismarck Model*

The SHI model (illustrated in Chapter 1) was first introduced in Germany in the late nineteenth century. In the decades that followed, numerous European and non-European countries followed the German example, promoting systems of protection against the risk of disease that were explicitly inspired by the Bismarckian model.

As it is easy to imagine, multiple variations of the original SHI model have been conceived in different countries over the decades (Saltman and Figueras, 1997; Busse et al., 2004; Wagstaff, 2010).

The first dimension in which national SHI systems may differ from one another concerns the criteria in which workers are assigned to the respective sickness funds (Saltman and Figueras, 1997). As a general criterion, membership to a sickness fund is established on the basis of profession. However, there are systems in which the criterion of geographical residence is used in addition to or as an alternative to the employment criterion. Therefore, multi-professional funds may exist to which workers who are residents in the same territory adhere. As we will see later, in some countries there are also company funds; for example, some large companies set up a fund that is exclusively intended for their employees.

In regulating an SHI system, a crucial dimension is the freedom of choice granted to users, and therefore, by the possibility (or not) that the sickness funds compete with each other. As mentioned in Chapter 1, the original Bismarckian model does not allow the worker to choose which sickness fund to enrol in. This is what still happens today in countries such as Austria or France, where sickness funds are not in competition with each other; so citizens have no margin of choice and are automatically assigned to the respective sickness fund.

A variant of the original model introduced in recent decades in some countries aimed to give users greater freedom of choice, while stimulating competition between the funds. Therefore, there are SHI systems in which citizens are granted freedom to choose the sickness fund, and so the funds compete with each other to attract the largest number of members.

Another relevant dimension, according to which the different SHI systems differ greatly, concerns the number of sickness funds operating in the country (Saltman and Figueras, 1997; Normand and Busse, 2002). There are countries in which hundreds of sickness funds operate. However, there are others in which there are only a few dozen sickness funds, or even less than ten. Then there are borderline cases of countries in which there is only one national sickness fund, unique for all workers. The latter case represents a *sui generis* social insurance system, in so far as one of the distinctive elements of the Bismarckian model – being a multi-payer system – thus, it evidently fails.

A further difference between the SHI systems concerns the extent and methods of paying sickness contributions (Busse et al., 2004). In many cases, the rate (i.e., the percentage of salary that the worker is required to pay) is the same for all funds. However, there are countries in which each fund is free to determine its own rate which must, however, be the same for all members of the fund.

In some countries, sickness funds are financed exclusively from contributions paid by workers and employers. In other cases, the State contributes – sometimes even in a substantial way – to the financing of funds by using resources deriving from taxes. There are also differences in the way in which healthcare contributions are distributed between employers and employees (Normand and Busse, 2002). The classic formula is a 50:50 division between employee and employer, which is what happens, for example, in Germany. However, there are countries where contributions are paid differently (Busse et al., 2004).

2.2.2 *Opting Out*

As seen in Chapter 1, various financing models involve mandatory adhesion to some sickness risk coverage scheme. In universalist systems, for example, all residents are obliged – through paying taxes – to contribute financially to the single national healthcare plan. In SHI systems some categories of workers are obliged to pay contributions regularly to a sickness fund.

In some national systems, however, certain categories of users are allowed, under certain conditions, to withdraw from the compulsory scheme and to subscribe to an "alternative" insurance coverage (usually a private insurance policy). This organizational variant – for which it is possible to not contribute financially to the compulsory scheme when subscribing to alternative coverage that is equivalent to the mandatory scheme – is called "opting out" (Mossialos and Thomson, 2004; Blomqvist, 2011).

In Germany, for example, employees with an income above a certain threshold are allowed to "leave" the SHI system, thus avoiding payment of the compulsory contributions to a sickness fund; however, those who "opt to exit" from SHI are required to take out a private insurance policy that covers the basic package guaranteed by the compulsory scheme.

In Spain, only a portion of public employees are allowed to leave the public universal scheme and to take advantage of the services offered by private insurance companies. In this way, civil servants no longer contribute to the financing of the *Sistema Nacional de Salud*. On the other hand, they are required to pay regular sickness contributions to a separate mutual fund dedicated to public employees.

As can be deduced from the examples given earlier, opting out can constitute a variant of both SHI and universalist health systems.

2.2.3   Co-payment versus Co-insurance

A further measure used to hybridize funding systems is represented by methods for sharing patient expenses. Charging part of the actual cost of the service to those who have directly benefited from it constitutes – at least logically – a mixed solution because in doing so, something similar to market price is inserted into the insurance models (both mandatory and voluntary). The debate has been raging for some time, both politically and academically, regarding the usefulness, or otherwise, of this tool (Mossialos and Le Grand, 1999; Zweifel and Manning, 2000; Robinson, 2002; Schokkaert and van de Voorde, 2011). According to those in favor of this solution, cost-sharing by consumers would have the advantage of limiting the incentive – which is inherent in all insurance schemes – to an excessive request for benefits. However, there is no lack of opinions to the contrary. According to its critics, the use of cost-sharing represents an unfair measure – it affects the sick and saves the healthy – which proves to be ineffective in reducing the overall demand for health services.

2.3 THE SEGMENTATION OF HEALTHCARE SYSTEMS

It is important to point out that cost-sharing can be of two types, specifically, "co-insurance" (Kutzin, 1998; Johnson et al., 2018) is when the patient pays a percentage of the actual cost of the services received. Instead, "co-payment" is when the patient is charged a flat rate for each service received (Kutzin, 1998; Schokkaert and van de Voorde, 2011). For example, in France, for some services the patient is required to pay 30 percent of the cost of the visit, which is a co-insurance measure. In various countries, including Israel and Sweden, to take advantage of some outpatient services, the patient is required to contribute a flat-rate payment, which is not proportional to the actual cost of the examination or the diagnostic test performed, which is an example of co-payment.

It is necessary to point out to the reader how forms of co-payment or co-insurance can be applied in all insurance financing models. Sharing of user expenses can, therefore, be requested in voluntary insurance systems, in SHI, in targeted programs, in mandatory residence insurance schemes, as well as in universalist systems.

2.3 THE SEGMENTATION OF HEALTHCARE SYSTEMS

To untangle ourselves from the jungle of hybrid systems, it may be useful to introduce the concept of segmentation, which is frequently used in studies on the welfare state, with special reference to the labor market (Reich et al., 1973; Korpi and Palme, 1998). The term segmentation, when adopted for the healthcare sector, indicates the presence of dividing lines by which the overall national system is broken up into subsystems in which different models of healthcare organization are applied (Toth, 2016a). There are two basic segmentation principles: (1) segmentation of healthcare services; (2) segmentation of the population.

The segmentation of healthcare services involves subdividing the entire range of healthcare services into different "packages." An example of the segmentation of healthcare services can lead to distinguishing between: (1) "essential" procedures (i.e., those deemed necessary and thus to be included in the basic insurance package);

(2) "supplemental/additional" procedures (those not considered strictly necessary); (3) "exceptional" procedures, related to "catastrophic" risks (for chronic or, in any event, highly disabling conditions, the costs of which would be financially unsustainable for the majority of the population). As we shall see shortly, the Dutch system segments healthcare into three categories similar to those explained earlier.

In many of the countries analyzed in this book, the government has defined a basic package of health benefits; in this way, healthcare is divided into two categories: essential and "additional" ones.

In Italy, for example, the government has defined the so-called Essential Levels of Assistance, that is, the services that the public health service deems fundamental and which it undertakes to guarantee to all residents (Toth, 2016b). The services that are not included in those that are "essential," including a large part of dental care and cosmetic surgery, some categories of drugs, lenses and glasses, outpatient physiotherapy, are instead paid for by the families, who can access them under market conditions or by taking out private insurance. In other countries too, the services included in the compulsory basic package have been precisely defined. Israel, for example, has a very explicit and detailed definition of the benefits included in the standard basket provided by national health insurance (Gannot et al., 2018).

The second type of segmentation regards the "population." This logic of segmentation involves the subdivision of residents into distinct groups associated with different funding schemes. The population can be segmented according to different criteria. The most common are: occupation (for example, a distinction is made between employees and self-employed workers, or between government and private employees); earned income; and age (there may be programs reserved only for the young or the elderly). In addition to these three, there are other possible criteria for segmenting the population; there may be programs dedicated exclusively to ethnic minorities, citizens suffering from certain medical conditions, prisoners, pregnant women and so on.

The following sections will briefly illustrate the methods for financing health services in four countries: the Netherlands, France, Germany and the United States. These four systems are all "segmented" according to different criteria.

2.4 THE NETHERLANDS

The Dutch healthcare system applies segmentation of healthcare services. Healthcare is subdivided into three distinct packages: (1) "exceptional" medical expenses; (2) the basic package for essential care; and (3) "complementary" procedures.

Exceptional expenses, related particularly to long-term care, are covered by a single compulsory national scheme (identified by the acronym WLZ), which covers the entire population. The second sector (ZVW), consisting of the basic package for essential care, is entrusted to a mandatory residence insurance system that, however, has some typical elements of SHI systems in terms of the insurance premium calculation method. The third segment consists of "complementary" care (mainly dental care for adults, glasses and physiotherapy). Complementary care fits under a typical, voluntary, private insurance system.

It is useful to provide some further details on these three segments in order to understand how they have evolved over time. Up until the end of the 1980s, a typical Bismarckian system was used in the Netherlands, which was established in 1941 during the German occupation. About two-thirds of the population were subject to a typical social health insurance scheme, while the remaining part of the population was free to take out private insurance. For those enrolled in the mandatory scheme, the benefit package was uniform, and contributions were paid in equal shares by employers and employees (Vonk and Schut, 2019). Healthcare providers were – and still are – independent of insurance companies and sickness funds, and were reimbursed by the latter

In addition to basic insurance (mandatory or voluntary), from 1968 onward, all Dutch residents can rely on additional insurance coverage for catastrophic risks. This long-term care insurance scheme, initially referred to as AWBZ, went through a profound reform in 2015, and was replaced by a less comprehensive insurance plan, referred to as WLZ (Alders and Schut, 2019). The public long-term care insurance scheme, unique and uniform for all residents, is financed through mandatory income-related contributions.

In the last three decades, the Dutch healthcare system has experienced various reform initiatives (Kroneman et al., 2016). The most important reform was implemented in 2006, and largely inspired by the recommendations contained in the 1987 Dekker Report (Maarse et al., 2016; Vonk and Schut, 2019). The 2006 reform introduced a unified mandatory insurance scheme and provided for a regulated competition system in order to promote the efficiency of the system and increase citizens' freedom of choice. Following the 2006 reform, all Dutch residents were obliged to purchase an insurance policy covering a standard, basic benefits package. Two categories of people were excluded from mandatory insurance (this is an example of population segmentation): (1) the military, as they have a dedicated targeted scheme; (2) people who refuse insurance for religious reasons or out of principle (they must nevertheless pay a contribution, that is deposited in a personal, medical savings account).

Citizens are free to choose their insurer, which may be changed every year. Virtually all health insurance companies in the Netherlands are nonprofit cooperatives. Insurers are in competition with each other, and they are strictly regulated (Toth, 2021). First, the insurers cannot select their registered patients. Instead, they are obliged to accept every person who applies for an insurance plan ("open enrolment"). Adults are required to pay an annual premium directly to their insurer. These premiums vary depending on the insurer, but cannot be calculated based on individual risk since they must be community rated (Stolper et al., 2019). The government pays the premiums due for minors through tax revenue. In addition to the fixed premium, subscribers pay an income-dependent contribution to a single national fund. The contributions collected by this fund are redistributed among all insurers on a risk-adjusted basis. Low-income families can apply for a fiscal subsidy to purchase basic health insurance (Okma and Crivelli, 2013).

There are two types of basic insurance packages: policies defined as "nature" ("in-kind policies") and so-called "restitutie" ("restitution policy"). With "in-kind" policies, the insured do not enjoy full freedom of choice as they can only choose between the providers that are under contract with their own insurance (if the insured use a non-contracted provider, they are required to pay compensation). On the other hand, the insured person must not make any advance payments because the supplier is paid directly by the insurer. The restitution policies instead guarantee the full freedom of choice of the providers; however, the insured is required to anticipate the cost of the services (paying it out of his own pocket), and then asking for the subsequent reimbursement from the insurer. Regardless of the type of policy, the basic insurance benefit package is uniform and determined by the national government (Stolper et al., 2019). It includes primary care, outpatient and hospital care, prescription drugs and dental care for children under eighteen (Maarse et al., 2016).

Healthcare services excluded from the basic package may be covered by voluntary private insurance. Four out of five Dutch citizens subscribe to complementary private insurance (Kroneman et al., 2016; Mossialos et al., 2017). With regard to complementary coverage, insurers are allowed to refuse applicants and calculate premiums based on individual risk.

2.5 FRANCE

The architecture of the French health system has traditionally mirrored – and reflects even today – both a logic of segmentation of benefits (distinguishing two packages of care, one basic and one complementary), and a logic of segmentation of the population (indicating a difference between workers and nonworkers). The French sickness insurance system is structured on two levels: a mandatory basic level (governed by SHI and targeted programs), and a complementary level provided by private insurance companies.

As for the basic package, all French workers are required to pay contributions regularly to a sickness fund, without the possibility of opting out. Part of the funding for the SHI scheme comes from taxes (Goujard, 2018).

French sickness funds are private nonprofit organizations, subject to stringent public regulation, and are not in competition with each other. The French – unlike what happens, for example, in Germany – cannot, in fact, choose the fund in which to register. Assignment takes place according to profession. The largest sickness fund is the Caisse Nationale de l'Assurance Maladie (CNAM), which assists over 90 percent of the population (employees in the industry and commerce sectors, and their families). For some years now, the self-employed and student funds have also joined the CNAM. The second largest in size is that of farmers (MSA), which covers about 7 percent of the population (OECD, 2019a). In addition to these two, other cases – about a dozen – of a much smaller size operate in France, assisting categories such as railway workers, the military, ministers of worship, parliamentarians, sailors (Chevreul et al., 2015; Nay et al., 2016).

Healthcare providers are independent entities from the sickness funds. The SHI members have maximum freedom to choose a doctor and a hospital. They can choose the preferred supplier knowing that the sickness funds will reimburse the expenses incurred. However, the mandatory SHI scheme does not fully cover the medical costs incurred. Depending on the type of treatment, the sickness funds usually reimburse between 70 percent and 80 percent of the expenses incurred (Chevreul et al., 2015). The remainder, (this is, therefore, a form of co-insurance), remains the responsibility of the patients. There are also services that are not covered by the compulsory scheme. To meet these extra costs, approximately nine out of ten French people take out complementary private insurance (OECD, 2019a). The majority of these insurance packages are underwritten through nonprofit insurance organizations (the *mutuelles*). Until a few years ago, complementary coverage was voluntary, although widely spread. Since 2016, however, it has become to some extent mandatory (Goujard, 2018). In fact, all private sector employers are obliged to offer their employees a complementary policy. Complementary policies are incentivized by the tax deduction of the premiums paid.

A characteristic of the French system is, therefore, to impose co-insurance measures on patients, with the explicit objective of limiting the demand for health services and to combat moral hazard. The deterrent effect of co-insurance is, however, largely offset by the fact that complementary insurance packages reimburse the cost-sharing of patients, and that the great majority of French people enjoy complementary coverage.

The mandatory SHI scheme, therefore, concerns workers (both active and retired), and covers their respective dependent family members. And how are those who do not work, or who carry out atypical or occasional work covered? Until 2000, those who did not pay contributions received no assistance from the SHI scheme. They could possibly purchase a private policy. Things have changed since 2000, with the introduction of the so-called *Coverture Maladie Universelle* (CMU). This reform established a targeted program, financed by general taxation, which reimburses medical expenses to residents who are not already enrolled in the mandatory SHI scheme. Again in order to protect the weaker sectors of the population, the CMU instituting law also provided that the State should furnish not only the basic package but also the complementary coverage free to less well-off citizens.

From 2000 onward, the French SHI system has undergone significant transformations. Thanks to the introduction of the CMU, it now guarantees coverage of the entire population, at least on paper. The SHI scheme is funded in part by contributions from workers and businesses, but it is subsidized in part by general taxation. The tax component has grown compared to twenty years ago (Chevreul et al.,

2015; Goujard, 2018). Recently, some health insurance funds have been merged into CNAM; which is also responsible for the residual scheme for low-income citizens. Thus CNAM ends up covering the vast majority of the population.

For all of these reasons, the French system must be considered as a particular type of SHI, which approaches the model of the single national fund, and which makes it resemble – in some respects – the separate universalist model (see Chapter 5).

2.6 GERMANY

The German health system has traditionally represented an interesting application of the principle of segmentation of the population.

Up to the early 1990s, Germany relied on a classic social health insurance system.[1] The Bismarckian system obliged most workers to make regular contributions to a sickness fund. Some categories of workers were exempt from this obligation and were excluded from the mandatory SHI scheme. Those belonging to the latter categories could have taken out a private insurance policy. The majority of those enrolled in the mandatory SHI scheme could not choose the sickness fund since enrolment automatically depended on profession. Healthcare providers were independent of the sickness funds (and still are today), and patients had ample freedom of choice with respect to both physicians and hospital facilities.

As a consequence of a series of reforms adopted in the last three decades, the original Bismarckian system has changed some of its distinctive features (Busse and Blümel, 2014; Giaimo, 2016). The major reforms, which have significantly changed the architecture of the system, were passed respectively in 1993 and 2007.

The 1993 Healthcare Structure Act was to open up the system to greater competition between sickness funds. This reform guaranteed the majority of German citizens the freedom to choose which

---

[1] In 1990, with the German unification, the SHI system adopted in West Germany was extended also to the Länder of former East Germany.

sickness fund to subscribe to. The new arrangement was put into practice in 1996. In order to discourage insurers from the discrimination of patients on the basis of risk, sickness funds were required to accept all subscribers (open enrolment). A new risk-adjusted compensation scheme, which would redistribute contributions equitably among the sickness funds, was established in 1994 (Greß et al., 2002; Busse et al., 2017).

The 2007 reform comprises a wide range of measures that, as a whole, have significantly modified the way the German healthcare system is regulated and financed. The most relevant change was the introduction of a universal insurance obligation. Starting in 2009, the obligation to take out insurance is no longer limited to some professional categories, but includes all German residents. Non-SHI subscribers are required to have a substitutive private healthcare insurance policy. Private insurers are obliged to offer their policyholders a basic tariff for the coverage of a benefit basket similar to the one guaranteed by the SHI (Busse and Blümel, 2014). A Central Reallocation Pool has been established in order to make the financing of sickness funds even more equitable and transparent. All mandatory contributions paid by SHI subscribers are now collected by this central fund, which in turn allocates them to individual sickness funds according to a morbidity-based risk-adjustment scheme (Kifmann, 2017). Another important change concerns the standardization of the contribution rate for SHI subscribers. Prior to the reform, contributions could have varied depending on the sickness fund. Following the 2007 reform, all sickness funds are financed through the same contribution rate. The latter was subsequently set at 14.6 percent of the worker's salary, to be paid in equal shares by employer and employee. Each sickness fund charges an additional contribution fee directly to its members. These additional contributions are income-related and currently amount to around 1 percent of the salary (Busse et al., 2017; Mossialos et al., 2017).

The reform of 1993, and even more that of 2007, both led to a change (at least partial) of the funding model. Therefore, the German system, the cradle of the Bismarck model, today presents some distinctive features of the mandatory residence insurance model. The SHI system has not been dismantled, but it has been modernized and incorporated into the new system. The financing system adopted today in Germany is, consequently, configured as a hybrid form. It is like a matryoshka, in which the previous system based on sickness funds becomes a component of a wider system of compulsory residence insurance. Health insurance is no longer mandatory for only given professions but applies to all residents. The mandatory contributions that were once collected by individual sickness funds are now collected and then allocated by a single national fund; the latter allocates the resources collected using a risk-adjusted capitation formula, which takes into account the age, sex and morbidity of the members of the individual sickness funds (Mossialos et al., 2017). The financing of the system has, consequently, become more centralized and equitable. Also, starting in the mid-1990s, SHI subscribers are entitled to choose the sickness fund they wish to adhere to, whereas in the past this was not possible. To date, the German system is based on competition between insurers, which are nonetheless subject to stringent public regulation. Approximately one hundred sickness funds and about forty private insurance companies currently operate in Germany (OECD, 2019b).

It is interesting, at this point, to reflect on the effects produced by the principle of population segmentation. Depending on family income and profession, residents in Germany end up being divided into different categories.

The first category is composed of those who are obligatorily subject to the SHI regime. This category includes private sector employees who earn less than a certain income threshold (in 2020 it was 62,550 euros per year), pensioners, farmers and recipients of unemployment benefits. Each year, those who belong to these categories must register with a sickness fund and pay the relative contributions. The benefits guaranteed by the sickness fund are not limited to the worker only, but also extend to the respective nonearning dependants.

A second category is made up of self-employed workers and employees with annual incomes that are higher than the above threshold. They are obliged to be insured, but they are granted the option of opting out in that they can decide whether to join the statutory health insurance scheme or take out a private policy. It is important to highlight that the underwriters of a private substitutive policy do not pay contributions in proportion to their income (as in the SHI scheme), but they pay an individual risk-rated premium, with separate premiums for dependants (OECD, 2019b). The option of private health insurance thus ends up being particularly attractive especially for young people with higher incomes, who are in good health, with no family members (Giaimo, 2016; Mossialos et al., 2017).

Both active and retired civil servants enjoy a special regime in which the government reimburses a large part of healthcare costs and they purchase a private policy to cover the remainder (Busse and Blümel, 2014). In addition to civil servants, other categories, including military and law enforcement personnel, are targeted through "special" programs (Busse et al., 2017). The government pays contributions for certain categories (such as the long-term unemployed), and finances a specific program to benefit refugees.

The overall result is that around 87 percent of the German population is covered by the statutory health insurance scheme; about 11 percent of the population (including civil servants) take out a substitutive policy with a private company; and the remaining portion is covered by the "special" program (OECD, 2019b).

2.7 THE UNITED STATES

The US healthcare system has been defined as a "patchwork" of different schemes and programs (Marmor and Oberlander, 2011). The different subsystems that make up the patchwork are the consequence of an articulated segmentation of the population, which has been consolidating over time. The US mosaic is made up in part of public programs (financed, in whole or, in any case, primarily by the government) and in part by private insurance schemes (mainly by families and businesses). In Chapter 1 reference has already been made to both public programs (typical examples of targeted programs) and private insurance coverage.

As the reader may have guessed, in the United States the type of health coverage available to the individual depends to a large extent on the socio-demographic characteristics of the individual. If you are more than sixty-five, you are eligible to enrol in the Medicare program. Low-income households fall under the Medicaid program. Minors belonging to poor families can be assisted through the Children's Health Insurance Program. War veterans are assisted through the Veterans Health Administration (VHA). The military on duty is covered by a different program, known as Tricare. This program assists not only military personnel on duty but also military retirees, reservists and their dependants. If you are a federal employee, you have access to the Federal Employees Health Benefits (FEHB) program. American Indians and Alaska Natives have a dedicated program called Indian Health Services. Then there are other public programs that vary from state to state. These programs assist, for example, the prison population or individuals with HIV.

Each of these programs has separate management, and has different criteria for enrolment and for accessing treatment. Some require a financial contribution from the assisted (this is the case with Medicare and the FEHB), while other programs do not involve fees (neither in terms of enrolment fees nor in the form of co-payment at the point of delivery) to be borne by the beneficiaries (this is the case for Medicaid clients and prisoners).

All those who legally reside in the United States, and who do not fall into one of the categories for which a public program is envisaged, have the opportunity to take out a private policy. Those who are not covered by either a public program or a private policy remain uninsured.

In short, compared to the risk of disease, the US population ends up fragmented into many distinct subgroups, each of which has different protection from sickness risks.

The majority of the US population has a private insurance policy, purchased individually or, more often, obtained through their employer (US Census Bureau, 2020). In order to encourage the purchase of a health insurance policy, the Obama reform approved in 2010 implemented both incentives and fines, according to a classic carrot and stick strategy. On the one hand, an economic incentive has been provided for both families and small businesses. Households with an income below 400 percent of the federal poverty level, as well as businesses with fewer than twenty-five employees, can enjoy special tax credits. On the other hand, pecuniary penalties were provided for those who, despite having the economic means, had decided not to take out health insurance. The fines[2] concerned only companies with at least fifty full-time employees as well as households with income above a certain threshold. At the federal level (although some states have maintained these), the individual mandate penalties, which entered into force in 2014, were reset in 2019. In the United States, there is therefore no formal individual insurance mandate. Some might argue that an "employer mandate" is in force. However, the financial penalties for employers are of modest entity (when compared to the actual cost of policies), and concern only a limited number of companies. In the Unites States, private insurance is spurred by financial incentives, but it is not made mandatory by regulatory instruments (Doern and Phidd, 1983; Vedung, 1998). Individuals remain free not to insure themselves, if they do not want to.

The Obama reform also provided for a more stringent regulation of the private insurance market in order to better protect buyers and prevent fraud and abuse by insurance companies. Insurers are now required to offer a minimum package of essential care, and they cannot refuse enrolment to individuals at particular risk. The Affordable Care Act establishes the principle of the adjusted

---

[2] A penalty of $695 per adult was imposed on individuals without a health policy. However, each household did not have to pay more than $2,085 in fines (or in any case no more than 2.5 percent of their income).

62 FUNDING HEALTHCARE: VARIANTS AND HYBRID SYSTEMS

community rating. Insurance companies must, therefore, offer the same contractual conditions (and also the same premium) to all those who belong to the same age group, and they cannot discriminate based on the gender or health conditions of the individual subscriber.[3]

Before the reform came into force, insurance companies were basically free to select which subjects to insure and which not ("cream skimming"). Consequently, each company could refuse a new policy or, even worse, deny the renewal of an existing one to the individuals considered to be most at risk, starting from those with serious, chronic or degenerative diseases. Insurance companies were also allowed to challenge the infamous preexisting conditions clause. Based on this clause, the insurer could refuse the reimbursement of medical expenses to one of his clients if he was able to demonstrate that the latter had symptoms or preexisting pathological conditions that were not declared at the time of signing the policy. The Obama reform put a stop to these opportunistic practices so that insurance companies are, in fact, forbidden to terminate the contract (or refuse to renew it) to individuals who have fallen ill in the meantime. Insurance companies are also prevented from refusing reimbursement of expenses incurred to their clients by invoking "preexisting conditions." Another novelty, also introduced by the Obama reform, allows children to remain covered by parental insurance up to the age of twenty-six.

2.8 COMPARING HEALTHCARE FINANCING SYSTEMS

After reviewing the seven pure models (Chapter 1) and some of the main organizational variants that have been made to these models (illustrated in the previous sections), we can now test the usefulness of the classification proposed by applying it to the twenty-seven OECD countries included in this study. In Table 2.1, for each country,

---

[3] Among individual plans, premiums for older adults cannot be more than three times higher than premiums for younger individuals. Higher premiums may be indicated for smokers.

2.8 COMPARING HEALTHCARE FINANCING SYSTEMS   63

both the predominant financing model and the other financing methods that are still used in ancillary form are indicated. As is also evident from the examples reported earlier, the seven "pure" models are not mutually exclusive. Thus, in the same country we see more than one model at work simultaneously.

Let us focus, in the first instance, on the prevalent model. If we reflect on this criterion, in the twenty-seven countries analyzed it is easy to identify some families of similar systems (these families will be analyzed in greater detail in Chapter 5).

The largest family is that of the countries that adopt, as a prevailing model, a universalist scheme (financed by general taxation). There are a dozen countries that fall into this category. However, some of them also adopt some form of social health insurance as an auxiliary function.

The second largest family is that of the SHI systems. There are about ten countries that use some form of social health insurance as the dominant model. To overcome the insurance coverage limits of this model, many of these countries fund some form of targeted programs.

The model of compulsory residence insurance is seen in Switzerland, Germany and the Netherlands. In the Netherlands, as we have seen, a universalist scheme against "catastrophic" risks also operates alongside the compulsory residence insurance system. While in Germany the compulsory residence insurance system that was introduced a few years ago has partially incorporated the traditional SHI system.

As is well known, the United States is a case in itself. The American system is a mix of private insurance and targeted programs. Greece and Israel are also peculiar cases, as will be better seen in Chapter 5.

This is what emerges if we focus on the column: "prevalent model." If we also consider the last column of Table 2.1, relating to auxiliary models, interesting elements emerge. In fact, it is confirmed that there is no country that uses only one of the seven models. All twenty-seven countries considered have hybrid health systems that make up at least three, if not more, different funding models.

Take New Zealand for example. In this country a universalist financing system operates through general taxation. Some services (especially dental care, optician services, physiotherapy sessions) are often purchased privately, on a market basis. Almost one in three New Zealanders also holds, in addition to the coverage provided by the public health service, an additional health policy (Goodyear-Smith and Ashton, 2019). In short, in New Zealand there is a mix of three systems: the universalist model, market and voluntary insurance.

Previously we focused on the French case: For the majority of the population there is a SHI system. However, citizens in economic difficulty are covered by a targeted program. Nine out of ten French individuals take out a voluntary insurance policy in addition to the mandatory coverage. And even in France, nothing prevents one from purchasing market-based health services. Therefore in France, four models are adopted.

As we have seen, a very special case is the Dutch system, which mixes five different models (if not six). In the Netherlands, the so-called exceptional medical expenses (mainly related to the care of the disabled and long-term care) are covered by a universalist scheme. The second sector, consisting of the basic package of essential care, is entrusted to a mandatory residence insurance system (which in some respects resembles SHI). Some categories (such as members of the armed forces or refugees) enjoy specific targeted programs. Finally, the services considered as "complementary" (dental care, physiotherapy, alternative medicine, cosmetic surgery, etc.) are left to market or voluntary insurance.

In summary, Table 2.1 ultimately ends up confirming the existence of two large families, already broadly outlined in the literature (OECD, 1987; Saltman and Figueras, 1997; Freeman, 2000; Rothgang et al., 2005; Freeman and Frisina, 2010; Blank et al., 2018): first, countries with a universalist system, and second, that of social health insurance systems. However, about a quarter of the OECD countries considered here do not belong to either family. Among the countries that are neither universalist nor SHI, we find systems that are halfway between the two models, mandatory residence insurance systems and systems based on a mix of private insurance and targeted programs (the United States).

Probably, the most interesting conclusion that emerges from the comparison of the twenty-seven countries concerns the mixed nature of health systems. In fact, for the funding of health services, all the countries analyzed mix at least three different models, and some countries also use four or five simultaneously.

An effective image used for commenting on these results – and to further highlight the composite nature of health systems – is that of cocktails. With the same basic ingredients, bartenders know how to create very different drinks, depending on which ingredients are mixed and in what proportions. By developing this metaphor, the individual national health systems can then be conceived of as cocktails, which mix – in different proportions and each according to a specific recipe – the seven pure financing models presented in Chapter 1.

The allegory of the cocktail highlights an additional aspect: Each cocktail has a basic ingredient, which must be used in greater quantities than the others. This basic ingredient identifies a "type" of cocktail, a family of drinks that is similar to each other. Within these large categories, however, it is the secondary ingredients, those that are added to the base, that confer the distinctive flavor of the drink. The same is true for health systems. Focusing on the prevailing model is important, because it allows you to group countries into families of similar health systems (for an analysis of these families, see Chapter 5). However, if you want to understand how the individual national system actually works, you cannot neglect the ancillary models and the ways in which they are mixed with the prevailing model.

3 Healthcare Expenditure and Insurance Coverage

In Chapter 1, seven different models of financing healthcare were illustrated. In the second chapter, we saw how individual countries can mix these financing models in different ways and in different proportions, having a multiplicity of organizational variants at their disposal. Over time, every single national system has developed its own specific formula to finance health services. It is interesting at this point to compare the different national "formulas," evaluating the effects they produce in reference to two variables which, in terms of financing healthcare, are of indisputable importance: (1) The overall cost of the health system (i.e., how much is spent overall on health in the individual countries); and (2) the percentage of the national population that is, for various reasons, covered against disease risks.

3.1 CURRENT EXPENDITURE ON HEALTH

Let us start with healthcare expenditure – understood as overall health spending in a country, covering both individual needs and population health. Two measures are usually used to compare levels of health expenditure across countries: health expenditure calculated as a percentage of the gross domestic product, and per capita health expenditure, adjusted for cost of living using purchaser power parities (Frogner et al., 2011). Both of these measures will be reported here.

Let us start with Table 3.1, in which health expenditure is expressed as a percentage of the country's gross domestic product. Three values are reported for each of the twenty-seven countries analyzed here. The first concerns overall health expenditure: It includes spending by all types of financing schemes (both governmental and private, both compulsory and voluntary) on medical services and goods, population health and prevention programs, as well as

Table 3.1 *Current expenditure on health, as a share of GDP*

(2019 or nearest year)

	All financing schemes	Government and compulsory schemes	Voluntary schemes and OOP payments
Australia	9.3	6.3	3.0
Austria	10.4	7.8	2.6
Belgium	10.3	7.8	2.5
Canada	10.8	7.6	3.2
Czech Republic	7.8	6.5	1.3
Denmark	10.0	8.4	1.6
Finland	9.1	7.0	2.1
France	11.2	9.4	1.8
Germany	11.7	9.9	1.8
Greece	7.8	4.6	3.2
Hungary	6.4	4.4	2.0
Ireland	6.8	5.1	1.7
Israel	7.5	4.9	2.6
Italy	8.7	6.4	2.2
Japan	11.1	9.3	1.8
Korea	8.0	4.9	3.1
Netherlands	10.0	8.3	1.7
New Zealand	9.3	7.4	1.9
Norway	10.5	9.0	1.5
Poland	6.3	4.5	1.8
Portugal	9.6	5.9	3.7
Spain	9.0	6.4	2.6
Sweden	10.9	9.3	1.6
Switzerland	12.1	7.8	4.3
Turkey	4.4	3.4	1.0
United Kingdom	10.3	8.0	2.3
United States	17.0	7.6	9.4

Source: OECD (2020); CMS (2019)

administration of the health system (OECD, 2020). The overall health expenditure consists of two parts. The first component is what we could define as "mandatory" health expenditure, the second is constituted by "voluntary" private expenditure. The mandatory component includes both government and private financing schemes imposed by law (including, for example, the social contributions provided for in the SHI systems, and the insurance premiums relating to the basic package in the mandatory residence insurance systems). The "voluntary" component, instead, includes out-of-pocket payments and the cost of private insurance policies purchased on a voluntary basis.

The data reported in Table 3.1 lends itself to multiple comments and conjectures. We limit ourselves to presenting three.

First, it emerges that some countries spend more on healthcare, others less. The country that spends the most is the United States, which allocates 17 percent of its gross domestic product to healthcare. The other countries with the highest healthcare spending are, in order: Switzerland (12.1 percent of the GDP), Germany (11.7 percent), France (11.2 percent) and Japan (11.1 percent). Among the twenty-seven countries considered in this paper, there are others that allocate a much lower percentage of GDP to healthcare. The country that spends the least is Turkey (just 4.4 percent of the GDP), followed by Poland (6.3 percent), Hungary (6.4 percent) and Ireland (6.8 percent). The average health expenditure of all OECD countries corresponds to 8.9 percent of the GDP, while that of the twenty-seven countries included in Table 3.1 is around 9.5 percent. Just for curiosity, we can compare the OECD countries with the so-called BRIC countries. In Brazil, the overall health expenditure corresponds to 9.4 percent of the GDP, in Russia to 5.4 percent, in the People's Republic of China to 5.0 percent, and in India to just 3.6 percent (OECD, 2020). This means that in Brazil the overall cost of the healthcare system is roughly in line with that of the countries considered in this study. In Russia, China and India, on the other hand, the incidence of health expenditure in proportion to the GDP is much lower than the average for OECD countries.

Table 3.1 suggests a second annotation. In the final part of Chapter 2, the "prevalent" financing model was indicated for each country (see Table 2.1). A dozen countries use the universalist model as their prevalent system. About ten countries apply the

SHI model. There are only a few countries, at least to date, in which mandatory residence insurance operates. At this point, it is natural to ask whether the overall cost of the healthcare system depends on the financing model adopted. The data reported in Table 3.1 do not seem to support this hypothesis. With reference to the twenty-seven countries considered here, those with a universalist system spend, on average, around 9.5 percent of GDP, while those with an SHI system spend, on average, around 8.8 percent. The difference is not striking, and seems to depend mainly on the per capita income of individual countries. The data available in the OECD database seem to confirm that – as a general rule – countries with a higher per capita income typically allocate a higher percentage of their GDP to healthcare (Newhouse, 1977; Culyer, 1989; Gerdtham and Jönsson, 2000). In other words, health expenditure grows more than proportionally to income. Among the twenty-seven countries considered here, there is one that constitutes an obvious exception to this general rule, which is Ireland. The latter, despite having a very high GDP per capita, spends only 6.8 percent of it on healthcare.

A third comment suggested by the data shown in Table 3.1 concerns the internal differences that are found within the two "families" just mentioned: that of universalist systems and that of SHI systems. These internal differences (i.e., between countries belonging to the same family) will be explored in Chapter 5. For the moment, we can take note of the differences between the universalist systems of Northern Europe (Denmark, Finland, Norway and Sweden) and those of Southern Europe (Italy, Portugal and Spain). Compared to their Southern European counterparts, the Nordic countries spend a much higher share of their GDP on healthcare. There are also marked differences between SHI countries, which seem to stem, to a large extent, from different levels of per capita income. SHI countries with higher per capita income (Austria, Germany, Belgium, France and Japan) spend more than 10 percent of their GDP on healthcare. Conversely, SHI countries with lower per capita income (Czech

Republic, Hungary, Poland and Turkey) spend 4.4–7.8 percent of GDP on healthcare.

3.1.1 Total Healthcare Spending Per Capita

The annotations developed starting from the data contained in Table 3.1 are confirmed even if the per capita health expenditure, expressed in US dollars, is taken into consideration (Figure 3.1). In order to make spending levels comparable between different countries, per capita health expenditure is usually converted into a common currency (US dollars) and adjusted to take account of the different purchasing power of the national currencies (OECD, 2019e, 2020).

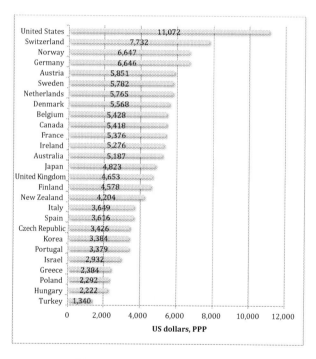

FIGURE 3.1 **Health expenditure per capita (USD PPP).**
(2019 or nearest year).
Source: OECD (2020)

Figure 3.1 shows even more clearly the differences, in terms of health spending, between one country and another. The United States appears to be, in this respect, decidedly "out of scale" compared to all the other countries, spending over $11,000 per capita. The second country to spend the most is Switzerland, where per capita health expenditure is just over $7,700. This means that the second in the ranking spends less than 70 percent of what the United States does. High-income countries like Belgium, Canada and France spend less than half of what the United States spends, while Italy and Spain spend less than a third. In 2019, the overall average of all OECD countries ($3,093) was less than 30 percent of the US figure. Not to mention Turkey, the lowest per capita spender among the countries considered here: Turks spend, on average, just 12 percent of what Americans spend.

3.2 THE GROWTH OF HEALTHCARE EXPENDITURES

Table 3.2 allows the placement of the data relating to healthcare expenditure in a diachronic perspective. In fact, the table shows the values of the overall healthcare expenditure (calculated as a percentage of the GDP), with reference to the years 1975, 1985, 1995, 2005 and 2015. The essential objective of this table is to focus on the trend – and in particular the growth – in healthcare spending over the last few decades.

What emerges clearly is that, in all the countries considered, without exception, over the last few decades healthcare spending has grown faster than has gross domestic product. In the average OECD country, the overall healthcare expenditure corresponding to 5.7 percent of the GDP in the year 1975, grew to 6.2 percent in 1985, to 7.1 percent in 1995, to 8 percent in 2005 and up to 8.7 percent in 2015.

In 2019 (or in the last year available), OECD countries spend on average about 8.9 percent of the GDP on healthcare. This figure is similar to that recorded in 2009. This means that, following the financial crisis that erupted in 2008, on average, the growth in healthcare spending remained in line with overall economic growth.

72 HEALTHCARE EXPENDITURE AND INSURANCE COVERAGE

Table 3.2 *Healthcare expenditure, as a share of GDP (1975–2015)*

	1975	1985	1995	2005	2015
Australia	5.8	6.1	6.9	8.0	9.3
Austria	6.5	6.0	8.9	9.6	10.4
Belgium	5.5	6.9	7.5	9.3	10.4
Canada	6.5	7.6	8.5	9.0	10.7
Czech Republic	n.a.	n.a.	5.7	6.4	7.2
Denmark	8.5	7.9	7.8	9.1	10.2
Finland	5.7	6.7	7.4	8.3	9.6
France	6.2	7.7	9.9	10.2	11.5
Germany	8.0	8.5	9.5	10.3	11.2
Greece	4.1	4.9	8.0	8.6	8.0
Hungary	n.a.	n.a.	6.7	8.0	6.9
Ireland	6.6	6.8	6.1	7.6	7.3
Israel	4.4	6.6	6.9	7.1	7.1
Italy	5.8	6.7	6.8	8.3	8.9
Japan	5.4	6.5	6.3	7.8	10.9
Korea	2.2	3.2	3.4	4.6	6.7
Netherlands	6.2	6.5	7.3	9.1	10.3
New Zealand	6.5	4.9	6.9	8.3	9.3
Norway	5.2	5.5	7.3	8.3	10.1
Poland	n.a.	n.a.	4.9	5.8	6.4
Portugal	4.7	5.4	7.2	9.4	9.0
Spain	4.2	5.0	7.0	7.7	9.1
Sweden	6.5	7.3	7.3	8.2	10.8
Switzerland	6.3	7.5	8.9	10.3	11.4
Turkey	2.2	1.5	2.4	4.9	4.1
United Kingdom	4.9	5.1	5.6	8.5	9.9
United States	7.2	9.5	12.5	14.6	16.7
OECD average	5.7	6.2	7.1	8.0	8.7

n.a. = not available.
Source: OECD (2020); Schieber and Poullier (1989)

3.3 THE COMPOSITION OF HEALTH EXPENDITURE

Overall healthcare expenditure can be broken down into three distinct components. The first – in analogy with what has already been seen in Table 3.1 – is constituted by the sum of public funding (which derives from taxation) and contributions to compulsory health insurance schemes. This is the component of health expenditure previously defined as "mandatory." The second component consists of insurance premiums intended for the purchase of a voluntary health policy. The third component is represented by out-of-pocket payments. The values for these three different components are reported for each of the twenty-seven countries under investigation, in Table 3.3. These values are calculated as a percentage of total health expenditure (THE). Let us analyze the three components one at a time.

3.3.1 The "Mandatory" Component

Let us start with the first component, the one fueled by taxes and compulsory contributions. Dwelling on this value allows us to understand which part of the healthcare expenditure is imposed by the State, and which is left to the discretion – and the pockets – of individuals.

The peculiarity of the American system immediately emerges. The United States is, in fact, the only country, among those considered, in which the formally "voluntary" component (given by the sum of VHI plus out-of-pocket expenses) exceeds the "mandatory" component. In all other countries the opposite is true. On average, OECD countries have a ratio of compulsory to voluntary expenditure of approximately 75 to 25.

The countries in which the mandatory component is higher are, in order: Norway (85.3 percent), Sweden (85.2 percent), Germany (85 percent) and Japan (84.1 percent). This suggests that in these countries the compulsory basic package – regardless of whether it is provided through a universalist or SHI scheme – is generous, and that, therefore, policyholders do not need to supplement it with a substantial private contribution. The voluntary expenditure is actually around 15 percent of the total expenditure.

The situation appears to be reversed in countries where the mandatory component is lower, primarily Greece (58.9 percent), the

Table 3.3 *Health expenditure by type of financing*

(2019 or the nearest year)

	Government/Compulsory schemes (% THE)	Voluntary health insurance (% THE)	OOP payments (% THE)
Australia	66.5	15.6	17.9
Austria	74.7	6.9	18.4
Belgium	75.8	5.1	19.1
Canada	70.4	14.9	14.7
Czech Republic	83.0	2.8	14.2
Denmark	83.8	2.4	13.8
Finland	76.9	4.7	18.4
France	83.7	7.1	9.2
Germany	85.0	3.0	12.0
Greece	58.9	4.7	36.4
Hungary	69.4	3.7	26.9
Ireland	74.3	14	11.7
Israel	65.7	12.4	21.9
Italy	74.1	2.8	23.1
Japan	84.1	3.2	12.7
Korea	60.8	7.8	31.4
Netherlands	82.7	6.9	10.4
New Zealand	79.2	7.9	12.9
Norway	85.3	0.4	14.3
Poland	71.5	8.1	20.4
Portugal	61.2	9.0	29.8
Spain	70.4	7.4	22.2
Sweden	85.2	1.1	13.7
Switzerland	64.5	7.5	28.0
Turkey	77.4	5.1	17.5
United Kingdom	77.8	5.5	16.7
United States	44.8	44.4	10.8

THE = total health expenditure.
Source: OECD (2020); CMS (2019)

Republic of Korea (60.8 percent) and Portugal (61.2 percent). In these countries the voluntary share, which corresponds to the private expenditure borne by the individual citizen, is around 40 percent. This suggests that in these countries the package guaranteed by the

3.3 THE COMPOSITION OF HEALTH EXPENDITURE   75

mandatory schemes is not very generous, and therefore, needs to be integrated privately, or with the purchase of supplementary policies or – more frequently – with the purchase of out-of-pocket services.

3.3.2   *The Expenditure for Voluntary Health Insurance*

A second source of funding comes from the premiums paid to take out a voluntary insurance policy. The relative value of this component of expenditures allows us to understand how developed the market for private voluntary insurance policies is in each country.

Also, from this point of view, the United States recorded an out-of-range value (higher than 40 percent of total healthcare expenditures), which deserves a brief explanation. The majority of the American population is covered by private policies, which are to be considered "voluntary" as in the United States there is no formal insurance obligation. In accordance with the definition given in Chapter 2, in the United States most of the voluntary policies are primary, while in the other countries the voluntary policies have an eminently complementary or supplementary function.

Apart from the United States, the countries where there is a higher spending on voluntary insurance are Australia (15.6 percent of total health expenditure), Canada (14.9 percent) and Ireland (14.0 percent). It should be noted that in these three countries the purchase of a voluntary health policy is subsidized by the government (Marchildon, 2013; Turner, 2015; Duckett, 2018). On the contrary, there are countries in which the turnover of the voluntary private insurance market appears much lower. The countries with the lowest values for voluntary health insurance are three Nordic countries: Norway (0.4 percent), Sweden (1.1 percent) and Denmark (2.4 percent).

3.3.3   *Out-of-Pocket Payments*

Finally, we come to out-of-pocket payments (Table 3.3, last column). The latter consist of payments incurred directly by households. They include the different forms of cost-sharing for patients and, in some countries, the estimations of informal payments to healthcare providers (OECD, 2019e). The out-of-pocket expense is the component of health expenditure not brokered by insurers, which therefore, does not provide for any form of risk pooling. Due to its "regressive" nature, a high percentage of out-of-pocket spending is considered by many authors, and also by the World Health Organization, as an element of inequity of the overall financing system (WHO, 2000).

Among those considered, the countries with the highest percentage of out-of-pocket payments are Greece (36.4 percent of total health expenditure), the Republic of Korea (31.4 percent), Portugal (29.8 percent) and Switzerland (28 percent). On the contrary, there are countries where the out-of-pocket share is decidedly lower, around 10 percent of the total expenditure, which is the case of France (9.2 percent), the Netherlands (10.4 percent) and United States (10.8 percent). In the BRIC countries – to have a point of comparison – there are high levels of out-of-pocket spending, such as, in Brazil it is 28 percent of total health expenditure, in China 36 percent, in Russia 41 percent, and in India even 62 percent (OECD, 2020).

3.4 PREVALENCE OF HEALTH INSURANCE COVERAGE: THE CURRENT SITUATION

As well as in terms of expenditure, it is important to evaluate the effects that the various financing systems produce in terms of insurance coverage for the population. The purpose of this and the next sections is to address the following questions. Which countries, among the twenty-seven analyzed here, guarantee health insurance coverage to the entire population and which, conversely, leave part of the resident population without coverage? In countries where part of the population is uncovered, how many people do not have health coverage, and what are their characteristics?

Before continuing and seeking answers to these questions, a disambiguation is necessary. Several studies propose to investigate the concept of health coverage (or universal health coverage), by unpacking it into three distinct dimensions (WHO, 2008, 2010,

2013; Lagomarsino et al., 2012; Kutzin, 2013; Boerma et al., 2014; Cotlear et al., 2015; OECD, 2018): the breadth (who is covered), the depth (what services are covered) and the height (what proportion of costs are covered) within insurance coverage. It is worthwhile to make clear that this and the next two sections focus exclusively on the first dimension, namely, the breadth of health insurance. The breadth of health insurance, also called "population coverage" (Abiiro and de Allegri, 2015; Dmytraczenko and Almeida, 2015; OECD, 2018), can be defined as the share of the population formally covered for a given set[1] of healthcare services under public programs and private insurance (OECD, 2018). This definition implies two clarifications. First, here, it is not important whether the insurance protection is public, private or obtained through a mandatory or voluntary healthcare plan. What counts is that residents are protected against health risks and do not pay completely out-of-pocket for the healthcare services they receive. Second, since the focus is on the breadth of coverage, we will only dwell on the percentage of the population[2] which is "formally covered" by some sort of insurance plan, with no reference to actual access to health services, quality of services or other dimensions of coverage. Hence, we will not mark out the difference between what citizens are granted on paper and what they are guaranteed in practice (Stuckler et al., 2010; Lagomarsino et al., 2012; Savedoff et al., 2012; Abiiro and de Allegri, 2015; Cotlear et al., 2015).

A further lexical clarification is appropriate. In the following, we will make a distinction between "universal" and "nonuniversal"

---

[1] The healthcare services or procedures that are considered "essential" (Stuckler et al., 2010; Boerma et al., 2014; O'Connell et al., 2014; Cotlear et al., 2015) vary from country to country, as the "basic package" is defined at the discretion of each national government (Boerma et al., 2014). In any event, in all the countries examined in this work, the insured are formally guaranteed a core set of services which usually include prevention, consultations with physicians, tests, diagnostic procedures and hospital care (Baeten et al., 2018; OECD, 2018).

[2] As a general criterion, the population coverage rates reported in the OECD database (OECD, 2020) concern all individuals "legally residing" in the country. In many countries, undocumented immigrants are not considered part of the population, and are, therefore, excluded from OECD statistics.

countries. Countries where all residents are formally holders of health insurance that covers essential healthcare will be referred to as being "universal." The "uninsured," instead, refer to individuals who do not have public or private primary health coverage, therefore, those who must pay for healthcare services out of their own pockets.

3.4.1 Universal, Quasi-Universal and Nonuniversal Countries

It is worthwhile to start from the analysis of the current situation (relative to 2019, or the last year available). Figure 3.2 shows, for each country, the percentage of population with basic health insurance, whether public or private.

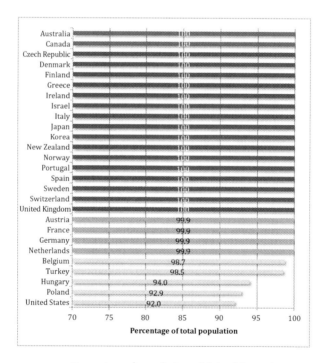

FIGURE 3.2 **Percentage of population with healthcare insurance coverage.** (2019 or the last year available).
Source: OECD (2020); US Census Bureau (2020)

Of the twenty-seven countries considered in this study, eighteen of them ensure universal coverage, four have what we can call "quasi-universal" coverage, whereas five countries do not attain universal coverage.

The eighteen countries with universal coverage (where 100 percent of the population is therefore covered) include: Australia, Canada, the Czech Republic, Denmark, Finland, Greece, Ireland, Israel, Italy, Japan, Korea, New Zealand, Norway, Portugal, Spain, Sweden, Switzerland and the United Kingdom.

According to the OECD data, four countries have coverage that can be considered "quasi-universal." In this work, we have considered those countries where the percentage of the uninsured is minimal to be quasi-universal, namely less than or equal to 0.5 percent of the population. When applying this classification criterion, the four quasi-universal countries are Austria, France, Germany and the Netherlands.

In the remaining five countries, universal coverage is not achieved. In these countries, the uninsured account for a minimum of 1.3 percent to a maximum of 8 percent of the population. These countries cannot be considered "quasi-universal" as they exceed the threshold of 0.5 percent; hence they will be referred to as "nonuniversal." The "nonuniversal" countries include: Belgium, Hungary, Poland, Turkey and the United States.

Although the problem is usually associated only to the United States, we find that other high-income countries do not provide healthcare coverage to the entire population. If, instead of the twenty-seven countries considered in this work, we considered all the countries belonging to the OECD, and all the member countries of the European Union (EU), the data would be even more striking (Toth, 2020b), in that more than a third of the OECD countries and half of the EU countries do not guarantee – to date – universal coverage. At present, the uninsured in European Union countries totals more than seven million, corresponding to 1.4 percent of the population. In absolute terms, the countries with the highest number of uninsured are

80 HEALTHCARE EXPENDITURE AND INSURANCE COVERAGE

Poland (2.7 million), Romania (2.1 million) and Bulgaria (0.8 million). Among the OECD member countries, the average percentage of the uninsured is even more pronounced: Out of an overall population exceeding 1.3 billion, there are approximately 47 million uninsured, accounting for 3.6 percent of the population. This high overall percentage of uninsured in the OECD countries is mainly attributable to the United States, which alone contributes almost twenty-six million, followed by Mexico (more than fourteen million).

3.5 HEALTH INSURANCE COVERAGE OVER TIME

To put these data into context, it is helpful to review the time sequence. Therefore, we will compare the data from 2015 with the data available for ten, twenty, thirty and forty years earlier, respectively.

Now, let us try to interpret the data shown in Table 3.4. In 2015, there were twenty-one countries with universal or quasi-universal coverage (to simplify matters, in our intertemporal comparison "quasi-universal" and "universal" countries have been combined). In the mid-1970s, universal coverage was ensured in only twelve out of twenty-seven countries. Since then, the number of countries with universal coverage has increased from the twelve countries in 1975 to sixteen countries in 1985, twenty in 1995 and twenty countries in 2005.

Over the last four decades, the percentage of the insured in the twenty-seven countries considered here has increased steadily. If we consider the aggregate population of the twenty-seven countries, in 1975 the uninsured corresponded to 13.3 percent. Since then, the percentage of the uninsured has dropped. In 1985 it was 10.5 percent, in 1995 it went down to 6.6 percent, in 2005 it reached 5.7 percent and in 2015 it decreased to 3.2 percent. The greatest reductions in the percentage of uninsured were, therefore, recorded in the decade from 1985 to 1995 and from 2005 to 2015.

Having understood the extent of the phenomenon, and how it has evolved over time, it is reasonable to ask which residents in the countries in consideration do not have any primary health insurance.

Table 3.4 *Percentage of population with healthcare insurance (1975–2015)*

	1975	1985	1995	2005	2015
Australia	100	100	100	100	100
Austria	96.0	99.0	99.0	98.0	99.9
Belgium	99.0	98.0	99.0	99.0	99.0
Canada	100	100	100	100	100
Czech Republic	100	100	100	100	100
Denmark	100	100	100	100	100
Finland	100	100	100	100	100
France	97.3	99.2	99.4	99.9	99.9
Germany	92.1	91.2	99.8	99.8	100
Greece	75.0	100	100	100	86.0
Hungary	100	100	100	100	95.0
Ireland	85.0	100	100	100	100
Israel	94.5	94.5	100	100	100
Italy	95.0	100	100	100	100
Japan	100	100	100	100	100
Korea	14.5	52.1	100	100	100
Netherlands	69.5	66.3	98.6	97.9	99.8
New Zealand	100	100	100	100	100
Norway	100	100	100	100	100
Poland	100	100	100	97.3	91.0
Portugal	60.0	100	100	100	100
Spain	81.0	97.1	98.6	98.3	99.8
Sweden	100	100	100	100	100
Switzerland	94.0	98.0	99.5	100	100
Turkey	33.6	42.1	65.0	86.6	98.4
United Kingdom	100	100	100	100	100
United States	86.9	85.5	83.7	83.6	90.9

Source: OECD (2020); European Observatory on Health Systems and Policies – country HiTs (various years); US National Health Statistics Reports (various years); Toth (2020b)

3.6 THE PROBLEM OF THE UNINSURED

The categories of uninsured residents vary depending on how the obligation of health insurance is regulated in the individual countries. National healthcare systems that do not guarantee health insurance coverage for the entire population can be subdivided into three groups. The first case is represented by countries without a mandatory health insurance scheme. The United States belongs to this category.

The second category of "nonuniversal" national systems includes countries that implement a mandatory health insurance scheme that does not apply to the entire resident population (Paris et al., 2016). This is the case for Austria, Belgium, France, Poland and Turkey. In these countries, part of the resident population is not obliged to subscribe to a social health insurance plan or a national insurance plan; therefore, if they do not voluntarily sign up for some coverage scheme (paying the related costs), they risk having no healthcare coverage.

Finally, the third category of countries is where all residents are formally required to pay healthcare contributions or to purchase a private policy. However, some individuals do not pay contributions (or premiums) on a regular basis, hence they are not guaranteed the health coverage required by government obligation (Baeten et al., 2018). Germany, Hungary and the Netherlands fall within this category.

Depending on the system adopted and the obligations enforced by each country, some specific categories of residents are more likely than others to be left without health insurance. In a number of countries, there may be no insurance coverage for some freelancers, atypical workers and precarious workers. This happens, for example, in Austria and Poland (Sagan et al., 2011; Bachner et al., 2018; Baeten et al., 2018). In other systems (including Austria, Germany and Turkey) the unemployed may not have adequate health insurance coverage, especially the long-term unemployed or those who are not eligible for unemployment benefits (Ökem and Çakar, 2015; Bachner et al., 2018; Johnson et al., 2018). Another category at risk is represented by those who work in the informal sector (Baeten et al., 2018). In several Eastern European countries (including Hungary and Poland), a considerable segment of the uninsured is of Roma ethnicity (Rechel and McKee, 2009; Sagan et al., 2011; FRA, 2012; Vilcu and

Mathauer, 2016): Those who do not have any identification documents or a permanent residence are usually excluded from the coverage offered by the mandatory scheme.

To complement this brief review on who the uninsured are, we should not forget to point out that in all the "nonuniversal" countries mentioned earlier, citizens without health insurance, however, receive a minimal package of medical care, usually provided by public facilities. In addition to emergency care, this minimal package often includes other benefits such as maternity coverage and/or the treatment (and prevention) of infectious diseases (Baeten et al., 2018). In all of the countries that have been examined, a healthcare "safety net" does exist, which provides emergency and minimal care to uninsured individuals as well (Paris et al., 2016).

3.6.1 The Problem of the Uninsured in OECD Countries and in the European Union

As the reader knows, in this book the health systems of twenty-seven OECD countries are compared, of which most are also members of the European Union. The cases considered in this paper, therefore, represent a large subset of both OECD and EU countries. Wanting to focus on the problem of uninsured in the most economically developed countries, it is advisable to temporarily make an exception, and extend the analysis to all OECD countries and to all member countries of the European Union. In this regard, it should be noted that the data reported here in reference to the breadth of coverage extends till the year 2019. For this reason, the composition of the European Union will be considered as being twenty-eight countries, thus, also including the United Kingdom (which formally left the EU at the end of January 2020). As for the OECD, the thirty-six countries that were members in 2019 will be considered here, except for Colombia which joined in 2020.

If we compare the prevalence of health insurance coverage in OECD countries (considered as a whole) and in the European Union (again as a whole), different trajectories emerge (Toth, 2020b). Over the last four decades, the thirty-six OECD member countries have registered a continuous evolution toward universal coverage. Compared to the mid-1970s, the number of countries with universal or "quasi-universal" coverage have indeed increased from nineteen to twenty-four, and the uninsured have decreased from 16.7 percent to the current 3.6 percent of the population. Conversely, if we consider the countries in the European Union,[3] the tendency toward universalism shows a fluctuating trend. Even in Europe, during the twenty-year period spanning from 1975 to 1995, the overall number of the uninsured dropped substantially, going from more than 28 million to just 1.5 million. Over the next twenty years (1995–2015), the uninsured European population has, nonetheless, started to increase again, and has currently reached 7.2 million.

We should reflect upon the circumstances that may have favored the drop in insurance coverage registered over the last two decades in EU countries. Two factors appear to have played a decisive role: (1) the healthcare reforms implemented in Eastern European countries following the fall of the Berlin Wall, and (2) the effects of the 2008 financial crisis.

Let us start from the first factor. Among the EU members, there are eleven Eastern European countries: Bulgaria, Croatia, the Czech Republic, Estonia, Hungary, Latvia, Lithuania, Poland, Romania, Slovakia and Slovenia. In the early 1990s, all of these countries provided – at least on paper – health insurance coverage for the entire population (Vilcu and Mathauer, 2016). Universal coverage was guaranteed by programs financed and managed directly by the national governments (Rechel and McKee, 2009). In the transition toward a democratic regime, all these countries reformed their healthcare systems – often in a radical way – leaving behind the socialist model in favor of some form of social health insurance or national insurance

---

[3] When referring to the insured and uninsured population in EU member countries over the past decades, the calculation includes all twenty-eight countries that were part of the European Union in 2019.

(Preker et al., 2002; Waters et al., 2008; Rechel and McKee, 2009). In some countries, these reforms led to a reduction in the rate of health insurance coverage for the population (Waters et al., 2008; Rechel and McKee, 2009; Vilcu and Mathauer, 2016). In 1985, all eleven Eastern European countries currently belonging to the EU guaranteed health insurance to 100 percent of the population. Thirty years later, only four countries out of eleven provided universal coverage.

The contraction in terms of insurance coverage in EU countries can also be attributed to a second factor, namely the global financial crisis, which erupted in 2008, although its effects spread primarily during the following years. As widely argued, the 2008 economic crisis had major repercussions on the healthcare systems of the more fragile economies (Karanikolos et al., 2013; Thomson et al., 2014; Kentikelenis, 2015; Morgan and Astolfi, 2015; Reeves et al., 2015).

Figures 3.3 and 3.4 can help determine to what extent the economic crisis has influenced the rate of health insurance coverage. Figure 3.3 reports the percentage of the uninsured in the OECD area from the year 2000 to 2019. Figure 3.4 shows the same data referring to the European Union member countries.

If we consider the thirty-six OECD countries as a whole (Figure 3.3), we can see how the number of the uninsured has gradually decreased over the last two decades. The trend follows a rather regular course, with the sole exception of the year 2009. The crisis appears to have had an impact for only one year, and as of 2010 the overall number of uninsured began to decrease again. From 2015 to 2019, the percentage of the uninsured remained almost stable.

The situation experienced in the European Union countries is rather different (Figure 3.4). In this case, no significant change in the rate of health insurance coverage was registered in the years immediately following the outbreak of the financial crisis. The effects of the crisis became evident as of 2011. Suddenly, in just one year, the uninsured rate doubled, peaking from 0.9 percent to 1.8 percent of the EU population. After a peak in 2013, the number of uninsured individuals dropped somewhat, also due to the reforms implemented

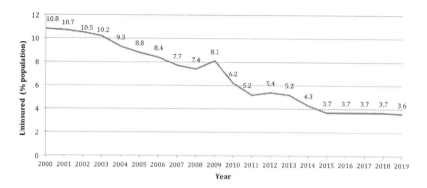

FIGURE 3.3 **The uninsured in the OECD countries (2000–2019).**
Source: OECD (2020); US Census Bureau (various years); US National Health Statistics Reports (various years); European Observatory on Health Systems and Policies – country HiTs (various years)

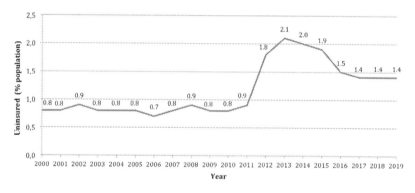

FIGURE 3.4 **The uninsured in European Union countries (2000–2019).**
Source: OECD (2020); OECD (2018); European Observatory on Health Systems and Policies (various years)

in Greece. Nevertheless, the number of individuals with no insurance coverage is currently twice as high as the figure recorded in 2006 (before the outbreak of the crisis).

Assessing the prevalence of health insurance coverage over the last four decades has thus brought to light two different trajectories. In OECD countries, there has been a constant reduction in the number of uninsured individuals over time, which has dropped from 16.7 percent in 1975 to the current 3.6 percent. Conversely, in EU countries, the trend has been discontinuous. Up to the mid-1990s, the number of uninsured decreased. In 1995, the uninsured in the EU-28 were as low as 0.3 percent of the population. However, a trend reversal took place and the number of the uninsured started to rise again from the second half of the 1990s, also due to the health reforms implemented in Eastern European countries. The percentage of the uninsured remained roughly stable for over a decade, from 2000 to 2011. During the two-year period of 2012–2013, the number of the uninsured doubled. At present, the uninsured in EU countries account for 1.4 percent of the overall population.

4 Healthcare Provision

Integrated versus Separated Systems

In the first three chapters, we have concentrated on the different systems for financing healthcare services, and the consequences in terms of expenditure (mandatory and voluntary) and coverage of the population they affect. In this chapter, we will deal with the provision system, that is, how the network of healthcare providers is organized. As stated above, providers are to be understood as individual professionals engaged in directly providing medical and healthcare services, as well as the facilities where such professionals carry out their services (hospitals, outpatient clinics, primary healthcare centers, private practices etc.).

In various studies and research (OECD, 1987; Rothgang et al., 2005; Lee et al., 2008; Wendt et al., 2009; Rothgang et al., 2010; Böhm et al., 2013), in order to classify healthcare delivery systems the traditional distinction between public and private providers is used. Within the private sector we can further distinguish between for-profit and not-for-profit providers (Rothgang et al., 2010; Böhm et al., 2013; Mossialos et al., 2017). Those who utilize this criteria evidently think that the providers' public or private nature deeply influences the behavior of the healthcare professionals and their relationship with patients.

The criterion of the providers' legal status is certainly a relevant element, but not the only one which can be used to describe how the provision system operates. In this chapter, an alternative criteria is proposed based on the method of integration of the healthcare provision system. To this end, we will present two rivaling models: on one hand, the integrated model and, on the other, the separated model (Toth, 2020a). We will proceed in a similar way to what has already been done regarding financing: The ideal production models will be presented first, then we will attempt to trace the individual, national systems.

Before we proceed, we ought to clarify an aspect so as to avoid dangerous misunderstandings. In the last three decades, much has been written on healthcare integration: Hundreds of reports and scientific articles have been published, and some journals have even been exclusively dedicated to further exploring this topic. Unfortunately, the tumultuous burgeoning of contributions on the subject has encouraged a lax and not very rigorous use of the concept of "integrated care." It is common opinion that this literary current lacks commonly shared definitions and conceptual coherence (Kodner and Spreeuwenberg, 2002; Suter et al., 2007; Thaldorf and Liberman, 2007; Kodner, 2009; Evans et al., 2013; Goodwin et al., 2017). Combing through the various contributions on the subject, we find that the concept of healthcare integration is applied to different levels of the system and has resulted in multiple subcategories. There is talk of "clinical integration," "functional integration," "organizational integration," "normative integration," "professional integration," "vertical integration," "horizontal integration," "system integration," "virtual integration" (Gillies et al., 1993; Conrad and Shortell, 1996; Robinson and Casalino, 1996; Burns and Pauly, 2002; Delnoij et al., 2002; Suter et al., 2007; Valentijn et al., 2013; Amelung et al., 2017). Yet, each of these labels is used differently, and there is no broad consensus as to how each concept ought to be used. Since, hereinafter, we will dwell on the concept of integration, an initial disambiguation is necessary. A fundamental boundary can be traced between organizational and clinical integration (Gillies et al., 1993; Shortell et al., 2000; Kodner, 2009; Valentijn et al., 2013). "Organizational" integration concerns the formal contractual agreements that bind healthcare providers together. "Clinical" integration, instead, evaluates to what extent different providers treating the same patient coordinate their efforts. Organizational integration, therefore, applies to the theoretical structure of the healthcare provision system. Clinical integration, instead, refers to the actual interaction of individual professionals, to the operational method used – in practice – to deliver care to patients. In this work we will deal solely with organizational integration, leaving out clinical integration. We should, in fact, point out that organizational integration and clinical integration are not necessarily related (Goodwin et al., 2017).

4.1 INTEGRATED MODEL VERSUS SEPARATED MODEL

If in terms of financing there were seven pure models (see Chapter 1), on the provision side there are essentially two archetypes from which to start off the discussion: the "separated" and the "integrated" models.

The "integrated" and the "separated" models should be considered ideal types, in the Weberian meaning of the term (Weber, 1922). Neither model expresses a principle that is in itself right or wrong; nor should we give them a preconceived positive or negative meaning. They simply represent two opposed models that embody two antipodal logics based on which the healthcare provision system can be structured. We will shortly see how the separated model seeks to coordinate the various healthcare providers through contractual relationships that are not necessarily stable and lasting. Conversely, the integrated model strives for coordination through internal organization, placing providers under a single proprietorship (Bazzoli et al., 1999).

4.1.1 The Separated Model

The separated model is characterized by: (1) utmost autonomy of the players; (2) contractual relationships between the parties; and (3) ample freedom of choice (both for patients and healthcare professionals). In such a model, the players are independent legal entities, which enjoy a high degree of autonomy. We should, therefore, expect a network of providers largely comprised of self-employed physicians and healthcare facilities (hospitals or outpatient clinics) that are independent from one another.

To a large extent, relationships between players are governed by contracts, which the counterparts are free to enter into at their sole discretion. Another peculiarity of the separated model is the great freedom of choice granted to the individual players: The parties meet and collaborate voluntarily, selecting one another on grounds of reputation and mutual trust. A minimum degree of pluralism is an essential prerequisite to ensuring that the players actually have power of choice. One must, indeed, always have the possibility to pick from several counterparts (i.e., patients should be able to choose from several specialists, physicians should be in a position to refer their patients to several hospital facilities and so on).

4.1.2   The Integrated Model

Unlike the separated model, which – in many respects – recalls a market system, the integrated model is more similar to an internal organization. A distinctive trait of the integrated model lies in the fact that the players are affiliated with the same organization; this entails adhering to a single role structure, supporting a shared culture and abiding by common rules. Over time, all these factors should lead the players to become increasingly homogeneous, and to share – at least in part – the same objectives. Internal cohesion is also favored by stable employment relationships between the organization and its employees. Relationships between the parties are, therefore, not governed by voluntary and occasional work contracts, as is the case with the separated model, but rather through the hierarchical structure and the internal policies of the organization. The latter define the form of cooperation between players, who are no longer free to choose their counterparty. The relationships, therefore, tend to be biunique, mandatory and permanent.

Compared with the separated model, the integrated model has opposite characteristics: (1) the players are not independent entities but are affiliated within the same organization; (2) relationships between the parties are governed by permanent employment contracts; and (3) freedom of choice is severely limited.

4.1.3 The Five Dimensions

Given their opposite characteristics, the integrated model and the separated model lend themselves to be conceived as the extremes of a "continuum" along which the twenty-seven national cases contemplated in this research can be placed, depending on their closeness to one ideal model or another.

In order to bring into focus the main differences between the integrated model and the separated model (Table 4.1), the use of the following dimensions is proposed:

(1) insurer–provider integration;
(2) primary and secondary care integration;
(3) the presence or absence of gatekeeping mechanisms;
(4) the greater or lesser freedom of patients in choosing their providers;
(5) the individual or group practice of general practitioners.

Each of these five dimensions will be analyzed separately in the following sections. We can, however, already point out that they not

Table 4.1 *Integrated model versus separated model*

Integrated model		Separated model
Insurers and providers are affiliated with the same organization	*Insurer–provider integration*	Insurers and providers are independent entities
Primary and secondary care is provided by the same organizations	*Primary and secondary care integration*	Primary and secondary care is provided by separate entities
Mandatory	*Gatekeeping mechanisms*	Discretionary
Limited. The patient uses the providers indicated by the insurer	*Patient's freedom of choice*	Extensive. The patient can choose any provider
Group practice	*Organization of general practitioners*	Solo practice

Source: Toth (2020a)

only involve the relationships existing among the various providers but also those established between the latter and the additional two actors of the so-called health triangle (see the Introduction), namely the insurers and the patients. The first dimension concerns the relationships between providers and insurers. Freedom of choice and, to some extent, gatekeeping have to do with the relationships between providers and their patients. The other dimensions are applicable to the relationships between different providers.

4.2   INSURER–PROVIDER INTEGRATION

The first dimension used to distinguish the different provision systems is a form of "vertical integration" (Shortell et al., 1994; Burns and Pauly, 2002; Thaldorf and Liberman, 2007), involving, in particular, the relationships between insurers and providers.

In integrated systems, health insurance and healthcare service provision are managed by the same organizations. In separated systems, they are instead dealt with by different, formally independent entities. In other words, in the "integrated" model, the entities that act as insurers (therefore, the public service, nonprofit sickness funds or private insurance companies) have their own healthcare facilities and staff, and through them provide most of the services required by their registered members. In such a model, insurer and provider thus coincide, as they form one single organization.

Conversely, in the "separated" model, the insurers do not have their own hospitals or outpatient clinics, nor do they employ medical and healthcare personnel. Healthcare is provided by third parties, and the insurers are only committed to reimbursing them. Hence, there is a substantial difference between the two models. In the separated model, relationships between providers and insurers are entertained by distinct entities and are regulated by contracts, while in the integrated model, exchange and production decisions are made within the same organization through a hierarchical structure.

What are, at least in principle, the advantages of these two organizational solutions? A high level of vertical integration should ensure greater insurance control over supplier activity. Thus, not only the transaction costs but also the production costs would be kept under control due to the lower friction between the parties and the possibility of achieving economies of scale and purpose (Evans, 1981; Robinson and Casalino, 1996; Bazzoli et al., 1999). On the other hand, the separate setup has the advantage of giving the actors broad autonomy of action and freedom of choice, as well as giving the system greater flexibility and competition (Robinson and Casalino, 1996; Bazzoli et al., 1999).

Let us now assess the level of "insurer–provider integration" within the twenty-seven national healthcare systems analyzed in this book. To divide the countries into separate classes, we will adopt the following operational criterion. A national system is to be considered "integrated" if the majority of physicians (general practitioners, outpatient and inpatient specialists) are affiliated with organizations that – in addition to provision activities – also provide insurance against health risks. Those systems where the majority of physicians work autonomously or within organizations that do not provide insurance coverage are instead considered as "separated."

Ten countries fall under the definition of an "integrated" system: Denmark, Finland, Ireland, Italy, New Zealand, Norway, Portugal, Spain, Sweden and the United Kingdom.

Conversely, the healthcare systems of Australia, Austria, Belgium, Canada, Czech Republic, France, Germany, Hungary, Japan, the Netherlands, Poland, the Republic of Korea, Switzerland, Turkey and the United States are "separated" systems.

Greece and Israel should be considered mixed systems since the providers are partly integrated and partly separate from their respective insurers (see Chapter 5).

Considering the two classes identified above, the reader could expect the systems with a insurer–provider integration to be those in which there is a single insurance entity (universalist single-payer systems) and, vice versa, the separate systems to be those with a multiplicity of insurers (social health insurance and private insurance systems). Yet, this is not necessarily true. Systems such as those implemented in Australia or Canada, for instance, do not rely on integration between insurer and providers, albeit their single insurance scheme, since physicians are reimbursed by the public insurance program, but do not have an employment relationship with Medicare.

In countries such as the United States, Switzerland and Israel, we find examples of the opposite phenomenon. Insurers and providers can be integrated even within a system characterized by a multiplicity of competing insurers. Some American and Swiss Health Maintenance Organizations (HMOs), similar to the Israeli health funds (such as Clalit), actually own some healthcare facilities (hospitals and outpatient clinics) and have medical and healthcare personnel on their payroll, with whom they guarantee an ample range of basic to highly specialized services (De Pietro et al., 2015; Rosen et al., 2015; Toth, 2016a).

4.3 PRIMARY/SECONDARY CARE INTEGRATION

The second dimension that differentiates the integrated from the separated model concerns the relationships between providers of primary and secondary care. Although the boundaries between these two spheres of activity are often blurred, "primary" care is understood as the basic procedures performed in response to the most common illnesses and problems. To a large extent, it is provided by general practitioners who follow the patient from a continuous and broad-spectrum perspective (Starfield, 1998; Starfield et al., 2005; Boerma, 2006; Valentijn et al., 2013). Primary care is provided in the consulting rooms of general practitioners, in outpatient clinics located in the area and, at times, even at the patient's home.

"Secondary" care is medical care of a specialized nature. Unlike primary procedures, secondary care requires advanced knowledge and more sophisticated equipment. Consequently, it is provided primarily in hospitals, by medical specialists who have a more sectorial approach to illnesses and whose relationships with patients are occasional and usually limited to single pathological episodes (Starfield, 1998; WHO, 2008; Blank et al., 2018).

An aspect peculiar to the "integrated" model is the close coordination that exists between primary and secondary care providers, ensured by the fact that general practitioners and hospital specialists are affiliated with the same organization. In other words, integrated systems revolve around organizations whose scope is to provide an entire range of medical and healthcare services, from basic to specialist levels.

Conversely, in the "separated" model, primary and secondary care are largely disjointed spheres of activity: Primary and hospital services are managed by different, independent entities. As for integration between insurers and providers, also in this case the discriminating factor between separated and integrated systems is whether or not the providers are affiliated to the same organization. To be more precise, the criterion by which to classify the individual national healthcare systems will be the following. We will consider those systems which meet both of the following requisites as being "integrated": (1) the majority of general practitioners work for organizations that also provide secondary care; (2) the majority of hospital doctors are affiliated with organizations that also provide primary care. In all other cases, the systems will be considered as being "separated."

Based on this classification criterion, Finland, Greece, Portugal, Spain and Sweden have integrated systems.

A separate category includes Denmark, Ireland, Italy, New Zealand, Norway and the United Kingdom. These six cases are formally less integrated than the others mentioned, in one respect, that is, in these countries, general practitioners are not employees of the public healthcare service, but they are self-employed professionals contracted to the public health service. Given the ensuing commitment and constraints, the contractual relationship creates a preferential and long-term bond between physicians and the public service. This bond is perhaps not comparable to an employment relationship, but is certainly quite distant from short-term contracts. We, therefore, propose that these five countries be regarded as "quasi-integrated."

Countries in which "separated" systems apply are: Australia, Austria, Belgium, Canada, the Czech Republic, France, Germany, Hungary, Israel, Japan, the Netherlands, Poland, the Republic of Korea, Switzerland, Turkey and the United States.

Some studies reveal that, in recent decades, and even in countries classified as "separated" in this discussion, there is a general trend toward integration between primary and secondary care (Rico et al., 2003; WHO, 2008; Amelung et al., 2017; European Commission, 2017).

4.4 GATEKEEPING

The relationships between patients, general practitioners and specialists vary depending on the presence or absence of a formalized gatekeeping mechanism (Delnoij et al., 2000; Rothgang et al., 2005; Calnan et al., 2006; Kroneman et al., 2006; Wendt, 2009; Reibling and Wendt, 2012). Over the past few decades, in most countries belonging to the European Union and the OECD, policy makers have tended to favor and reinforce gatekeeping mechanisms (Reibling and Wendt, 2012; European Commission, 2017). Let us try to understand the reasons behind this trend.

Gatekeeping is the principle by which access to specialist healthcare is possible only through referral by general practitioners. This principle influences many aspects of the provision system: the patient's freedom of choice; the relationship between family doctors and their patients; the overall demand for specialist services; as well as the connection between primary and secondary care.

In a mandatory gatekeeping system, the general practitioner (GP) is the patient's "primary contact" with the health system, with an exception being made for emergency cases for which citizens can go directly to the emergency room; family doctors are called upon to provide a wide range of primary care services and refer patients to specialists for all examinations and procedures that do not fall within their sphere of competence. The GP, therefore, plays a fundamental role in sorting and filtering healthcare needs. On one hand, the GP has to recommend the most suitable specialist to the patient following an initial diagnosis. On the other hand, GPs must ensure access to specialist care to only those patients who have a real need for it.

The gatekeeper physician is also assigned an additional task: advising and guiding patients throughout their care process within the health system. In essence, the mission of the general practitioner would be to remedy the disconnect that easily occurs between different healthcare providers (Kodner, 2009). It is a commonplace situation, that of being examined by a number of different specialists, none of whom have an overview of the entire diagnostic and therapeutic process undertaken by the patient. Hence, the family doctor should coordinate the different specialist services, ensuring continuity of treatment.

Depending on the extent of his functions, the figure of the gatekeeper doctor lends itself to two different interpretations, one of a more limited scope and the other of a broader scope. The more limited interpretation, above all, underlines the role of the family doctor as a guardian of the appropriateness of the treatments. Hence the image of the "gatekeeper," that is, of one who controls the entrance gates to the "health care fortress" (Willems, 2001). Gatekeeping, for this reason, is considered by many to be the most effective tool for reducing inappropriate demand for specialist services. The second interpretation goes beyond mere checking and sorting tasks, and instead, highlights the function of "integrator" that the family doctor is called to perform (Calnan et al., 2006). The latter acts as a connecting element between primary and secondary care.

If applied correctly, the gatekeeping mechanism promises a plurality of benefits in that it reduces unnecessary specialist visits; promotes continuity of care; and strengthens coordination between primary and specialist care. This is only in theory, since in practice it is easy to imagine that the picture can be less than idyllic. In many systems the filtering done by the general practitioner is easily circumvented by the patients, who resort directly to the emergency room. Another way to get around gatekeeping is the so-called inverse referral (Saltman and Figueras, 1997). Instead of going to the specialist on the advice of the general practitioner, in many countries it is common practice to contact a paid specialist directly, then the general practitioner is consulted only afterward, and then formally prescribed as already recommended by the specialist.

That gatekeeping has both advantages and disadvantages also emerges from the research which has aimed to evaluate the effects produced by the introduction of this mechanism (Garrido et al., 2011). These studies agree on the effectiveness of gatekeeping regarding the rationing of services. In general, it leads to a reduction in the demand for specialist care, which, in turn, translates into a lower cost of the provision system as a whole (Martin et al., 1989; Delnoij et al., 2000). However, it is also true that gatekeeping limits the patient's freedom of choice (Kroneman et al., 2006) and the quality of care does not always increase (Halm et al., 1997).

Health systems are, therefore, divided between those that adopt the principle of gatekeeping, and those that grant "direct access" to secondary care (Kroneman et al., 2006). The presence of a mandatory gatekeeping mechanism for the majority of the population, and for most of secondary care, is typical of the "integrated" model. The absence of mandatory and formalized gatekeeping mechanisms is quite typical of the "separated" model.

Countries with mandatory gatekeeping are: Australia, Denmark, Finland, Ireland, Israel, Italy, the Netherlands, New Zealand, Norway, Portugal, Spain and the United Kingdom.

There are, by contrast, healthcare systems in which most of the population has free access to specialist care without any referral by the general practitioner. To avoid any doubt, we should immediately point out that some form of gatekeeping exists in these countries also. It is simply not mandatory, and in any event it does not apply to most of the population, nor to most of specialized care procedures. The countries belonging to this second group are Austria, Belgium, the Czech Republic, France, Germany, Greece, Japan, the Republic of Korea, Sweden, Switzerland, Turkey and the United States.

In countries such as the United States and Switzerland, the gatekeeping mechanism is only implemented by some insurance plans (like HMOs). However, individual users are free to subscribe or to not subscribe to these insurance plans. In countries such as Belgium, France and Germany, in order to promote some forms of gatekeeping – which are nonetheless still discretionary – economic incentives are granted to patients who access secondary care following referral by their general practitioner.

Canada, Hungary and Poland raise classification issues, and will thus be considered as mixed systems. In Canada, gatekeeping is not formally defined as mandatory, but the majority of the population behaves as if it were. The Canadian system provides for effective economic incentives in favor of gatekeeping, making it convenient for patients. In other words, in most Canadian provinces, general practitioners act largely as gatekeepers (Marchildon, 2013; Mossialos et al., 2017). In Poland, it is customary for general practitioners to act as gatekeepers even if referral by a general practitioner is required only for a portion of specialized care. We should also recall that some categories of Polish patients are not required to present a referral by the general practitioner, and so they can access specialist care directly (Sagan et al., 2011). Also in Hungary, a referral from the family doctor is formally requested for only some specialist services (Gaál et al., 2011; Kringos et al., 2015).

4.5 PATIENTS' FREEDOM OF CHOICE FOR PROVIDERS

Healthcare provision systems can be distinguished according to the greater or lesser freedom of choice granted to patients (Reibling and Wendt, 2012; Blank et al., 2018). A distinctive feature of the "separated" model is the ample freedom given to patients to choose the physician and the hospital that will provide healthcare services. The citizens – if covered by an insurance scheme – may freely choose from all providers operating throughout the country.

Conversely, in the "integrated" model, the patient's freedom of choice is somewhat limited. The physician and hospital are identified by the insurer (the insurance company, the sickness fund or the public service) and the patient can, at most, choose from a subset of available providers.

As we will see in Chapter 7, during the last three decades we have witnessed a generalized tendency toward a strengthening of the freedom of choice granted to patients in OECD countries (Saltman and Figueras, 1998; Toth, 2010a; Reibling and Wendt, 2012; Victoor et al., 2012).

Where granted, the patient's right to freedom of choice may be exercised at different levels. It may, indeed, relate to the general practitioner, the medical specialist, the hospital and also the individual physician within the chosen healthcare facility.

As for the choice of a general practitioner, there is no need for lengthy consideration. The right to choose one's family doctor is, in fact, recognized – at least in theory[1] – in all of the twenty-seven countries examined in this study (Kringos et al., 2015; OECD, 2016a). It is, however, worth dwelling on the greater or lesser freedom accorded to patients in the selection of a specialist and a hospital. On this front, the differences among the various health systems are noteworthy.

There are systems where the choice of provider is essentially "free," meaning that patients have the right to choose from all the specialists and hospitals in the country, whether public or private.

---

[1] Although formally recognized, in some countries the freedom of choice of the GP is, in fact, limited by two factors. The first is the different concentration of doctors between urban and rural or mountain areas. In the latter, the circle of professionals from which patients can choose is generally more restricted. The second factor is the maximum number of patients that a family doctor can take charge of. In many countries, in fact, a ceiling is set beyond which a doctor cannot accept new patients. Citizens' freedom of choice is then restricted to professionals who have not already reached this maximum limit (i.e., the least requested).

The countries where insured citizens can freely choose their healthcare providers are: Australia, Austria, Belgium, Canada, Czech Republic, France, Germany, Japan, the Netherlands, Norway, the Republic of Korea, Sweden and Turkey. In some of these countries it is not always possible to choose the individual physician once the hospital of choice has been determined (OECD, 2016a). Despite this, patients in the aforementioned countries enjoy an extensive freedom of choice. In the Netherlands, the choice of provider is, in part, limited for only those citizens who voluntarily subscribe to an "inkind policy" (Kroneman et al., 2016).

On the contrary, there are countries where the freedom enjoyed by the majority of patients is somewhat limited. In these systems, patients can only choose from healthcare providers that are "vertically integrated" or who have entered into a service supply agreement with their insurer. Some private insurance companies, for example, impose on the insured a list of "preferred providers" with which they have executed a specific agreement. Programs funded through general taxation often limit patient choice to public providers and, at most, to private providers who are under contract with the public service (hence, only some private providers).

The countries where the patients' right of freedom of choice is somehow limited are: Denmark, Finland, Greece, Hungary, Ireland, Israel, Italy, New Zealand, Poland, Portugal, Spain, Switzerland, the United Kingdom and the United States. In all of these countries, for one reason or another, the majority of the population cannot freely choose a hospital or a specialist for the health treatments they need. This is confirmed by the fact that each of these systems includes a wide array of private providers whose services, when requested, impose on the patient additional costs, if not the full cost of the service.

Many countries, therefore, recognize freedom of choice (total or partial) of a doctor and a hospital as a patient's right. It is good to specify that this right – affirmed on paper – can then, in practice, be to some extent disregarded. Long waiting lists threaten patients' actual freedom of choice especially in public health services. Because of this, patients often find themselves forced to give up their favorite provider, turning to lesser-qualified specialists or private facilities for which an additional price must be paid. Waiting lists aside, limitations on patients' freedom of choice can take different forms. In some countries (including Hungary, New Zealand, Portugal and Switzerland), the choice of a hospital may be limited only to facilities that fall within the patient's area of residence. Looking at the United States, it is widely believed that the American system guarantees citizens, once insured, great freedom of choice of the provider; but this is not the case, at least for the vast majority. Of course, in the United States it is possible to take out insurance policies that allow those who subscribe to them the maximum freedom of choice. These insurance schemes – traditional "indemnity plans" – are, however, very expensive and are underwritten by a small minority of the population (Kaiser Family Foundation, 2019). Most American families, on the other hand, have insurance packages that constrain the patient's freedom of choice. The patient has the right to only choose from doctors who work under contract with the insurance plan. Patients are required to pay extra if they intend to go to a specialist or to a hospital facility that is not included in the network of "preferred providers."

4.6 GENERAL PRACTITIONERS: SOLO VERSUS GROUP PRACTICE

Let us now look into the manner in which general practitioners are organized. There are, again, two rival models. In the first model, GPs practice separately, each in their own consulting room. This is referred to as "solo practice." In the second model, general practitioners are associated (group practice), sharing common spaces and equipment. This second model expresses – at least on a structural level – a higher degree of integration with respect to solo practice. We can, therefore, consider solo practice to be typical in the separated model, whereas group practice exemplifies the integrated model.

The main advantage of group practice is to be found, not so much in the economic benefit of sharing the expenses with colleagues, but rather in the possibility of expanding – through team work – the range and quality of services offered. The members of an associated study can, in fact, consult with each other in relation to the most problematic cases; the tasks can be divided, each developing a different specialization; they can buy equipment that a professional alone could not afford; they can agree on shifts, so as to extend the opening hours. Obviously, we should not expect that it is enough to set up an associated medical practice to achieve all the advantages listed above. In practice it often happens that doctors simply share the consulting room, without any other form of cooperation (Boon et al., 2004).

To somewhat synthesize the issue, we can define solo practice as the traditional way of organizing primary care. Conversely, group practice is the emerging model, which has been gradually supplanting the traditional model for at least twenty years now (Rico et al., 2003; Saltman et al., 2006; Damiani et al., 2013; European Commission, 2017). Indeed, among GPs, group practice has become the most common mode in most OECD countries (OECD, 2016a). Australia, Canada, Denmark, Finland, France, Greece, Ireland, Israel, Italy, the Netherlands, New Zealand, Norway, Poland, Portugal, Spain, Sweden, Turkey, the United Kingdom and the United States are all countries where GPs practice mainly in an associated form.

Healthcare systems in which solo practice still prevails are a minority. They are operative in Austria, Belgium, Czech Republic, Germany, Hungary, Japan, the Republic of Korea and Switzerland.

Let us make one last reflection on the subject of group practice. In some countries, (Finland, Greece, Israel, Spain, Portugal, Sweden and Turkey) primary care is organized in primary care centers. The latter differ from other forms of group practice because of their multidisciplinary nature. Indeed, these facilities comprise not only general practitioners, but also other professionals including medical

Table 4.2 *Integration versus separation: national cases compared*

	Insurer–provider integration	Primary/secondary care integration	Gate keeping	Patient's freedom of choice	Solo versus group practice
Australia	Separated	Separated	Yes	Free	Group
Austria	Separated	Separated	No	Free	Solo
Belgium	Separated	Separated	No	Free	Solo
Canada	Separated	Separated	Mixed	Free	Group
Czech Rep.	Separated	Separated	No	Free	Solo
Denmark	Integrated	Quasi-integrated	Yes	Limited	Group
Finland	Integrated	Integrated	Yes	Limited	Group
France	Separated	Separated	No	Free	Group
Germany	Separated	Separated	No	Free	Solo
Greece	Mixed	Integrated	No	Limited	Group
Hungary	Separated	Separated	Mixed	Limited	Solo
Ireland	Integrated	Quasi-integrated	Yes	Limited	Group
Israel	Mixed	Separated	Yes	Limited	Group
Italy	Integrated	Quasi-integrated	Yes	Limited	Group
Japan	Separated	Separated	No	Free	Solo

Table 4.2 (*cont.*)

	Insurer–provider integration	Primary/secondary care integration	Gate keeping	Patient's freedom of choice	Solo versus group practice
Korea	Separated	Separated	No	Free	Solo
Netherlands	Separated	Separated	Yes	Free	Group
New Zealand	Integrated	Quasi-integrated	Yes	Limited	Group
Norway	Integrated	Quasi-integrated	Yes	Free	Group
Poland	Separated	Separated	Mixed	Limited	Group
Portugal	Integrated	Integrated	Yes	Limited	Group
Spain	Integrated	Integrated	Yes	Limited	Group
Sweden	Integrated	Integrated	No	Free	Group
Switzerland	Separated	Separated	No	Limited	Solo
Turkey	Separated	Separated	No	Free	Group
United Kingdom	Integrated	Quasi-integrated	Yes	Limited	Group
United States	Separated	Separated	No	Limited	Group

Source: Kringos et al. (2015); OECD (2016a); Toth (2020a)

4.7 THE INTEGRATION-SEPARATION CONTINUUM

specialists, nurses, physiotherapists and auxiliary personnel. Precisely because of their ability to allow different professional figures to work together within the same structure, these multidisciplinary centers represent the organizational solution that should best embody the principle of integration.

If we combine the five dimensions reviewed in the foregoing section, we can arrange the twenty-seven national cases along a "continuum" that has the integrated model and the separated model at the two opposite poles. To do this, it is sufficient to compare the properties of each single national system (Table 4.2) with the five elements which characterize each of the two models (see Table 4.1).

The placement of countries along the Integration-Separation continuum is obtained by introducing a simple "integration index," the value of which may vary between 0 and 5. Zero indicates maximum separation, while 5 stands for maximum integration. The value 1 was attributed to each of the five characteristics of the integrated model. The value 0 was assigned to each characteristic element of the separated model. With respect to the second dimension, pertaining to the relationship between primary and secondary care, the countries classified as "quasi-integrated" were assigned the value 0.5. In relation to the first dimension, (the integration of insurer-provider) and to the third (gatekeeping), the "mixed" cases were also given half a point. For each country, the overall integration index is given by the sum of the scores related to the five dimensions analyzed.

In Figure 4.1, the twenty-seven countries are listed in descending order of organizational integration. At the top we find the national systems that are closest to the ideal of the integrated model, while at the bottom are the countries that primarily adhere to the separated model.

As shown in Figure 4.1, healthcare systems that more closely embody the principles of the integrated model are those

HEALTHCARE PROVISION: INTEGRATED VERSUS SEPARATED SYSTEMS

Integration index		
5	Finland, Portugal, Spain	
4.5	Denmark, Ireland, Italy, New Zealand, United Kingdom	Highly integrated systems
4		
3.5	Greece, Israel, Norway	Moderately integrated systems
3	Sweden	
2.5	Poland	Mixed
2	Australia, Netherlands, United States	Moderately separated systems
1.5	Canada, Hungary	
1	France, Switzerland, Turkey	
0.5		Highly separated systems
0	Austria, Belgium, Czech Republic, Germany, Japan, Republic of Korea	

FIGURE 4.1 **The Integration Index:** twenty-seven **countries compared**

implemented in Finland, Portugal and Spain. Indeed, these three countries have all five of the characteristics found in the ideal model. Conversely, the separated model is rather well represented by countries such as Austria, Belgium, the Czech Republic, Germany, Japan and the Republic of Korea. These six national systems indeed have all the distinctive features of the separated model. Apart from these pure cases, the other countries considered in this study are spread over the intermediate positions included between the two extremes.

Although the countries are scattered along the continuum, it is not difficult to divide the national healthcare systems analyzed in this work into different classes. The first group of countries comprises Finland, Portugal, Spain, Denmark, Ireland, Italy, New Zealand and the United Kingdom. This eight countries are to be considered "highly integrated" in that they have at least four of the five characteristics of the integrated model (they have, therefore, an integration index value greater than or equal to 4).

Four other countries have at least three of the five characteristics of the integrated model. They are Greece, Israel, Norway and

Sweden. To differentiate them from the first seven, we might label these five countries as "moderately integrated."

At the opposite end, we can identify a group consisting of Austria, Belgium, the Czech Republic, Germany, Japan, the Republic of Korea, France, Switzerland and Turkey. These nine countries are to be considered "highly separated" as they have at least four distinctive features of the separated model.

Similar to what was done previously, we could identify a group of countries that can be categorized as "moderately separated" due to the fact that they have at least three (but not four) elements that are characteristic of the separated model. These countries are Canada, Hungary, Australia, the Netherlands and the United States.

The only country left, Poland, is to be considered as a perfect mixed system, since it combines – in roughly equal parts – some typical features of the integrated model with characteristics of the separated model.

The reader should be made aware that the classification illustrated in the foregoing section is a simplification of an otherwise overly complex scenario. For each of the five dimensions analyzed herein, the individual national systems were in fact classified based on the country's "prevailing" organizational model, namely the model used for the majority of the population and for most healthcare services. The provision systems of each country have, therefore, been considered as homogeneous within themselves. But we acknowledge this to be a simplification: As stated in Chapter 2, the individual national systems are segmented into different subsystems, and the latter can present different levels of organizational integration. Let us take the United States as an example. Within the American system there coexist subsystems with a high level of organizational integration (such as the Veterans Health Administration or the staff-model HMOs) and other subsystems that are in large part separated (like the Medicaid program or the traditional "indemnity plans"). As a further example, we can state that in most countries with a universalist model it is possible to refer to private providers by spending out-of-pocket. In these countries, the public provision system is usually more integrated, whereas the private system more closely resembles the separated model.

These examples above serve to confirm that, similar to what happens in financing systems, the systems for the provision of healthcare services can also be "segmented." And the different subsystems can present different degrees of organizational integration.

In closing this chapter, it is opportune to recall what has already been discussed in the previous pages. The classification proposed does not pertain to the clinical integration of the different healthcare systems, but rather to organizational integration. The integrated and separated models embody two different and rivaling strategies on how to structure, as a whole, the healthcare provision system. These strategies refer to the formal relationships between the different healthcare providers.

A high level of "organizational" integration does not necessarily imply a higher level of "clinical" integration. It may happen that two health professionals belonging to the same organization and involved in delivery of healthcare services to the same patient do not coordinate their activities. In such a situation, organizational integration is not matched by clinical integration. Of course, the opposite situation may arise, in that two professionals who are either self-employed or working with different companies may, however, coordinate their respective activities for a patient's care. In the latter case, there will be clinical integration, despite the absence of organizational integration. As mentioned above, organizational and clinical integration are two distinct properties, and this research only deals with the former.

5 Financing and Provision

Four Families and a Few Outliers

In the first two chapters, and in particular in Table 2.1, the twenty-seven countries covered by this study were classified according to the prevailing financing model. In Chapter 4 (see Figure 4.1 for a summary), the national healthcare delivery systems have been cataloged with reference to their degree of integration/separation. The dimensions of funding and healthcare provision can now be combined with each other (see Table 5.1).

From the intersection of these two dimensions, four families of healthcare systems stand out: two large ones (each containing a dozen countries) and two smaller ones. The two larger families reflect the traditional contrast between "Bismarck" systems and "Beveridge" systems (OECD, 1987; Rothgang et al., 2005; Wendt et al., 2009; Freeman and Frisina, 2010; Blank et al., 2018). One of the two largest families is, in fact, made up of the Social Health Insurance countries in that all these countries (with the partial exception of Poland[1]) have a separate provision system. The other larger family is made up of "integrated" universalist systems. Healthcare systems with these characteristics are properly defined as National Health Service (NHS). The National Health Service should, therefore, be understood as a single-payer public system, financed according to the universalist model, which directly delivers the treatments through its own structures and staff.

The two smaller families are made up, respectively, of countries that have a "separated" universalist system and countries that adopt

---

[1] Poland, as seen in Chapter 4, has a provision system that is exactly halfway between the integrated and the separated models. In Table 5.1 the Polish system is, as a whole, considered as being separated, because it does not present elements of integration between insurer and provider, nor between primary and secondary care.

Table 5.1 *Financing and provision*

		Provision system	
		Integrated	Separated
Prevalent financing model	*Universalist*	Denmark, Finland, Ireland, Italy, New Zealand, Norway, Portugal, Spain, Sweden, United Kingdom	Australia, Canada
	SHI		Austria, Belgium, Czech Republic, France, (Germany), Hungary, Japan, Korea, Poland, Turkey
	Mandatory residence insurance		(Germany), Netherlands, Switzerland
	Others/Mixed systems	Greece, Israel, United States	

the mandatory residence insurance model. The latter all have a separated delivery system.

From the four families just outlined, three countries are excluded (Greece, Israel and the United States) due to their mixed and peculiar characteristics, therefore, it seems appropriate to treat them as "outliers."

In the following sections, the four families of healthcare systems, as well as the outlier countries, will be presented separately. For each cluster of countries, both elements of similarity and differences across countries belonging to the same family will be highlighted.

5.1 THE SHI COUNTRIES

Of the twenty-seven countries analyzed in this study, there are ten that belong to the Social Health Insurance family. Germany is also included in this group, although the German system – as has already been anticipated in the second chapter, and as will be repeated even later – is a hybrid system that combines SHI and mandatory residence insurance. The other nine SHI countries are: Austria, Belgium, the Czech Republic, France, Hungary, Japan, the Republic of Korea, Poland and Turkey.

From a geopolitical point of view, seven of these ten countries are located in Central (or West Central) Europe, and are adjacent to each other. To these are added Turkey and the two Far East countries considered in this paper (Japan and Korea).

As we have already had occasion to argue in Chapter 2, the original Bismarckian model of the late nineteenth century has gone through – over the decades, and in the various countries that have been inspired by it – many reworkings. There are, therefore, various versions of the Social Health Insurance model. The SHI systems differ from each other in a plurality of aspects, which we will try to briefly review.

5.1.1   Single Fund versus Multiple Funds

A first, yet fundamental, dividing line can be drawn in relation to the number of sickness funds operating in the country. There are, in fact, two subgroups in the SHI countries which should be kept separate: (1) the systems in which only one sickness fund operates that is unique for the whole country; (2) the systems in which multiple funds operate. It is evident that the choice of having a single national fund is a "strong" variant, which distorts the original Bismarckian model. In fact, the latter is, by definition (see Chapter 1) multi-payer.

There are four SHI countries where a single sickness fund operates: Hungary, Korea, Poland and Turkey. In the majority of these countries (Korea, Poland, Turkey), the classic formula of multiple funds was first tried out, but later it was preferred to proceed – by legislative means – to the unification of the many previously operating sickness funds (Yıldırım and Yıldırım, 2011; Ökem and Çakar, 2015; Lee et al., 2017; Polak et al., 2019).

Six out of ten countries adopt an SHI system in which multiple funds coexist. However, the number of funds varies significantly from one country to another. The most funds operate in Japan, where there are more than three thousand (Sakamoto et al., 2018; Kato et al., 2019). In Germany, there are more than a hundred *krankenkassen* (OECD, 2019b). In Belgium there are just more than fifty (Thomson et al., 2013). In Austria there are eighteen funds, while in France there are about fifteen (Bachner et al., 2018; Rodwin, 2018). There are currently seven sickness funds in the Czech Republic (Alexa et al., 2015).

5.1.2 Funds: Freedom of Choice

A second relevant dimension concerns freedom to choose or to not choose the sickness fund from which to be assisted. This option of choice – strictly speaking – can only exist in systems in which multiple funds operate. In Austria, France and Japan, citizens have no choice and are automatically assigned to a specific sickness fund. This means that the sickness funds do not compete with each other. In Belgium, the Czech Republic and Germany, SHI members are given the freedom to choose a health insurance fund, and the funds compete with each other to attract clients.

It should be noted that in the vast majority of SHI countries, opting out is not contemplated. This opportunity (i.e., the possibility of not joining the mandatory scheme and of subscribing, instead, to a substitutive private policy) is granted only in Germany and Austria, and only to certain categories (which constitute a minority of the population). In all other countries, opting out is not allowed.

5.1.3 Risk Adjustment Mechanisms

In systems where multiple funds operate, the presence or absence of a risk compensation mechanism among insurers is relevant. In several countries (including Austria, Belgium, the Czech Republic and Germany) an explicit risk adjustment mechanism redistributes funds. The principle of large-scale risk sharing is inherent and, therefore, not necessary in systems with a single national fund in which the risk pool already coincides with the entire population.

5.1.4 Occupational, Territorial and Corporate Funds

A distinctive feature of SHI systems – also in this case, the distinction makes sense only for systems with multiple funds – is the criteria according to which workers are assigned to the respective sickness funds. In general, membership of a fund is established on the basis of the profession performed or the place of residence.

In France, both professional funds (most of them) and territorial funds (in Alsace and Moselle) operate. In Austria, Germany and Japan, in addition to occupational and territorial funds, we also find some corporate sickness funds. In the Czech Republic there is only one company fund (the automobile manufacturer Škoda), while the others are based on employment (Alexa et al., 2015). The Belgian system is particular since the mutual funds – from which workers have the right to choose – are also connoted on the basis of political or religious orientation. The Belgian funds are, in fact, grouped into five "alliances": Christian, socialist, neutral, liberal and the "free and professional" mutualities (Gerkens and Merkur, 2010).

5.1.5 Calculation of Contributions

An important feature of SHI systems, which concerns both systems with multiple funds and those with a unitary fund, regards the amount of mandatory contributions to be paid to sickness funds, and how they are divided between employees and employers.

Let us start with the amount of the contribution. As stated in Chapter 1, the distinctive characteristic of the contributions of SHI is that they are calculated in proportion to earned income. In most countries, the contribution rate is the same for all funds and is set by the government. In this respect, Japan is an exception: The one sickness fund is free to determine its own rate (however, it must be the same for all members of the same fund).

Of the ten countries considered here, Korea would appear to be the one with the lowest contribution rate since Korean workers have to pay approximately 6.5 percent of their salary to the single national fund. In other countries the rate is much higher. In the Czech Republic it amounts to 13.5 percent, in Germany to 14.6 percent (Alexa et al., 2015; Busse et al., 2017). In comparing these rates, however, at least two important factors must be taken into account. The first factor is public subsidies. In all ten countries analyzed here, the SHI system is also partially financed by the state budget, through taxes. Therefore, in some countries the rate could be lower because the component derived from tax revenue could be more substantial. The second factor to keep in mind concerns the formula with which health contributions are shared between workers and businesses. In Austria, Germany, Japan and Korea health contributions are paid in equal parts (50:50) by the employee and their respective employer. In Belgium and the Czech Republic, the worker pays one-third of the contributions, while the remaining two-thirds go to the company. In Turkey, again the formula is different: The worker pays two-fifths of the contributions and the employer pays the remaining three-fifths (Tatar et al., 2011).

5.1.6 Population Coverage

A characteristic of the original Bismarckian model is that it is purely occupational and that it is only anchored to income from work. As a consequence, it inevitably ends up excluding "economically inactive" individuals. Unless they are the family members of a worker who is registered with social insurance, the latter are likely to remain with no insurance coverage. As mentioned in Chapter 1, SHI systems do not guarantee – by nature – universal coverage of the population unless the State introduces particular corrective measures, for example, by financing typical targeted programs that cover those who are excluded from the compulsory social insurance system.

In all of the ten countries considered, the State uses part of the public budget to cover categories of people who would otherwise be excluded from the mandatory SHI scheme. In some countries, these "corrective" measures prepared by the government end up guaranteeing coverage for the entire population. In other countries, however, universal coverage is still not achieved and so part of the population remains uninsured.

As already seen in Chapter 3, the Czech Republic, Japan and Korea formally reach 100 percent population coverage. Following the terminology used previously, Austria, France and Germany can be considered "quasi-universal" countries. In the remaining four countries (Belgium, Hungary, Poland and Turkey), universal coverage is not achieved; the percentage of residents who are formally with no health insurance is high especially in Poland and Hungary.

5.1.7 *Public Subsidies and Targeted Programs*

At this point, it is only natural to ask which tools are used in the different SHI countries to address the problem of those who are uninsured. In France, Germany and Korea, the individuals who are excluded from the mandatory SHI system are covered by typical targeted programs. We have already mentioned the residual programs in France and Germany (see Chapter 2). In Korea, the government funds a specific targeted program (called the Medical Aid Program) to guarantee healthcare protection for the poorest sections of the population (Kwon et al., 2015).

In other SHI countries, instead of setting up real "targeted programs," with legal entities and separate management from other sickness funds, another route was preferred in which the government undertakes to pay the contributions on behalf of certain categories who end up being assisted not by "ad hoc" public programs, but by "normal" sickness funds, which also assist other categories of workers. Specifically, the underlying principle remains that of targeted programs (the State, through tax revenue, pays for the healthcare of certain "weak" or "deserving" categories), but the organizational solution is different.

In the Czech Republic, for example, the State pays health contributions to economically inactive individuals, including children, students, the unemployed, pensioners, people below the poverty line, women on maternity leave. The Czech case, in reality, appears most particular in this respect because the inactive individuals – for whom the State pays – are actually more than half of the population (Alexa et al., 2015). In Turkey, the State pays contributions for certain categories, including the poor, provisional village guards, the unemployed (for a few months only), war veterans and Olympic sports champions (Tatar et al., 2011; Yıldırım and Yıldırım, 2011). And the examples could continue, since in other countries as well, (Austria, Belgium, Hungary, Japan, Poland), the State subsidizes specific categories of people who are considered at risk, or in any case, those having low incomes (Gerkens and Merkur, 2010; Gaál et al., 2011; Matsuda, 2016; Bachner et al., 2018; Sakamoto et al., 2018; Sowada et al., 2019; Szigeti et al., 2019).

5.1.8 Similarities and Differences

So, let us try to wrap up what has been said so far regarding the family of SHI systems. Considering the differences that exist between one national system and another, it would be concluded that there is more than one single standard model, since SHI today is made up of a family of variegated systems, which – inspired by the original Bismarckian model – share some fundamental, common characteristics: (1) the compulsory scheme (although it may be partially fueled by taxes) is financed mainly through sickness contributions that are proportional to income; (2) unless the State fills the gap with targeted programs (or subsidies in favor of the "economically inactive"), not all residents are covered by the SHI systems, but only those who regularly pay contributions (including their dependant family members); (3) sickness funds are always independent from healthcare providers. Regarding this last aspect, it is curious to note that none of the ten SHI countries apply insurer–provider integration. Sickness funds reimburse medical care and treatments, however, they do not provide them directly through their own structures and staff.

If these are the elements of similarity, it is worth noting once again, the element that most of all seems to differentiate the systems of SHI, namely, the contrast between single-fund systems and multiple funds systems. In fact, single-fund systems end up resembling – at least in some respects – separate universalist systems. This is especially true for single-fund systems, such as in Korea, where it is possible to guarantee coverage of the entire population, thanks to the action of targeted programs.

5.2 THE NHS COUNTRIES

The second large family of health systems is made up of countries adopting the National Health Service model. Ten of the twenty-seven countries analyzed in this volume can be traced to this model: Denmark, Finland, Ireland, Italy, New Zealand, Norway, Portugal, Spain, Sweden and the United Kingdom. An eleventh could be added to these ten countries, which would be Greece, where a national health service (called ESY), established in 1983, officially operates. However, the Greek system is a mixture of NHS and SHI, and so, it is more appropriate to catalog it as a mixed system. Looking at the geographical layout of the NHS-equipped countries, one of them (New Zealand) is located in Oceania, while all the others are in Europe. The NHS model has taken root in the Nordic countries, Southern Europe and the British Isles.

If we consider the organizational variants used, the NHS family of countries may appear, at first glance, to be more homogeneous than the family of SHI systems. But, on closer inspection, some noteworthy differences also emerge by comparing countries with a National Health Service. So, at this point, the focus will be on the main elements of similarity and difference found within the NHS countries.

5.2.1 Funding and the Possible Presence of SHI Schemes

Let us start with the aspect of financing. All ten NHS have a single-payer scheme that is unique for the entire population. This system is financed – either exclusively, or in any case predominantly – through taxes. The public scheme guarantees a basic package of healthcare benefits to all residents, and also to economically inactive individuals who – for one reason or another – do not pay taxes. All of these ten countries formally reach 100 percent population coverage.

A distinctive element of some NHS countries is the presence – in addition to the prevailing universalist scheme – of also an ancillary scheme of SHI, which is fed through wage-related contributions. In addition to Greece, there are three NHS countries (Finland, Portugal and Spain) in which separate schemes referable to the SHI model also operate.

In Finland, there is an insurance scheme called National Health Insurance, which is financed by social contributions and linked to the more general social security system of the country (Saltman and Teperi, 2016; Keskimäki et al., 2019). This scheme guarantees health benefits (including the reimbursement of medicines, private visits and rehabilitation services) not only to workers, but to all residents. Since it covers the entire population, we could consider this SHI scheme as "reinforcing" the universalist model.

On the other hand, the Spanish and Portuguese cases are different, where SHI schemes end up generating differences in treatment within the population.

In Portugal, some particular categories of workers, (civil servants, the armed forces, employees of the banking and insurance sectors, employees of the postal and telecommunications services), are required to pay contributions to their respective sickness funds. These funds, financed through the obligatory contributions of employees and employers, are called "subsystems" (*subsistemas de saúde*), and cover about one-fifth of the Portuguese population (Simões et al., 2017). These special SHI schemes provide enrolled workers (and their family members) with additional coverage beyond that provided by the NHS. It could, therefore, be argued that in Portugal the SHI schemes are "supplementary" or "complementary" to the public service. In Spain – which will be better explained in a moment – the SHI schemes are, instead, "substitutive" when compared to the NHS. A minority of the Spanish population is, in fact, covered by SHI funds instead of the coverage provided by the NHS.

5.2.2 The Provision of Services

All ten NHS countries have a predominantly public healthcare delivery system. This means that the vast majority of healthcare workers are civil servants, and that the majority of hospital and outpatient facilities are publicly owned. On the provision front, the main elements of dissimilarity among NHS countries concern the employment relationship of family doctors, and the presence or absence of a mandatory gatekeeping mechanism.

As previously mentioned, in many NHS countries family doctors – unlike hospital doctors – are not public employees, but they are private contractors who are under an agreement with the public healthcare service. Family doctors are independent providers in most NHS countries, such as Denmark, Ireland, Italy, New Zealand, Norway and United Kingdom. In contrast, in Finland, Portugal and Spain, general practitioners are public service employees. In Sweden, primary care units, to which family doctors belong, can be both public and private (Kringos et al., 2015; Mossialos et al., 2017).

A second discriminating element concerns the presence or absence of a mandatory gatekeeping system (see Chapter 4). In most NHS, (Finland, Ireland, Italy, New Zealand, Norway, Portugal, Spain and the United Kingdom) there is a mandatory gatekeeping system. In Sweden, in contrast, family doctors do not have a formal role as gatekeepers (Mossialos et al., 2017). In Denmark, citizens are free to choose between two regimes (gatekeeping or direct access); and as a result, 98 percent of Danes opt for gatekeeping (Pedersen et al., 2012; Mossialos et al., 2017).

A further element that can influence access to care in NHS systems concerns any cost-sharing methods for patients. In Chapter 1 it was mentioned that, in principle, universalist systems should provide healthcare that is considered essential in a free or semi-free form.

In most NHS countries (Finland, Ireland, Italy, New Zealand, Norway, Sweden), forms of cost sharing are applied, usually in the form of co-payments. Depending on each case, co-payment may cover outpatient visits, hospital treatments or both (OECD, 2016a). In three countries (Denmark, Spain and the United Kingdom), on the other hand, both primary and specialist care are free at the time of use, although some form of cost sharing may be required for certain drugs or dental care. In Portugal, modest co-payments, so far, have been applied to both primary care and specialist visits. A recent resolution of the Portuguese parliament, however, provides for the abolition of co-payment when the service is referred by an NHS doctor.

5.2.3 Centralized versus Decentralized NHS

A relevant dimension, in which the NHS systems differ, concerns the degree of centralization or decentralization of the system. Some countries, in fact, have an essentially centralized NHS, which means that the system is funded predominantly by national taxes, and that the reins of the system are in the hands of the central government. England, Ireland, Portugal and New Zealand have a centralized NHS. This does not mean that in these countries there are no territorial administrative articulations since all NHS have territorial divisions, but these – in centralized countries – respond to the national government (and are financed by it). In Ireland, the management of public health services is attributed to a government agency, called the Health Service Executive (HSE), which reports to the Department of Health. The New Zealand territory is divided into twenty District Health Boards (DHBs), which are financed by the national budget and whose leaders are appointed by the Minister of Health (Goodyear-Smith and Ashton, 2019). In Portugal, too, the management of the *Serviço Nacional de Saúde* (SNS) is centralized, although the government has divided the country into five regional health administrations. The leaders of the latter are not, however, an expression of local governments, instead, they are appointed by the national government and report to the Minister of Health (Simões et al., 2017).

In matters of centralization/decentralization, the United Kingdom is a special case. Since the late 1990s, the responsibility for organizing healthcare services has, in fact, been devolved to the four nations that make up the United Kingdom. The organization of healthcare is today entrusted to four separate bodies: NHS England, NHS Scotland, NHS Wales and the system called Health and Social Care (HSC) in Northern Ireland. Funding for these four systems is the responsibility of the UK government, while the health ministers of Scotland, Wales and Northern Ireland are responsible for healthcare services in their nations, and the healthcare policy for England is decided directly by the UK government (Cylus et al., 2015). Of the four "health nations," the largest is, by far, the NHS England. The latter remains a centralized system, which is, in fact, managed and financed directly by the UK government and does not have a significant regional level (Stewart et al., 2020).

The organization of healthcare services in Norway could be defined as a semi-decentralized NHS (Hagen and Kaarbøe, 2006; Ringard et al., 2013) since healthcare responsibilities are divided between national and local levels. The State is responsible for providing specialist care, (the country is divided into four regional health authorities, which operate as state-owned enterprises), while the municipalities provide primary care.

The other three Nordic countries are decentralized. In Finland, most of the healthcare competences are attributed to municipalities, and most of the funding also comes from local taxes (Keskimäki et al., 2019). In Sweden, healthcare responsibilities are mainly assigned to counties,[2] while municipalities are assigned school health services, elderly care, care for the disabled, home care (Anell et al., 2012). The Swedish public health service is funded mainly by taxes collected locally (Mossialos et al., 2017). In Denmark, the management of healthcare services is mainly assigned to the regions (Olejaz et al.,

---

[2] In Sweden, the counties are grouped into six medical regions, which are mainly entrusted with the management of tertiary care (Anell et al., 2012).

2012), while the municipalities are responsible for prevention, health promotion and long-term care, therefore, for most of the social health activities. However, most of the funding comes from national taxes (Christiansen and Vrangbæk, 2018).

A structure similar to that found in Denmark is also found in Italy. The financing of the system predominantly comes from the national level, but the management and planning of health services are assigned to regional governments. The Italian government has the power to set the general regulatory framework, but the organization of services is highly regionalized (Toth, 2014, 2015a).

Also in Spain, responsibilities in the health sector are devolved to Autonomous Communities, which enjoy great autonomy in managing healthcare in their own territory. The government of Madrid, which is responsible for the overall coordination and monitoring of the system, devolves taxes to individual regions, and uses compensation funds to guarantee adequate resources for all Autonomous Communities.

To summarize, we may conclude that England, Ireland, New Zealand and Portugal have basically a centralized management of the NHS, headed by the national government. Denmark, Italy, Spain and Sweden have a public healthcare service organized primarily on a regional basis. In Finland, the public health service is organized on a municipal level. Finally, Norway is an intermediate case, which is partly decentralized (for primary care) and partly centralized (for specialized care).

The data reported above require a brief comment. Identifying which level of government has been attributed responsibility for managing health services is not just a formal question of "constitutional engineering." In substance, it makes a great deal of difference if the system is governed in a uniform way from the center or if it is organized on a local basis. In the first case we can expect greater uniformity of the services offered and the organizational models adopted, while in the second case greater differentiation and localistic adaptation.

It is perhaps also for this reason that in the Nordic countries, the term "National Health Service" is not officially used to describe their healthcare system. It is expressly used in the United Kingdom, in Italy (*Servizio Sanitario Nazionale*), in Spain (*Sistema Nacional de Salud*), in Portugal (*Serviço Nacional de Saúde*), even in Greece (Εθνικό Σύστημα Υγείας, or ESY), but not in Northern European countries. The latter do not declare, in official documents, to have a "national health service." The question of terminology seems to derive from a substantial reason, which is, since they are largely decentralized, the public health systems of Northern European countries cannot be defined as "national" since they do not constitute a unitary and uniform service in the entire territory. In short, avoiding an NHS label would indicate their decentralized nature.

I would not want this last comment to confuse the reader. Using or not using the NHS label in the various countries is not decisive. There are, in fact, countries – think of Spain or Italy – which, while declaring to have an NHS, however, have highly differentiated health services at regional levels, and therefore, they are far from uniform when comparing the various areas of the country.

5.2.4   Nordic Countries versus Southern Europe?

Also on the basis of the differences already highlighted, some authors, (Petmesidou and Guillén, 2008; Magnussen et al., 2009; Toth, 2010b; Lyttkens et al., 2016), have tried to investigate whether – within the NHS family – it is possible to identify a typical Nordic health model (which unites Denmark, Finland, Norway and Sweden), and – conversely – a distinctive health model for Southern Europe (which includes Greece, Italy, Spain and Portugal).

In addition to the elements already highlighted, (including the presence of any SHI schemes, and the degree of decentralization of the system), the Nordic and Southern NHS are distinguished by the degree of "publicness" of the system and what we could call the "generosity" (Toth, 2019) of public health services.

In Northern European countries, the public health system is financed more generously, and – at least with reference to specialized care – it provides more in-house services, without resorting to contracted private providers. The high level of public spending ends up leaving less room for the private sector. In Southern European countries, on the other hand, the NHS receive lower levels of funding. The public health service, thus, ends up leaving some health needs unmet (Eurostat, 2020), and in order to fulfill these health needs citizens have to pay out of their own pockets. As seen in Chapter 3, the level of out-of-pocket spending is much higher in Southern European countries than in the Nordic countries. In the countries of Southern Europe, not only is the level of private spending higher but also the public health service tends more to outsource part of the care to private "affiliated" providers. Consequently, the Southern European NHS end up being less "public" than their counterparts in Northern Europe.

Data from the OECD Health Statistics database (OECD, 2020) can support what has just been stated. In the four Nordic countries, the financing of the NHS, (we are talking about the public service only, not the health system as a whole), absorbs on average 8.4 percent of the GDP. In the southern countries (Italy, Spain and Portugal) the NHS costs on average 6.2 percent of the GDP, (if we also included Greece in the calculation, the average would drop to 5.8 percent). The difference is already evident. However, it becomes even more impressive if it is expressed as a per capita expenditure (at purchasing power parity). In the Nordic countries, the public health system spends more than \$4,700 for each resident; whereas, in Southern Europe the per capita share is approximately \$2,445, (which becomes \$2,190, when including Greece). In Northern Europe, the public component corresponds to about 83 percent of total health expenditure. In Southern Europe, public spending is around 69 percent (66 percent when including Greece).

Let us also take a quick look at the structure of the healthcare offer, considering the indicator – a bit rudimentary, but still useful for revealing the relationship between the public and private sectors – of hospital beds. In Nordic countries – on average – 89 percent of beds are in public hospitals (therefore, just over 10 percent remain in private for profit and nonprofit hospitals). In Southern European countries, beds in public hospitals represent 67 percent of the total bed available (therefore, private hospitals manage almost a third of the beds). This confirms that in Southern European countries, the provision of healthcare is much more open to the private sector.

5.2.5 Spain and Ireland

Among the NHS countries, two are particular in that they are exceptions when compared to the other members of the family. So much so, that someone could go so far as to claim that they are not technically NHS. These two countries are Spain and Ireland.

The Spanish system is anomalous compared to the others because it allows a small minority of the population to be able to "leave" the NHS. Those who may enjoy right to opt out are some categories of public employees, compulsorily registered with the respective mutual funds. In fact, it should be noted that at the time when the Spanish NHS was established (in 1986), not all the previously operating sickness funds were abolished (Toth, 2010b). Some special regimes survived and are still active today. The funds MUFACE (*Mutualidad General de Funcionarios Civiles del Estado*), MUGEJU (*Mutualidad General Judicial*) and ISFAS (*Instituto Social de las Fuerzas Armadas*) respectively assist State civil servants, the staff of the Ministry of Justice and the armed forces and the police. These three mutual funds are financed in a smaller part by contributions paid by public employees and in a greater part by taxes (Bernal-Delgado et al., 2018). Members of these three mutual funds – about 5 percent of the population – enjoy privileged treatment compared to other working categories, being able to choose, every year, whether to be treated by the national health service (as with the rest of the population) or through private insurance companies. The majority of the members of these mutual funds opt for private care

(Bernal-Delgado et al., 2018). Therefore, in Spain a segmentation of the population is carried out, and so not all residents enjoy the same health coverage.

In the NHS family, Ireland is also an exception to the rule, in addition to Spain. Ireland is anomalous for having a "two-tier" health system (Johnston et al., 2019; OECD, 2019c), and for "segmenting" the population into multiple categories.

Irish residents are in fact divided – mainly on the basis of income, through means testing – into three categories (Connolly and Wren, 2017; Johnston et al., 2019). The first category is made up of low-income individuals who hold a medical card, which guarantees that they can take advantage of primary care, hospital care and prescription medicines for free. A second category are individuals who hold a GP visit card. They do not pay for the family doctor's examinations, but they are required to pay the user charges for hospital treatments. The third category is made up of those who, having neither a medical card nor a GP visit card, are subject to user charges for hospital care and are required to pay for the general practitioner's visits in full. According to recent data (OECD, 2019c), about 32 percent of the Irish have a medical card, 10 percent have a GP visit card, while the remaining 58 percent have to pay out-of-pocket expenses for the family doctor. Thus Ireland is the only European country not to guarantee universal access for primary care (OECD, 2019c; Wren and Connolly, 2019).

The Irish healthcare system is also considered as two-tier due to another characteristic, which is the vast diffusion of voluntary private health policies. The latter are subsidized by the State, and are partly complementary and partly supplementary in that they allow you to skip waiting lists, access private providers, take advantage of private rooms in public hospitals and get reimbursements for visits to GPs and for physiotherapy sessions (Turner, 2015; Connolly and Wren, 2017). About 45 percent of the Irish population buys a private policy (OECD, 2019c), which is a very high percentage for a NHS country.

5.3 SEPARATED UNIVERSALIST SYSTEMS: AUSTRALIA AND CANADA

Of the twenty-seven countries considered in this book, only two fall into the category of separated universalist systems: Australia and Canada.

The architecture of the Australian and Canadian health systems is similar in many respects (Gray, 1998; Duckett, 2018). A single public insurance scheme operates in both Canada and Australia, which covers the entire resident population and which is financed through tax revenues. In both countries, this scheme is called Medicare. The Australian Medicare program was established in 1984. In that year, the Canada Care Act was also approved, which is the founding law that still governs Canadian Medicare, as well as the relationship between provinces and the federal government in the health field. In both countries, the financing of the system and the competences in health matters are shared between the federal government and the governments of the individual states or provinces. In both Australia and Canada, healthcare providers are separate entities from Medicare, and are reimbursed by the latter.

The main elements of difference between the two countries concern: hospital management; user fees; the regulation of private insurance; the balance of competences between the federal government and state and provincial governments. In Canada, the majority of hospitals are private nonprofit corporations (Fierlbeck, 2011). In Australia, however, public hospitals are in the majority and they account for about two-thirds of all beds (Duckett, 2018). In Canada, as required by the Canada Health Act, Medicare healthcare must be free and cannot involve patient co-payments. In Australia, on the other hand, there are forms of co-payment, which are payable by the patient for outpatient care and for medicines. Australians are also required to pay out of their own pockets to access private hospitals or to be treated as private patients in public hospitals. A further difference between the Australian and the Canadian systems concerns private insurance and how it is regulated. In Canada, supplementary private policies in some provinces are prohibited, and in the remaining provinces, however, they are strongly discouraged (Marchildon, 2013). In Australia, on the other hand, private insurance – even the supplementary type that ends up also covering benefits included in the Medicare package – is encouraged through tax incentives (Connelly et al., 2010). Finally, it should be pointed out that the overall governance of the Australian healthcare system is less decentralized than that found in Canada (Gray, 1998; Duckett, 2018). In fact, the Australian federal government has greater regulatory powers, and takes on a greater share of the financing of the system. This means that Australian Medicare – unlike the Canadian equivalent – guarantees a greater degree of uniformity across the country (Gray, 1998).

5.3.1 Australia

The Australian Constitution divides the competences in the field of healthcare between the federal government (Commonwealth) and the individual state governments (Duckett, 2018), but in reality – on most issues – it is the federal government that defines the line (Gray, 1998). Medicare funding is also split between the federal government and the individual states. The Commonwealth transfers the necessary resources to states to pay for primary and outpatient care, medicines (those included in the Pharmaceutical Benefits Schedule), aged care services and about 40 percent of public hospital funding (Duckett, 2018). In addition to transfers from the federal government, individual states must contribute to the financing of the system with their own funds.

Public hospitals are owned by state governments, although operational coordination is delegated to Local Hospital Networks (LHNs). Public hospital facilities are allowed and even encouraged to admit private patients (Cheng et al., 2013). In fact, privately treated patients pay out of their own pockets, which leads to extra income for public facilities. Outpatient medical care is provided by independent doctors (not employed by the government), who are remunerated mainly on a fee-for-service basis. Medical specialists are allowed to practice in both the public and private sectors, and most of them work in both (Cheng et al., 2013).

About one out of two Australians holds private health insurance (Duckett, 2018). The private insurance policy market is highly regulated (Hall, 1999). In fact, insurers are required to comply with both the open enrollment and community rating constraints. A risk-adjustment mechanism also operates across the various private insurance companies (Connelly et al., 2010). Private insurance policies play both a supplementary and complementary role to Medicare. In fact, they cover the costs of both the excluded services (such as optometry, physiotherapy, dental treatment) and those included in the Medicare package. Having a private policy allows policyholders to seek treatment privately in both private and public hospitals. Private insurance allows a greater choice of hospital specialists, higher levels of hospital comfort (e.g., a single room) and skipping waiting lists in public hospitals (Hall, 1999; Connelly et al., 2010). The purchase of a private insurance policy is encouraged with a mix of "carrot and stick." On one hand, tax rebates are provided, commensurate with income, for the purchase of a private health policy; on the other hand, there is a tax penalty (the Medicare Levy surcharge) for taxpayers with medium-high incomes who do not subscribe to a private policy (Connelly et al., 2010; Mossialos et al., 2017).

5.3.2 Canada

The structure of the Canadian healthcare system is highly decentralized (Gray, 1998; Geva-May and Maslove, 2000; Fierlbeck, 2011). Although the federal government imposes a common regulatory framework throughout the country, Medicare is managed at a provincial level. The overall governance of the system is essentially based on financial leverage since the Canadian Constitution guarantees the autonomy of the provinces insofar as healthcare matters are concerned, and the Ottawa government uses financial transfers to "convince" the provinces to implement the federal objectives (Evans, 2000; Marchildon, 2019).

The Medicare scheme is financed through general taxation. The provinces raise the majority of funds through own-source revenues and receive roughly a quarter of their healthcare budget from federal transfers (Geva-May and Maslove, 2000; Marchildon, 2013).

The Medicare scheme guarantees "medically necessary" care to all Canadian residents, without deductibles or co-payments (Evans, 2000). There is no official list of services guaranteed by Medicare, established at federal level. The benefit baskets are defined at the provincial level. Coverage includes hospital care and most outpatient specialist care, primary care and long-term care.

For services that are not included in the Medicare package, two-thirds of Canadians subscribe to private complementary insurance (Martin et al., 2018). As previously stated, supplementary private policies are prohibited or strongly discouraged (Flood and Haugan, 2010; Marchildon, 2013). Conversely, the purchase of a complementary private policy is incentivized through tax exemption on insurance premiums. Most private insurance policies are paid by employers, unions or professional associations under a group contract (Marchildon, 2013; Mossialos et al., 2017).

From the early 1990s, the Regional Health Authorities (RHAs) have been established in most Canadian provinces. These agencies were not introduced through a federal reform, but were established at different times and in different ways by the individual provinces.[3] RHAs have been delegated by provincial ministers of health to oversee hospitals, long-term facilities, home care and public health services within defined geographical areas. The RHAs are entitled to provide these services directly or by contracting with other healthcare organizations and providers. The main purpose of the RHAs is to make the system more integrated (Marchildon, 2019).

---

[3] Ontario has not established RHAs, but Local Health Integration Networks (LHINs) that have functions that are partially different. Recently, some provinces have replaced RHAs with a single provincial health authority.

Something similar has also happened in Australia, with the establishment – beginning in 2011 – of the Local Hospital Networks and subsequently – starting from 2015 – of the Primary Health Networks (PHNs). Local Hospital Networks are separate statutory authorities to which state governments delegate the management and funding of public hospitals. The Primary Health Networks, on the other hand, aim to make the primary care network more integrated, with particular reference to the treatment of chronic diseases.

The regional health authorities in Canada, as well as the PHNs and LHNs in Australia, have the declared objective of integrating the network of public providers in certain geographical areas. These innovations at the forefront of service delivery manage to make the Australian and Canadian systems, (especially in the provinces where the RHAS own and manage first-hand most of the healthcare facilities), more integrated than in the past and, therefore, more similar to the NHS.

5.4   MANDATORY RESIDENCE INSURANCE

Only two countries fully belong to the mandatory residence insurance family: the Netherlands and Switzerland. Germany can be added to these two cases, even if the German system – as already specified in Chapter 2 – combines the mandatory residence insurance model with the preexisting one of the SHI.

Israel also has some characteristic features of mandatory residence insurance, hybridizing them – as will be discussed shortly – with both the SHI and the universalist model. In this chapter, it was chosen – for the reasons that will be presented later – to categorize the Israeli case among mixed systems. Therefore, it will not be considered as belonging to the mandatory residence insurance family.

Geographically, if we exclude Israel and include Germany, the members of the family are contiguous countries of Western Europe.

The essential features of the Swiss healthcare system have already been presented in Chapter 1, while a brief description of the German and Dutch financing systems has been provided in Chapter 2. Taking

134 FINANCING AND PROVISION: FOUR FAMILIES AND A FEW OUTLIERS

into account what has been stated above, in this chapter we can limit ourselves to recapitulating the elements of similarity and to underline the main differences among the countries belonging to this family.

5.4.1 A Recent Model

The first feature to be highlighted concerns the relative "youthfulness" of this model of mandatory residence insurance, which is, in fact, a model that has established itself more recently than the others analyzed in this chapter. As we know, the first SHI systems date back to the late nineteenth century. Targeted programs, especially for the benefit of the poor, were adopted by many European countries well before the Bismarckian-inspired reforms. The first universalist system was introduced in New Zealand in 1938.

Mandatory residence insurance only appeared on the international scene in more recent times, starting from the mid-1990s. Switzerland led the way by introducing this model in 1994. Previously, in Switzerland, there was a voluntary health insurance system. The Netherlands officially entered a mandatory residence insurance system in 2006, which came from a Bismarckian system introduced in the early 1940s. In Germany, the SHI system, with over a century of history behind it, has been adapted (and incorporated) into a mandatory residence insurance system since the 2007 reform. It has previously been pointed out that Israel can be considered to have a system of mandatory residence insurance only partially. Just for completeness of information: Israel introduced a system that is in some respects similar to the Swiss system, in the same year, 1994. Previously in Israel there was a voluntary, nonprofit sickness fund system (Clarfield et al., 2017).

In short, these dates confirm that the principle of mandatory residence insurance has been fully applied – at least in OECD countries – in only the last three decades. Therefore, it proves to be a more recent model than the others. It is easy to think that other countries may, in the near future, be inspired by this model, perhaps by re-adapting the current SHI or voluntary health insurance systems.

5.4.2 *Similarities*

The main elements of similarity between the systems in Germany, the Netherlands and Switzerland compose the distinctive and qualifying elements of the ideal model of mandatory residence insurance. In these three countries, the obligation to obtain basic health coverage rests with all residents in the country. The coverage is thus universal or quasi-universal (see Chapter 3). Insurance coverage is not provided directly by the State but by a plurality of competing insurers. We are, therefore, in the presence of multi-payer systems in which the individual resident has the right to choose the subject (sickness fund or private insurance company) with which to insure.

Regarding the basic insurance package, in all three countries the regulation of insurers is stringent (the regulatory constraints are, on the other hand, decidedly more relaxed in relation to supplemental private insurance). In both Switzerland and the Netherlands, insurers are required to comply with the principles of open enrollment and community rating. To make competition between insurers more equitable, a risk-adjustment mechanism operates across them, which is managed at national (the Netherlands) or cantonal (Switzerland) level. These regulatory constraints are also applied in Germany, but only to the sickness funds belonging to the SHI scheme. These rules do not apply to substitutive private insurance.

5.4.3 *Differences*

If those listed above are the main elements of similarity between Germany, the Netherlands and Switzerland, let us now focus on the differences that – again at the level of system financing – are found between these three national systems.

The main difference concerns Germany, where the principle of mandatory residence insurance applies to only a minority of the population, while the majority of Germans are subject to a SHI system. In fact, two schemes operate in Germany, the first is SHI (called GKV) and the second is private health insurance (PKV), which are not connected to each other and which operate according to different rules (Kifmann, 2017). Only a small part of the population has the right to choose (through opting out) which scheme to follow. Of the two schemes, only the private health insurance (PKV) scheme responds to the mandatory residence insurance model. The freedom of choice granted to citizens is confined within the single scheme, as the SHI members can only choose from sickness funds (*krankenkassen*), while private health insurance members can only choose from private insurers.

Let us consider the legal nature of the insurers. In Switzerland, insurers must act as nonprofit entities in the provision of the basic, mandatory package, but they can operate as for-profit entities in the sale of complementary packages (De Pietro et al., 2015). In the Netherlands, almost all insurers are nonprofits (Stolper et al., 2019). In Germany, the krankenkassen who belong to the SHI scheme are compulsorily nonprofit, while the insurers who offer private policies can be both for profit and nonprofit (Kifmann, 2017; Mossialos et al., 2017).

Another element of discrepancy between the three countries regards the methods of contribution. In Switzerland, each resident pays their own insurance premium (De Pietro et al., 2015). In the Netherlands, the payment is mixed, as such, both a fixed premium and income-dependant contributions are paid (Schut and Varkevisser, 2017). In Germany, SHI members pay sickness contributions proportional to income, while private insurance members pay a premium (Kifmann, 2017).

Further differences concern the ways in which the State supports the categories most at risk. First of all, it should be reiterated that in all three countries, the state significantly subsidizes the compulsory scheme by helping economically the weakest categories, and the poorest sections of the population. In Switzerland, the State provides economic support to low-income citizens to pay their insurance premium (Mossialos et al., 2017). In the Netherlands, the State pays the premium for minors, and provides subsidies for

5.5 THE OUTLIERS: GREECE, ISRAEL AND THE UNITED STATES

low-income individuals (Kroneman et al., 2016). In Germany, the State pays contributions for some categories, while for others it finances specific targeted programs (Busse and Blümel, 2014; Mossialos et al., 2017).

All the differences listed above seem to confirm what has already been anticipated at the beginning of this section: Switzerland and the Netherlands are closer to the ideal model of mandatory residence insurance, and are more similar to each other than is the case with Germany.

5.5 THE OUTLIERS: GREECE, ISRAEL AND THE UNITED STATES

Of the twenty-seven countries analyzed in this book, three remain excluded from the four "healthcare families" described above. The three countries are Greece, Israel and the United States.

5.5.1 Greece

The Greek healthcare system cannot be cataloged as either a NHS or as a SHI system, since it is a mixture of these two models (Grigorakis et al., 2016; Economou et al., 2017). When the Greek National Health Service (known as ESY) was established in 1983, the preexisting sickness funds were, in fact, not abolished but they continued to operate in parallel with the ESY (Mossialos et al., 2005; Toth, 2010b). Therefore, up to 2010 multiple occupation-based sickness funds operated in Greece. The SHI system was characterized by a variety of schemes with differences in contribution rates, in benefits offered by the various funds, thus resulting in inequalities in access to health services (Mossialos et al., 2005).

The Great Financial Crisis of 2008 had a devastating effect on Greek healthcare (Simou and Koutsogeorgou, 2014). In the years that followed the outbreak of the crisis, several reforms were approved to try to remedy the failure of the health system. The main reforms involved the merger of most of the sickness funds (including those that covered salaried employees in the private sector, the self-employed, civil servants and farmers) under the EOPYY, the National Organization for the Provision of Healthcare Services. The benefit packages of the various SHI funds were standardized to provide a common benefits package under EOPYY (Economou et al., 2017). Another important step was taken in 2016 in which the government re-established universal coverage of the population, including more than two million people who had lost their health coverage during crises due to job losses and inability to pay contributions (OECD, 2019d).

Despite recent reforms, the Greek health system continues to be characterized by the overlapping of two mandatory schemes today: the universalist (largely integrated) system and SHI (largely separated). The universalist component is made up of ESY, which covers the entire population. Not only public hospitals but also health centers and rural units belong to the ESY. The staff of these public facilities are paid from the state budget. The SHI component is embodied by EOPYY. The latter is financed by compulsory social contributions paid by workers and their respective employers, according to a typical SHI model.[4] EOPYY, which does not have its own health facilities, is assigned the function of commissioning healthcare on behalf of its clients. EOPYY, therefore, stipulates agreements with a variety of public and private suppliers (doctors, diagnostic centers, private clinics, etc.). EOPYY covers the medical expenses of the vast majority of the Greek population (Grigorakis et al., 2016). EOPYY is not the only sickness fund operating in Greece since there are others which are smaller (such as those covering bank employees, public accountants and media workers).

The overlap of NHS and SHI determines differences in the levels of access to medical care. Those who are not registered with EOPYY

---

[4] Employees in the private sector pay 7.1 percent of their salary (with one-third of the contributions paid by the worker, and two-thirds by the employer). The self-employed pay 6.95 percent. Civil servants pay 7.65 percent of their wages (one-third is paid by the worker and two-thirds are paid by the State). Retirees contribute 6 percent of their pension (Economou et al., 2017).

can only access public ESY facilities (where forms of co-payment are not foreseen), or they must pay out of their own pocket the full price of the service, if they wish to use private suppliers. Those covered by EOPYY, on the other hand, can have both public structures and private providers affiliated with EOPYY. The use of private suppliers contracted with EOPYY usually involves a shared cost on the part of the patient. It should be borne in mind that public facilities are not uniformly distributed throughout the country, and that some services have very long waiting times (Grigorakis et al., 2016; Economou et al., 2017). The Greek system, therefore, can be considered a two-tier system in which the minority of the population that is not registered with SHI ends up having more limited freedom of choice than those who are also covered by SHI.

Another peculiarity of the Greek healthcare system is traditionally represented by the high level of private spending, and in particular, the out-of-pocket component (Grigorakis et al., 2016; OECD, 2020). The high level of private spending is due to co-payment for drugs, services not included in the basic benefit package, visits to private providers and informal payments, which are still widespread in Greece (Grigorakis et al., 2016; OECD, 2019d).

At the level of financing, the Greek system, therefore, is composed of three components, that are roughly equivalent in size, which are the NHS (universalist and financed through taxes), the SHI contributions and out-of-pocket private spending. The healthcare provision system is also tripartite, where primary and specialist care are provided by a mix of public structures, private providers who are contracted with EOPYY, and private providers (not affiliated with EOPYY) operating under direct market conditions.

5.5.2 Israel

The Israeli health system is also difficult to classify. The financing methods of national health insurance adopted in Israel combine the characteristics of at least three models, namely SHI, mandatory residence insurance and the universalist model. The delivery system is also mixed in that it is partially integrated and partially separated, with significant variations found between one sickness fund and another.

Let us start with financing methods. Beginning with the National Health Insurance Law, passed in 1994 and in force the following year, in Israel there is a mandatory insurance scheme that covers the entire population. It is partly financed through general taxation, partly through a "health tax." The latter consists of an earmarked payroll tax, which can vary from 3 percent to 5 percent of the salary depending on the job category and the income received.

All citizens and permanent residents in Israel are covered by national insurance.[5] Each client is free to choose between four sickness funds, called "Health Plans" (or, in Hebrew, *Kupat Holim*), which are in competition with each other. These four "Health Plans" consist in nonprofit sickness funds, which existed before the 1994 reform. The four nationwide Health Plans are: *Clalit, Maccabi, Meuhedet* and *Leumit*. Of these four, the one that traditionally has the highest number of members is Clalit, which covers about half of the population (Gannot et al., 2018).

The four Health Plans must provide the same basic benefits package, which is established and periodically updated by the government (Rosen et al., 2015). Based on its share of the population, each healthcare plan receives a risk-adjusted per capita payment from the government, with which it must guarantee the supply of the standard basket of services to the respective clients. Members of each sickness fund can switch to a different fund once a year. The Health Plans are bound by the requirement of open enrollment, as such they must accept all applicants.

When compared with other OECD countries, Israel has high levels of both out-of-pocket spending and spending on the purchase of private policies. Voluntary private insurance is particularly

---

[5] Undocumented immigrants, temporary residents, foreign workers and tourists are not covered by national insurance. The military, on the other hand, is covered by a program dedicated to them, managed by the Israel Defense Forces.

widespread in Israel. It can be offered either by the Health Plans themselves to their respective beneficiaries (of course, with an additional contribution), or by commercial insurance companies. Approximately four out of five Israelis have "supplemental" coverage provided by their health plan; and about one in two Israelis purchase a commercial policy, often in addition to the supplemental coverage provided by their Health Plan (Rosen, 2018).

In Israel, the delivery system is also hybrid, being partly integrated and partly separated. In Clalit, most primary and outpatient care is provided in clinics that are owned and operated by the plan, where even doctors are salaried employees. Clalit also owns its own hospital facilities. However, the system is not fully integrated since Clalit also stipulates contracts with some independent providers (Rosen et al., 2015). The other three Health Plans use a mixture of proprietary clinics and independent providers. The mix between in-house production and the use of contracted independent providers varies from one health plan to another (Rosen et al., 2015; Mossialos et al., 2017). Maccabi owns a network of private hospitals, while the other two funds do not directly manage hospitals. A mandatory gatekeeping system is adopted by Clalit, but not by the other health plans.

As will be understood from this brief presentation of the Israeli system, it turns out to be a hybrid, both in terms of financing and production. Regarding financing, it presents some characteristics of SHI, some characteristics of mandatory residence insurance and still others of the universalist model. The Israeli system resembles SHI systems because it operates through multiple nonprofit sickness funds and because it is partly funded by contributions that are calculated as a percentage of income from work. However, it is not a typical SHI system because the funds are in competition with each other and because the insurance obligation is for all residents. The Israeli case could be categorized as a mandatory residence insurance system since all residents have an obligation to be insured. It is true, however, that residents do not pay a premium. There are only four sickness funds that are nonprofit. In addition, all residents are still covered by national insurance, regardless of whether they pay the health tax or not. The Israeli system also has some typical traits of the universalist model. National health insurance is, in fact, financed through taxes and covers the entire population. Here too, however, it is difficult to categorize the Israeli system as a typical universalist system, since it is not single-payer (but organized in competing sickness funds, from which citizens can choose).

For all these reasons, it has been decided to not include Israel in one of the families of health systems presented above, considering it, instead, as a separate case.

5.5.3 United States

Several elements of the American health system have already been outlined in the previous chapters. In Chapter 1 and especially in Chapter 2, the various insurance schemes (both public and private) have been illustrated, as well as the composite architecture of the American system and the multiple lines of segmentation that make it a patchwork of poorly integrated subsystems. In Chapter 3, the high number of Americans with no health insurance was highlighted. In Chapter 4 a quick reference was made to the forms of managed care. The points that have been previously mentioned will not be repeated. What we want to reiterate here are the peculiar characteristics of the US system and its eclectic and fragmented nature.

When compared with other OECD countries, the US system represents an anomalous case in many respects. We can begin by reiterating that the United States is the only OECD country that has not introduced a compulsory insurance scheme for the majority of the population. However, the majority of the population is covered by a mix of voluntary insurance and targeted programs. The United States, as seen in Chapter 3, is the country that, by far, spends the most on healthcare. It allocates more than 17 percent of its GDP to healthcare, which corresponds to over $11,000 per capita (Hartman et al., 2020). Despite the high level of overall spending, the United States turns out to be, among the OECD countries, the one with the highest number of non-insured, not to mention the problem of the "underinsured" (Schoen et al., 2011; Collins et al., 2019). The United States is also the only OECD country in which the private component of the health expenditure exceeds the public expenditure (Hartman et al., 2020).

It is easy to associate all these "abnormal values" with the high fragmentation of the American system, in which private policies can be purchased from a thousand insurance companies that are competing with each other; the majority of providers are independent subjects from the insurers; and primary and specialist care are weakly linked. Also, regarding public financing, dozens of government agencies are involved in various capacities in financing healthcare, promoting medical and health service research as well as regulating and monitoring the various aspects of the healthcare delivery system (Shi and Singh, 2017).

Having been already broadly diagnosed (Andersen et al., 2011; Marmor and Oberlander, 2011; Shi and Singh, 2017; Johnson et al., 2018), the American health system is a patchwork, a complex mosaic, made up of many different pieces. It is a potpourri of subsystems, inspired by different models and principles.

As Kieke Okma and Ted Marmor (2015) argue, within the American system we find – in part, applied to only a subgroup of the population – almost all the financing models that are used in other countries and that were illustrated in Chapter 1. The Medicare program, fueled by social contributions paid during one's working life, recalls the European systems of SHI. The Medicaid program is a typical targeted program (which can be linked to the European Poor Law tradition). Large part of the population is covered by a voluntary health insurance system. The Veterans' Health Administration is a sort of miniature NHS (financed by taxes, with care provided directly by salaried staff and facilities owned by the VHA), reserved for only veterans. Then, there are the uninsured, who rely on the market and private charity. Finally, in the United States, it is possible to open a medical savings account on a voluntary basis.

The American system appears to be a colorful mosaic, made up of many different pieces. Due to the complexity with which it is designed and the heterogeneity of the different subsystems, it is unique in the international panorama. Therefore, it should be considered as an outlier, not resembling any of the other countries that have been considered in this study.

6 Hospitals, Doctors and Nurses

In Chapter 4, national healthcare provision systems were categorized according to their proximity to the integrated or separated model. In this chapter, we will deepen the analysis of care delivery systems, focusing on three relevant categories of healthcare providers: hospitals, doctors and nurses.

6.1 THE HOSPITALS

Let us start with the availability of hospital beds. The first, interesting variable to investigate concerns the number of hospital beds available in individual countries. Table 6.1 shows the number of total hospital beds, calculated for every thousand inhabitants, in each of the twenty-seven countries analyzed here. By "total hospital beds," we mean all beds, in both public and private hospitals, which are regularly staffed and immediately available for patient care (OECD, 2020). They include acute care and rehabilitative care beds in general hospitals, psychiatric hospitals and other specialty hospitals. On the other hand, neither the residential long-term care beds nor the beds for same-day care are included in the calculation. Although this indicator may be considered gross, the stock of available beds provides an indication of the resources that can be used for the care of inpatients (OECD, 2019e).

With regard to this indicator, the differences between countries appear to be considerable. In fact, it varies from a minimum of 2.1 beds (in Sweden) to a maximum of 13 beds per thousand inhabitants (in Japan), against an OECD average of around 4.6 beds (OECD, 2020). Within the twenty-seven countries examined, the healthcare model adopted in the individual countries seems to play an important role. In the NHS countries there are, on average, 2.9 beds per thousand

146 HOSPITALS, DOCTORS AND NURSES

Table 6.1 *Hospital beds*

(2019 or last year available)

	Total hospital beds per thousand population	% beds in publicly owned hospitals	% beds in privately owned hospitals
Australia	3.8	66.6	33.4
Austria	7.3	69.5	30.5
Belgium	5.6	26.2	73.8
Canada	2.5	n.a.	n.a.
Czech Republic	6.6	84.7	15.3
Denmark	2.6	93.7	6.3
Finland	3.6	94.8	5.2
France	5.9	61.5	38.5
Germany	8.0	40.7	59.3
Greece	4.2	65.6	34.4
Hungary	7.0	96.9	3.1
Ireland	3.0	n.a.	n.a.
Israel	3.0	68.2	31.8
Italy	3.1	66.6	33.4
Japan	13.0	27.2	72.8
Korea	12.4	10.0	90.0
Netherlands	3.2	0.0	100.0
New Zealand	2.6	85.0	15.0
Norway	3.5	76.0	24.0
Poland	6.5	80.1	19.9
Portugal	3.5	68.1	31.9
Spain	3.0	68.2	31.8
Sweden	2.1	n.a.	n.a.
Switzerland	4.6	n.a.	n.a.
Turkey	2.9	76.4	23.6
United Kingdom	2.5	n.a.	n.a.
United States	2.9	21.5	78.5

Source: OECD (2020)

inhabitants. In the SHI countries, the average number of beds is much higher, equal to 7.5 (always per thousand inhabitants). Note that since the year 2000, the number of beds per capita has decreased in nearly all the countries, with the exception of Turkey and the Republic of Korea.

Still on the subject of hospital beds, the second dimension that deserves to be explored concerns the division of beds between publicly owned and privately owned hospitals. Actually, there are countries that are characterized by a predominantly public hospital offering system, and countries with a predominantly private offering.

On this front too, there is a large gap between the NHS and SHI countries. In NHS countries, on average, more than 80 percent of beds are in publicly owned hospitals. In SHI countries, on average, 57 percent of the beds are in public hospitals and 43 percent in private facilities. This difference between the two families of health systems is not surprising: The NHS are in fact, by definition, integrated public systems, therefore, it is natural that the majority of hospitals are publicly owned.

It should be noted that in many SHI countries, hospitals are predominantly publicly owned. This is particularly true in the countries of Eastern Europe (Hungary, the Czech Republic and Poland) and in Turkey. In the four countries just mentioned, beds in public facilities are more than 75 percent of the total.

This data suggests a more general reflection. It cannot, therefore, be assumed that countries with a universalist financing system necessarily have a prevalently public provision system, and that conversely the SHI or mandatory residence insurance systems necessarily have a mainly private provision system. Things can get mixed up. Just as there may be universalist systems with a private delivery system, there are also countries in which financing through SHI is combined with a prevailing public (hospital, but also outpatient) supply system. The three countries of Eastern Europe and Turkey are included in the latter category.

148 HOSPITALS, DOCTORS AND NURSES

Within the private hospital sector, it would be worthwhile to keep for-profit structures separate from not-for-profit structures. Unfortunately, this data is not available for many of the countries considered, so it is not possible to make a systematic comparison. Just out of curiosity, in countries such as Belgium, Korea and the Netherlands, all (or almost all) private hospitals are not-for-profit. On the contrary, in countries such as the Czech Republic, Greece, Italy, Poland or Turkey, the great majority of private hospitals are profit-making organizations.

6.2 PAYMENT METHODS FOR HOSPITALS

Thinking about the overall governance methods of the hospital system, a crucial element is the way in which hospital care is reimbursed. Although there are multiple variants, subcategories and further alternative formulas, the ways in which hospitals are paid can be essentially traced back to five different principles (Aas, 1995; Barnum et al., 1995; Langenbrunner and Wiley, 2002; Mathes et al., 2014; Berenson et al., 2016; OECD, 2016b): (1) pay-for-procedure; (2) payment per day; (3) case-based reimbursement; (4) global budgeting; (5) pay-for-performance.

Let us start with the first method, "payment for procedures" (also called fee-for-service, or fee-for-item). This is based on the principle that every single service provided to the patient is paid for. Therefore, the patient bill is made up of the sum of the prices for each procedure actually completed during the hospital stay.

Payment per day (*per diem*) occurs – as the reader can easily guess – when hospitals are paid a daily charge multiplied by the number of days a patient spends hospitalized. Therefore, this method provides for a fixed charge that is independent of the procedures delivered. Payment per day is a widely used method in the past (Aas, 1995), which, however, is gradually giving way to other methods of remuneration.

With "case-based" reimbursement, the hospital is paid a previously established lump sum for each admission or for each episode of illness. This lump-sum reimbursement is independent of the number and type of procedures actually provided. The most well-known and most widespread pay-per-case mechanism at an international level is the system of Diagnosis Related Groups (DRGs). It consists of a patient classification system, the purpose of which is to group patients who have similar conditions together and require a similar intensity of treatment into the one category (OECD, 2016b). Patients are assigned a specific category – the system currently in use provides several hundred DRGs – based on the diagnosis. A flat per-discharge payment is typically associated with each DRG (Berenson et al., 2016).

With "global budgeting," a hospital receives a lump sum to cover all specified services in a given period (Barnum et al., 1995). Once established, this budget does not vary according to the number of patients treated and the volume of services actually provided. Global budgets can be calculated and negotiated on the basis of various criteria (Aas, 1995; Barnum et al., 1995): in proportion to the population residing in a given geographical area; by taking into consideration the historical costs and, therefore, the budgets of the previous years; by dividing hospital expenses into different expense items (staff salaries, drugs, catering service, equipment maintenance, etc.), and assigning a certain amount of resources for each line item; or also, based on the number of beds or departments in the hospital.

To the four main payment methods just mentioned, a fifth can be added: "pay-for-performance." This method follows a different logic than the previous ones, in that it intends to reward the outcome, the achievement of predefined quality and effectiveness objectives. Therefore, this system provides financial incentives (or penalties) based on the hospital's ability to meet certain performance targets (Berenson et al., 2016). It is good to immediately clarify that in none of the countries considered in this book is the method pay-for-performance currently the principal remuneration method. It should, therefore, be considered as an "add-on" (Mathes et al., 2014; OECD, 2016b), which is used in some countries to complement another remuneration system.

As will be explained later, also with regard to the different ways of remunerating health professionals, there is no perfect payment method since each of them has advantages and disadvantages (Mathes et al., 2014; OECD, 2016b). With the payment for procedures there is an incentive to increase the volume of services and to increase the intensity of care, providing more procedures than would be appropriate or necessary (Langenbrunner and Wiley, 2002). Daily rates provide an incentive to extend the length of hospitalization, and thus, also to expand bed capacity. Both the "per procedure" and "per day" payments must be considered as "retrospective" methods (Aas, 1995; Kutzin, 2001), in the sense that they do not allow to determine in advance the overall cost of a hospital structure since the total cost is determined only afterward, based on the activity actually carried out.

The main advantage of case-based reimbursement should lie in the incentive to contain the cost per case. However, this system can push hospitals to select patients, so as to only accept patients for whom the default reimbursement exceeds the expected cost of the services that are expected to be provided. The payment per case can also provide an incentive for up-coding, that is, to code patients into high-cost diagnostic categories (Barnum et al., 1995; Mathes et al., 2014).

The global budget should be, among all the methods presented here, the most "prospective" (Kutzin, 2001), as in fact, it allows the purchaser to know in advance the total cost of a hospital for a given period of time (for example, for a full year of activity). With this system, however, hospitals can be incentivized to under provide services, to lower the quality of care provided or to ration services (Barnum et al., 1995; Langenbrunner and Wiley, 2002). Even the pay-for-performance method risks generating some perverse incentives. It can induce providers to risk selection, preferring to take charge of healthier patients, in order to attain better performance (Mathes et al., 2014).

Once the different payment methods for hospitals have been presented, let us now see which of them are used in different

Table 6.2 *Hospital payment methods*

	Prevalent payment method
Australia	Case-based (DRGs) + Global budget
Austria	Case-based (DRGs)
Belgium	Global budget + Pay-per-procedure
Canada	Global budget
Czech Republic	Case-based (DRGs) + Global budget
Denmark	Global budget + Case-based (DRGs)
Finland	Case-based (DRGs)
France	Case-based (DRGs)
Germany	Case-based (DRGs)
Greece	Case-based (DRGs)
Hungary	Case-based (DRGs)
Ireland	Global budget + Case-based (DRGs)
Israel	Per diem + Pay-per-procedure
Italy	Case-based (DRGs) + Global budget
Japan	Pay-per-procedure
Korea	Pay-per-procedure
Netherlands	Case-based (DRGs)
New Zealand	Global budget
Norway	Global budget + Case-based (DRGs)
Poland	Case-based (DRGs) + Global budget
Portugal	Global budget + Case-based (DRGs)
Spain	Global budget
Sweden	Global budget + Case-based (DRGs)
Switzerland	Case-based (DRGs)
Turkey	Global budget + Pay-per-procedure
United Kingdom	Case-based (DRGs) + Global budget
United States	Case-based (DRGs)

Source: European Observatory on Health Systems and Policies – country HiTs (various years); OECD (2016a, 2016b)

countries. In Table 6.2, the prevalent method is indicated for each national system.

In the twenty-seven countries examined, there are two prevailing methods of remuneration for hospitals: case-based reimbursement, (which is declined, almost everywhere, according to the principle of DRGs), and global budgeting. Nine countries only use DRGs, ten countries adopt a blended formula of DRGs and global budgets. Three countries only adopt global budgeting. There are five countries that use pay-per-procedure (either alone or mixed with other methods).

The choice of payment method seems to derive, to a large extent, from the organizational model adopted in the country and from the nature (public or private) of the hospital system. Countries with a universalist system, but also some of the SHI with a largely public hospital supply system, tend to use the global budget, alone or mixed with case-based criteria. The countries of SHI and mandatory residence insurance, (many of which are based on competition between public and private hospitals), instead prefer, as an exclusive or prevalent method, the system of DRGs. The pay-for-procedure method finds fertile ground only in some SHI countries, especially Japan and Korea. The Israeli case is particular, where a mixture of pay per day and pay per procedure is used.

6.3 THE NUMBER OF PRACTICING PHYSICIANS

Having briefly presented the characteristics of the hospital offer, let us now focus on the medical profession. A first variable worth considering is the number of practicing physicians in the various countries. Table 6.3 lists the number of practicing physicians in each country in relation to the resident population. "Practicing physicians," as defined by the OECD database, include all those who actually practice as doctors and who have direct contact with patients. The calculation includes foreign doctors who work in the country, while doctors who are in retirement, unemployed and dentists are excluded. Unfortunately, for some countries the data concerning "practicing physicians" is not available.

With reference to Ireland, the Netherlands (only for some years) and Turkey, some of the values shown in Table 6.3 concern the so-called professionally active physicians. This category includes, in

6.3 THE NUMBER OF PRACTICING PHYSICIANS 153

Table 6.3 *Number of practicing physicians (2000–2019)*

(per thousand inhabitants)

	2000	2005	2010	2015	2019
Australia	2.5	2.8	3.1	3.5	3.8
Austria	3.9	4.3	4.8	5.1	5.2
Belgium	2.8	2.9	2.9	3.0	3.1
Canada	2.0	2.1	2.3	2.6	2.7
Czech Republic	3.4	3.6	3.6	3.7	4.0
Denmark	2.9	3.3	3.7	3.9	4.2
Finland	2.5	2.6	3.0	3.2	3.2
France	3.0	3.1	3.0	3.1	3.2
Germany	3.3	3.4	3.7	4.1	4.3
Greece °	4.4	5.1	5.8	5.9	6.1
Hungary	2.7	2.8	2.9	3.1	3.4
Ireland	n.a.	2.7*	2.7	3.1	3.3
Israel	3.5	3.2	3.3	3.1	3.2
Italy	3.4	3.7	3.8	3.8	4.0
Japan	1.9	2.0	2.2	2.4	2.5
Korea	1.3	1.6	2.0	2.2	2.4
Netherlands	2.4*	2.7*	3.0*	3.5	3.7
New Zealand	2.2	2.1	2.6	3.0	3.4
Norway	3.4	3.6	4.1	4.4	4.9
Poland	2.2	2.1	2.2	2.3	2.4
Portugal °	3.1	3.4	3.9	4.6	5.2
Spain	3.1	3.6	3.8	3.9	4.0
Sweden	3.1	3.5	3.9	4.2	4.3
Switzerland	3.5*	3.7	3.8	4.2	4.3
Turkey	1.3*	1.5*	1.7*	1.8*	1.9*
United Kingdom	2.0	2.4	2.7	2.8	3.0
United States	2.3	2.4	2.4	2.6	2.6

Note: ° Values referring to doctors who are "licensed to practice."
* Values referring to doctors who are "professionally active."
Source: OECD (2020)

addition to practicing physicians, also those who, although they do not directly provide care to patients, occupy administrative, management and research positions for which a medical degree is required. The figure for "professionally active" doctors is usually slightly higher than that of practicing physicians.

For two countries, Greece and Portugal, the only data made available by the OECD regards physicians who are "licensed to practice." With this definition we are referring to all those who are formally authorized to carry out the medical profession; which includes, in addition to professionally active doctors, also retired doctors, those unemployed and those who carry out jobs for which a degree in medicine is not necessary. The number of "licensed to practice" is obviously much higher than that of "practicing physicians." Thus, the values of Greece and Portugal – for Table 6.3 only – are not comparable with those of the other countries.

Table 6.3 lends itself to two readings: one in a diachronic key (to understand how the number of doctors has changed over time), the other in a synchronic key, by focusing, in particular, on the last available year.

A diachronic reading of the data shows that in almost all the countries considered the number of doctors (per thousand inhabitants) is constantly growing. If we consider, as a whole, all the twenty-seven countries included in the table, from 2000 to 2019, in just under twenty years, the number of practicing doctors increased on average by 34 percent, that is, more than a third. The only country bucking the trend is Israel, where the density of practicing physicians has decreased since the year 2000.

Let us move on to the synchronic analysis, focusing on the last column of Table 6.3, relating to the density of practicing physicians in 2019 (or in the most recent year available). Most countries have between three and four practicing physicians per thousand inhabitants. However, there are profound differences between the health systems analyzed. If we temporarily exclude from the comparison Greece and Portugal, (whose values, as mentioned above, are not comparable to the others), the country with the highest density of practicing physicians is Austria (5.2 doctors per thousand inhabitants), followed by Norway (4.9), Germany, Sweden and Switzerland (4.3). On the other hand, the country where the concentration of doctors is lower is Turkey (only 1.9 doctors per thousand inhabitants); but also in the Republic of Korea (2.3), in Poland (2.4), in Japan (2.5) and in the United States (2.6) there is a low number of practicing physicians. The differences between countries are, therefore, significant, and are perhaps even more evident if we express them in the following way. In Turkey there is one active doctor for every 526 inhabitants; in Austria there is one practicing doctor for every 192 inhabitants. As striking as they are, the differences between countries do not appear to be strictly related to the healthcare model adopted in the country. Within each of the families identified in Chapter 5 there is great variance.

The number of doctors who are active in each country is an important element to consider, as it affects the overall organization of the system of care delivery, the relationships between doctors and other health professions and the remuneration of doctors.

In countries where there are fewer doctors, we can assume that certain "advanced clinical activities" (Maier and Aiken, 2016) are carried out by different professionals (such as nurse practitioners). And plausibly a whole series of administrative and management activities will also be entrusted to professionals who do not have a degree in medicine. Consequently, doctors are freed from the tasks that can be delegated to other professional figures, so they can concentrate on the activities of their exclusive competence, such as diagnosis and prescription of treatments.

The number of doctors working in each individual national context usually also has an impact on the prestige and earning potential of the medical profession. In general, in health systems where there is a high density of doctors, they earn less on average. The incomes of doctors tend, conversely, to be higher where there are fewer practitioners (Fujisawa and Lafortune, 2008; Toth, 2009).

And this appears not only plausible, but perhaps even obvious, in that, if there are few doctors in a country, they will be in greater demand and they may, therefore, require higher fees. By increasing the number of practicing doctors, according to the law of supply and demand, the rates should instead decrease. This is why in many countries the associations representing doctors are generally in favor of limiting access to the profession and imposing the *numerus clausus* in medical schools.

6.3.1 The Shortage of Doctors and Recruitment from Abroad

It was, therefore, noted that in the vast majority of OECD countries, with the sole exception of Israel, the number of doctors is constantly growing. From the 1960s onward, the number of practicing physicians has progressively increased, both in absolute terms and in proportion to the resident population (OECD, 2019f). It can, therefore, legitimately be said that – at least in OECD countries – there have never been as many practicing doctors as today (OECD, 2016c).

Despite this objective data, in many countries, for some time now, there have been strong concerns about a (current or in any case imminent) shortage of doctors (Lafortune et al., 2016). One naturally wonders how this could be possible. If the number of doctors is growing almost everywhere, how can there be a shortage of doctors?

Concerns about a possible shortage of doctors are fueled by some contributing factors. The first factor concerns the progressive aging of the population and the growing demand for healthcare (Lafortune et al., 2016). If, in the past, a certain proportion between practicing doctors and the population to be assisted could have been considered adequate, this may not apply in the future. In the years to come – this is the forecast – we will need more doctors than in the past, especially in some specialties.

A second element of concern is regarding the age composition of the medical profession itself. A problem that unites many countries is the high number of doctors from the "baby-boom" generation who are coming to retirement age (and will arrive in the next few years) (Ono et al., 2013; OECD, 2019f). The fear, in these countries, is that the number of new medical graduates entering the profession is not sufficient to compensate for the numerous doctors who are retiring.

In order to maintain or even increase the availability of doctors within their territory, the governments of the OECD countries have adopted a variety of countermeasures. Some national governments have intended to extend the working life of doctors, extending the retirement age or providing specific incentives for doctors to postpone their retirement (Lafortune et al., 2016). Many governments have intervened with the *numerus clausus*, by increasing the number of students enrolled in medical education (Moreira and Lafortune, 2016). There are numerous countries in which, in addition or as an alternative to the previous measures, it was decided to focus on the recruitment of professionals from abroad (Ono et al., 2013). The strategy of recruiting health professionals from abroad may concern not only doctors but also other professional figures (such as nurses) who are deemed to be insufficient in number to meet the national demand for healthcare. On the latter phenomenon, that is, on the percentage of doctors and nurses recruited from abroad, it is possible to provide some data.

Table 6.4 shows the percentage of doctors and nurses who have been trained abroad. Before commenting on the data, it is appropriate to dedicate a few words on the variable used, in order to avoid possible misunderstanding. To evaluate the weight of foreigners on the total healthcare workforce, one could consider the number of workers who were "born abroad." In doing so, however, one would end up considering even those who have lived in the country for many years as foreigners, and who, perhaps in the meantime, have obtained citizenship; or those who emigrated at an early age with their respective parents to a country, and completed their entire schooling there. To avoid this, the OECD believes it is more indicative to consider not the country of origin of the workers, but instead, the place of their education and training. The values shown in Table 6.4 refer to

158 HOSPITALS, DOCTORS AND NURSES

Table 6.4 *Foreign-trained doctors and nurses*

(2019 or last year available)

	Foreign-trained doctors (% of practicing physicians)	Foreign-trained nurses (% of practicing nurses)
Australia	32.5	18.1
Austria	6.0	n.a.
Belgium	12.4	3.9
Canada	24.5	8.3
Czech Republic	7.4	n.a.
Denmark	9.4	1.9
Finland	19.9	1.8
France	11.5	2.9
Germany	12.5	8.7
Greece	19.9	2.5
Hungary	8.1	1.5
Ireland	41.3	n.a.
Israel	57.8	9.8
Italy	0.9	4.8
Japan	n.a.	n.a.
Korea	n.a.	n.a.
Netherlands	2.7	1.3
New Zealand	42.5	26.2
Norway	41.0	6.2
Poland	1.9	0.1
Portugal	12.0	1.8
Spain	9.4	2.1
Sweden	27.9	3.1
Switzerland	35.4	25.0
Turkey	0.2	0.3
United Kingdom	30.3	15.4
United States	25.0	6.0

Source: OECD (2020)

foreign-trained professionals (doctors and nurses). This indicator should be interpreted with caution since not all doctors and nurses who trained abroad are necessarily foreigners; among the professionals "trained abroad" there are also those born in the country who have decided to study medicine or nursing abroad, and then return to their origin country to practice (Merçay et al., 2016).

If we consider the proportion of doctors trained abroad, the differences between the countries are enormous. At one extreme we find Israel, where doctors who were trained abroad even reach 58 percent of the total. But also in Ireland, New Zealand and Norway, more than 40 percent of the doctors graduated abroad; in Switzerland and Australia doctors trained abroad are about one-third of the total. If these are the countries with the largest percentage of foreign-trained doctors, there are others where doctors with degrees from abroad constitute a small minority. In Italy and Turkey, there is less than 1 percent of doctors with degrees from abroad and there is less than 2 percent in Poland.

As for nurses, the percentage of those who were trained abroad is highest in New Zealand (26.2 percent), Switzerland (25 percent), Australia (18.1 percent) and United Kingdom (15.4 percent). The countries where, on the other hand, the number of foreign-trained nurses is lower are Poland and Turkey. In these two countries, foreign-trained nurses make up less than 1 percent of practicing nurses. On average, the proportion of foreign-trained nurses is much lower than that of foreign-trained doctors.

The above data cannot be considered all that surprising, because to a large extent they reflect the demographic composition of the respective countries. In general, the presence of foreign doctors and nurses is higher in countries where a high percentage of the population is immigrant, and vice versa. The highest proportion of foreign-trained doctors and nurses is, therefore, found in what we can consider the main settlement countries (Australia, Canada, Israel, New Zealand, United States) and in European countries, such as Switzerland, traditionally accustomed to strong incoming flows of migrants (OECD, 2019b). Likewise, the countries with the lowest percentage of health personnel (both doctors and nurses) trained abroad are those of Southern Europe and Eastern Europe, in which foreign-born population rates are traditionally lower.

160 HOSPITALS, DOCTORS AND NURSES

6.3.2 Women Doctors

Continuing our "radiography" of the medical profession, it is interesting to take a look at how many women there are, as a percentage of the total number of practicing doctors. This data is reported in Table 6.5, with reference to the year 2000 (or the closest year) and to the year 2019 (or the last available year).

Also in this case, we can start from an inter-temporal comparison. The diachronic trend is toward a progressive and generalized feminization of the medical profession (Kilminster et al., 2007; Adams, 2010; Bleakley, 2014). From 2000 to date, in all the countries considered, without exception, the percentage of female doctors has increased, in some cases considerably. If we put together all twenty-seven countries included in our sample, in 2000 women made up just 30.8 percent of the doctors in practice. In 2019, the percentage of female doctors rose to 41.6 percent. The increase – in less than two decades – was, therefore, considerable.

In the year 2000, in only three countries – the Czech Republic, Hungary and Poland, all Eastern European countries – female doctors were in the majority compared to their male colleagues. In 2019, the countries where women were in the majority became nine: Czech Republic, Denmark, Finland, Hungary, the Netherlands, Norway, Poland, Portugal and Spain.

If we focus on the values relating to the most recent year available, Finland stands out as the country where female doctors are in the highest percentage (reaching almost 58 percent of practicing physicians).

But the most surprising data – at least for external observers, who are not familiar with these national contexts – concerns the two Far East countries included in our sample, namely Japan and South Korea. In these two countries, the percentage of female doctors is very low. In Japan, there are less than 22 percent women doctors (actually, about one doctor for every four men), in Korea there are less than 24 percent (therefore, less than one woman for every three men). Also

6.3 THE NUMBER OF PRACTICING PHYSICIANS   161

Table 6.5 *Female practicing physicians (2000–2019)*

(as a percentage of practicing physicians)

	2000	2019
Australia	30.0	41.8
Austria	36.8	47.6
Belgium	27.7	44.0
Canada	31.3	44.1
Czech Republic	51.6	56.3
Denmark	36.2	52.9
Finland	49.9	57.7
France	36.5	45.3
Germany	36.0	47.1
Greece	33.9	42.1
Hungary	50.1	56.1
Ireland	36.5	45.0
Israel	38.8	41.5
Italy	30.2	43.4
Japan	14.3	21.8
Korea	n.a.	23.6
Netherlands	35.3	55.5
New Zealand	32.9	45.7
Norway	33.5	50.6
Poland	54.2	56.8
Portugal	45.6	55.7
Spain	36.8	56.2
Sweden	39.7	46.8
Switzerland	29.1	42.7
Turkey	32.0	37.5
United Kingdom	36.0	48.6
United States	25.0	36.6

Source: OECD (2020)

in the United States (36.6 percent) and Turkey (37.5 percent) the percentage of female doctors is comparatively rather low. The ratio is roughly one female doctor for every two male colleagues. In short, it can be concluded that in the four countries just mentioned, despite

162 HOSPITALS, DOCTORS AND NURSES

the ongoing feminization process, the medical profession still remains a predominantly male profession.

6.3.3 Generalists versus Specialists

The OECD database provides a further interesting element concerning the composition of the medical profession: the distinction between generalists and specialists (Table 6.6). Values relating to Japan are not available because in that country the generalist-specialist distinction has little meaning and is not usually formalized (Blank et al., 2018).

Looking at the data, it can be seen that in some countries the share of generalists is very low. This is the case in the United States (which has just 0.3 generalists per thousand inhabitants), Greece (0.4) and Poland (0.4). On the contrary, the country that appears to have the highest density of generalists is Portugal[1] (with 2.7 generalists per thousand inhabitants), followed by Ireland (1.8 generalists per thousand inhabitants). Ireland and Portugal are the only two countries in which general practitioners are predominant when compared to their specialist colleagues. In all the other national systems, the number of specialists outnumbers – sometimes by quite a lot – that of generalists. As a general trend, in the NHS there is a greater presence of generalists (on average, 1.2 per thousand inhabitants) than in SHI countries (on average, 0.9 generalists per thousand inhabitants). As for the specialists, there are no particular differences between the two families.

The ratio between specialists and generalists is shown in the last column of Table 6.6. There are cases, such as Australia and Canada, in which the number of specialists is slightly higher than that of generalists (the specialist/generalist ratio is in fact 1.1). In other national systems, specialists are in clear prevalence. In the United States there are 7.5 specialists for each general practitioner,

---

[1] However, it should be noted that the data relating to Portugal, as well as that relating to Greece, refers to "licensed to practice" doctors and not to "practicing physicians."

6.3 THE NUMBER OF PRACTICING PHYSICIANS 163

Table 6.6 *Number of practicing generalist and specialist doctors*

(2019 or last year available)

	Generalist doctors (per thousand inhabitants)	Specialist doctors (per thousand inhabitants)	Specialist/ generalist ratio
Australia	1.6	1.8	1.1
Austria	1.7	2.6	1.5
Belgium	1.2	1.9	1.7
Canada	1.3	1.5	1.1
Czech Republic	0.7	3.2	4.9
Denmark	0.8	1.8	2.3
Finland	1.3	1.9	1.6
France	1.4	1.8	1.2
Germany	1.0	3.3	3.3
Greece	0.4	5.1	12.6
Hungary	0.7	2.7	3.7
Ireland	1.8	1.5	0.8
Israel	1.0	2.3	2.3
Italy	0.9	3.1	3.6
Korea	0.7	1.7	2.7
Netherlands	1.7	2.0	1.2
New Zealand	1.4	1.9	1.4
Norway	0.9	2.1	2.4
Poland	0.4	2.0	4.7
Portugal	2.7	2.6	1.0
Spain	0.8	2.6	3.4
Sweden	0.6	2.3	3.5
Switzerland	1.1	2.6	2.3
Turkey	0.6	1.3	2.1
United Kingdom	0.8	2.2	2.8
United States	0.3	2.3	7.5

Notes: Some of the values reported in Table 6.6 do not coincide with those reported in Table 6.3. This is due to the fact that in some countries there are a number of doctors who cannot be classified as either generalists or specialists.
Source: OECD (2020)

while in Greece the ratio is over 12 to 1. It should also be kept in mind that in most of the countries, in recent decades, the proportion of specialists in relation to generalists has increased (Blank et al., 2018; OECD, 2020).

The ratio of medical specialists to generalists seems to be connected, at least in part, to the organizational model (in the NHS this ratio assumes lower values on average than in the SHI systems), but even more to the presence or absence of a gatekeeping mechanism in the individual countries (see Chapter 4). In countries that adopt a mandatory gatekeeping system, the specialist/generalist ratio has an average value of 2, while in countries that allow direct access, this ratio is 3.9, almost double.

In short, the division between generalists and specialists seems to reflect a different vision as well as a different organization of the overall system of healthcare delivery (Ono et al., 2013). In countries where greater importance is given to primary and territorial care, and the role of "first contact" and "gatekeeper" attributed to the family doctor is more valued, we should tend to find a greater presence of generalists. On the contrary, in systems where the direct access rule is in force and where the level of primary care is less structured, we should find, in proportion, a greater number of specialists.

With the aim of strengthening the provision of primary care, several national governments (including Belgium, Canada, Czech Republic, France, Germany, Hungary, Poland, Switzerland, United Kingdom and United States) have recently introduced incentives to encourage more students to choose general medicine (Lafortune et al., 2016). In fact, it is good to point out that in most countries – at least in OECD countries – specialist doctors on average obtain higher remuneration (sometimes even much higher) than that of general practitioners (Fujisawa and Lafortune, 2008; Lafortune et al., 2016). This may, at least in part, explain why in many countries medical graduates prefer to pursue the career of the specialist rather than devote themselves to primary care.

The issue of doctors' remuneration, which has just been mentioned, constitutes a strategic element in the governance of every health system, thus, it deserves an in-depth study.

6.4 PHYSICIAN PAYMENT METHODS

As has been done previously with regard to hospitals, it is interesting to think about the methods by which doctors are paid. There are three main ways of remunerating doctors (Moreno, 1990; Robinson, 2001; Greß et al., 2006; Christianson and Conrad, 2011): (1) fee-for-service; (2) capitation; and (3) salary.

The fee-for-service (FFS) method – in a similar way to the pay-per-procedure applied to hospitals – requires each doctor to be paid in proportion to the type and quantity of services actually provided. Since each service is paid a certain rate, the most productive doctors – or those who provide the services with the most profitable rates – will be the ones who earn the most. Depending on the version, the rates can be the same for everyone (determined, for example, by doctors' associations, or through negotiation between insurers and providers), or set at the discretion of the individual professional.

A second remuneration mechanism is that of capitation. This system assumes that patients are attributed to a particular doctor, or to a group of professionals, for a specific period of time (for example, for a year). The logic of capitation provides that doctors are rewarded based on the number of patients they care for, regardless of how many treatments or the type of care each patient actually receives (Blank et al., 2018). The capitation fee (corresponding to each patient taken into care) can be uniform for all clients, or it can be weighed, taking into account some variables, such as the age or health conditions of the patients (Greß et al., 2006). In practice, as will be seen shortly (Table 6.7), it is rare for a single specialist physician to be remunerated with the capitation method; this payment model is applied above all to family doctors or to groups of multidisciplinary providers. In some versions of this payment system, to prevent professionals from buying up patients – arriving at an excessive number of them so that they are

Table 6.7 Remuneration methods for doctors

	General practitioners	Outpatient specialists	Hospital doctors
Australia	FFS + EB	FFS + EB	Salary + PP
Austria	Capitation + FFS	FFS	Salary + PP
Belgium	FFS	FFS	FFS
Canada	FFS	FFS	FFS
Czech Republic	Capitation + FFS	Salary	Salary + PP
Denmark	FFS + Capitation	FFS	Salary + PP
France	FFS + EB	FFS + EB	Salary + PP
Finland	Salary + Capit. + FFS	Salary + PP	Salary + PP
Germany	FFS	FFS	Salary
Greece	Salary or FFS	FFS or Salary	Salary + PP
Hungary	Capitation + FFS	Salary + PP	Salary + PP
Ireland	Capitation + FFS	Salary + PP	Salary + PP
Israel	Capitation or Salary	Capitation + FFS	Salary + PP
Italy	Capitation	Salary or FFS	Salary + PP
Japan	FFS	FFS	Salary

Korea	FFS	FFS	Salary
Netherlands	Capitation + FFS	FFS	Salary or FFS
New Zealand	Capitation + FFS	Salary + PP	Salary + PP
Norway	FFS + Capitation	Salary + FFS	Salary + PP
Poland	Capitation + FFS	FFS	Salary + PP
Portugal	Salary	Salary + PP	Salary + PP
Spain	Salary + Capitation	Salary + PP	Salary + PP
Sweden	Capitation + FFS	Salary	Salary + PP
Switzerland	FFS	FFS	Salary + PP
Turkey	Salary + Capitation	Salary + FFS	Salary + FFS
United Kingdom	Capitation + FFS	Salary + PP	Salary + PP
United States	FFS	FFS	FFS or Salary

EB = extra-billing; FFS = fee-for-service; PP = private practice.

168 HOSPITALS, DOCTORS AND NURSES

not able to follow them all – a maximum number of clients per doctor is set. In several countries there is a ceiling for the total number of patients per GP (Fujisawa and Lafortune, 2008).

A third method of payment is the fixed salary. Doctors undertake to observe a certain working schedule, for which they are rewarded with a previously agreed amount, regardless of both the number of patients and the services actually provided.

To summarize, it can be said that the fee-for-service method pays the providers for performance, the capitation method pays according to the number of patients, the salary method pays the doctors for their time (Greß et al., 2006). Each remuneration method incorporates incentives that can affect the behavior of the professionals (or organizations) receiving the payment (Christianson and Conrad, 2011). As previously commented on hospitals, even in terms of payment of providers there is no perfect method; each system inevitably has both pros and cons (Moreno, 1990). At least on paper, the fee-for-service method should be the system that stimulates productivity the most, as it rewards the most productive and most sought-after suppliers by patients. At the same time, however, it provides an incentive to increase the total volume of services provided, to also provide services that are not strictly necessary and to choose, with the same effectiveness, the most expensive therapeutic procedures (Moreno, 1990; Robinson, 2001). A further characteristic of the fee-for-service method is that it is a "retrospective" method (Kutzin, 2001) in that it does not allow the total amount of doctors' remuneration to be determined in advance, as the other two payment methods, salary and the capitation, instead, consent to do.

Compared to fee-for-service, remuneration through a fixed salary provides incentives in the opposite direction. If on one hand it discourages the overproduction of medical services, on the other hand it does not provide any premium for the productivity of the individual professional, who is paid the same if a large volume of work is done or if they are not very productive (Robinson, 2001). A difference that is often highlighted with respect to the fee-for-service method concerns customer orientation and the provision of high quality services (Christianson and Conrad, 2011). In the fee-based system, every doctor has an interest in seeking the satisfaction of his clients (so that they return or, in any case, speak well of the service received). Not having a direct economic incentive in this sense, the salaried doctor could, instead, take the patients' judgment less into consideration, treating them with less attention and kindness (this is what public healthcare services are often accused of).

Capitation can be conceived of as an intermediate solution with respect to the two previous methods. Like the fee-for-service method, it invites doctors to seek user satisfaction (patients can abandon professionals with which they do not feel satisfied); whereas, like the fixed salary system, the capitation quota system also allows the overall earnings of doctors to be kept under control and does not offer economic incentives for the provision of unnecessary services. To a greater extent than in the other two systems, the capitation method should also ensure the stability of the doctor–patient relationship and, therefore, the continuity of care (Moreno, 1990). Obviously, even the capitation method has some contraindications, in that this mechanism can induce doctors to select patients (Barnum et al., 1995; Robinson, 2001; Christianson and Conrad, 2011), accepting the less demanding ones (younger or healthier) and leaving those in need of more care to others (this is the "cherry-picking" mentioned in Chapter 2). Under a capitation system, since doctors do not have financial incentives to provide many services, the risk is that patients are undertreated (Aas, 1995).

Fee-for-service, capitation and fixed salary methods are, therefore, the three basic methods by which doctors can be paid. In reality, these methods are often found combined with each other. It is common for doctors' incomes to consist of several components, each of which is calculated according to a different payment mechanism (Greß et al., 2006). The use of mixed remuneration formulas can be considered an intentional choice by policy makers or purchasers of healthcare services, who hope – by mixing the different systems – to dilute (or balance) the perverse incentives that each of these payment methods tends to stimulate (Aas, 1995; Kutzin, 2001; Robinson, 2001).

Those illustrated above are the three most widely used remuneration models, even if they are not the only ones used. Recently, some countries have been experimenting with innovative forms of payment for doctors (as well as hospitals). Among these new payment mechanisms is that of rewarding the achievement of a set of performance and quality objectives (in a similar way to what can be done for hospitals). "Pay-for-performance" mechanisms have been introduced in several countries, including Australia, Czech Republic, France, Hungary, the Netherlands, United Kingdom and the United States (Fujisawa and Lafortune, 2008; OECD, 2016a). However, in countries where it was introduced, performance-based remuneration is still used as a minority component and accompanies other payment formulas.

To complete the picture, in addition to the three basic methods, the pay-for-performance schemes, and the mixed formulas, two further variants should be mentioned: the so-called extra-billing (Schokkaert and van de Voorde, 2011), and the possibility for employed doctors to practice privately as well.

The first of these two variants, "extra-billing," may exist in fee-for-service systems in which medical services are subject to a standard rate set at the national or local level. In fact, extra-billing consists, very prosaically, of the possibility granted to doctors to apply rates that are higher than the standard fees. Since, in general, the standard rates are those that insurers (private insurance, sickness funds, public schemes) agree to reimburse, the price difference is paid by the patients. In France, for example, doctors can choose whether to belong to "*secteur 1*" or "*secteur 2*" (Choné, 2017). Those belonging to "sector 1" accept the standard rate agreed with the social health insurance, and in exchange are entitled to some benefits in terms of social security and sickness contributions. Instead, doctors who opt for "sector 2" forgo these benefits, but in return they can ask their patients for higher rates than those negotiated nationally (Rodwin, 2018).

6.4 PHYSICIAN PAYMENT METHODS 171

The second variant is represented by "private practice" (also called dual practice), which is found only in systems in which doctors are employees. It is the faculty granted to these professionals to also practice independently. British hospital doctors, for example, despite being employees of the National Health Service are traditionally given the possibility – outside of their working hours – to also practice freelance (Cylus et al., 2015; Blank et al., 2018).

6.4.1 How Doctors Are Paid in Individual Countries?

Once the basic models and the most frequent variants have been presented, it is now possible to take a look at how doctors are paid in the different national systems (Table 6.7). In addition to the presence of mixed formulas, the picture is complicated by the fact that within the same country not all doctors are remunerated according to the same criterion. It will therefore be necessary to distinguish between: (1) general practitioners; (2) outpatient specialists; and (3) hospital doctors. The prevailing remuneration method is indicated for each of these categories, that is, the one applied to the majority of those belonging to the category.

Looking at the data contained in Table 6.7, it stands out that by far the most used method to pay hospital doctors is the salary, and this applies both to countries where an NHS operates, and to those that adopt a different model. The main deviations from this general pattern are Belgian and Canadian hospital doctors, who are paid mainly on a fee-for-service basis. In short, for the hospital doctors, the picture is rather homogeneous.

Let us move on to the payment methods of GPs and outpatient specialists. On the basis of what has been argued so far, we might expect: (1) that in countries with an NHS even nonhospital doctors are, for the most part, employees who are remunerated through a fixed salary and (2) that in all other systems the prevailing payment method is the fee-for-service. Observing the data, this second expectation is generally confirmed, thus, the fee-for-service (possibly mixed, as regards family doctors, with a component on a capitation basis) is actually the payment method most used in SHI systems, in separated universalist systems, in mandatory residence insurance countries and in the United States. Three countries with SHI (Czech Republic, Hungary and Turkey) are exceptions, where the production system is largely public. This seems to explain why out-of-hospital doctors are remunerated through salary, or with a mix of capitation and salary.

Contrary to expectations, it is not, however, true that family doctors and outpatient specialists working in NHS countries are predominantly salaried employees. In six out of ten NHS countries (Ireland, Italy, New Zealand, Norway, Sweden and the United Kingdom), family doctors are paid primarily on a capitation basis. This is justified by the fact that in these countries (with the exception of Sweden) – as mentioned in Chapter 4 – family doctors are not public employees, but freelancers contracted with the public service. Particular among the NHS countries is the Danish case, in which both family doctors and outpatient specialists are paid to a large extent by the fee-for-service method.

This leaves only three NHS countries (Finland, Portugal and Spain) where both outpatient specialists and family doctors are paid mainly through salary. It is also interesting to note how in all ten NHS countries hospital doctors are allowed to carry out, in addition to their institutional activities, even private practice.

The healthcare systems of Greece and Israel are confirmed as "mixed" also as regards the remuneration methods for doctors. The Israeli case has a peculiarity: It is the only one among the twenty-seven countries analyzed here to apply capitation not only to general practitioners but also to outpatient specialists. It should be noted that in Israel, a distinction is made between "active capitation" and "passive capitation." Some health plans use the former, while others use the latter (Rosen et al., 2015). "Passive capitation" is when the doctor receives a refund for each patient, regardless of whether or not the doctor has visited the patient in a certain time interval (usually a quarter – three months). In "active capitation," however, the payment is made only if the doctor has visited the patient at least once during the quarter (Mossialos et al., 2017).

6.5 THE NURSES

In analyzing the healthcare workforce, we began with doctors, because they are traditionally considered "dominant" (Freidson, 1970) in the sector, in terms of prestige and power. However, the numerically largest professional component is not made up of doctors, but of nurses.

6.5.1 The Number of Practicing Nurses

As was done previously for doctors, also in relation to nurses it is interesting to look at the data regarding their number, and how it has changed over the last two decades. The values relating to the number of practicing nurses (calculated per thousand inhabitants) in the various countries, in relation to the period 2000–2019, are reported in Table 6.8.

As has been observed for doctors, the number of nurses is also constantly growing, (both in absolute terms and in relation to the resident population), in most of the countries considered. In absolute terms, between 2000 and 2019, therefore in less than two decades, the number of nurses in the twenty-seven countries considered here increased on average by more than 40 percent. In some cases (Poland, United Kingdom, Czech Republic), the growth in absolute terms, during the last two decades, has been limited (less than 10 percent). In other countries, on the other hand, the absolute number has grown considerably, more than 150 percent in twenty years. This is the case of the Republic of Korea and Turkey. Two countries go against the trend, Israel and the United Kingdom, in which in 2019 there was a lower density of nurses than that recorded in the year 2000.

If we focus on the total number of practicing nurses in 2019 (or in any case, in the most recent year available), there are very marked differences between one country and another. The nation with the

174 HOSPITALS, DOCTORS AND NURSES

Table 6.8 *Practicing nurses (2000–2019)*

(per thousand inhabitants)

	2000	2005	2010	2015	2019
Australia	10.1	9.8	10.2	11.4	11.9
Austria	5.6	6.0	6.5	6.8	6.9
Belgium	n.a.	9.0	9.6	10.8	11.2
Canada	n.a.	8.7	9.4	9.9	10.0
Czech Republic	7.6	8.1	8.1	8.0	8.1
Denmark	9.3	9.6	9.8	9.9	10.1
Finland	10.7	12.6	13.9	14.3	14.3
France*	6.7	7.6	8.5	9.9	10.8
Germany	10.0	10.7	11.5	12.7	13.2
Greece	2.8	3.3	3.5	3.2	3.4
Hungary	5.3	6.0	6.2	6.5	6.6
Ireland*	n.a.	12.2	13.5	12.4	12.9
Israel	5.4	5.2	4.7	4.9	5.0
Italy	n.a.	5.0	5.2	5.4	5.6
Japan	8.4	8.8	10.1	11.0	11.8
Korea	3.0	3.8	4.6	5.9	7.2
Netherlands	7.8	8.2	8.4	10.5	11.1
New Zealand	n.a.	9.0	10.1	10.3	10.3
Norway	12.1	13.6	16.1	17.3	18.0
Poland	5.0	5.1	5.3	5.2	5.1
Portugal*	n.a.	4.4	5.7	6.3	6.9
Spain	3.5	4.4	5.2	5.3	5.9
Sweden	9.6	10.5	10.8	10.9	10.9
Switzerland	11.6	12.7	14.6	16.6	17.6
Turkey*	1.1	1.1	1.6	2.0	2.3
United Kingdom	8.2	9.2	8.4	7.9	7.8
United States*	10.2	10.4	10.9	11.3	11.9

Note: * The value refers to professionally active nurses.
Source: OECD (2020)

highest density of nurses is Norway (18 practicing nurses per thousand inhabitants), followed by Switzerland (17.6) and then Finland (14.3). By contrast, the country that makes the least use of nurses is Turkey (just 2.3 practicing nurses per thousand inhabitants), followed by Greece (3.4), Israel (5.0) and Poland (5.1). Between the country with the highest density and the one with the lowest density of nurses, the distance is truly astounding. In Norway there is one nurse for every fifty-five inhabitants; in Turkey the ratio is 1 to 435. In Switzerland, there is a concentration of nurses that is five times higher than that recorded in Greece.

Therefore, the differences between one country and another are marked. They could, to some extent, also depend on the organizational model adopted. On average, there are 10.4 practicing nurses per thousand inhabitants in NHS countries, compared to an average of 7.9 in SHI countries.

6.5.2 *The Relationship between Doctors and Nurses and the Topic of Task Shifting*

Table 6.9 shows an interesting variable used to understand the relationships between the different health professions. This table shows the numerical relationship between practicing nurses[2] and practicing doctors. As well as the ratio between specialist doctors and generalists (analyzed in Table 6.6), also the nurse to doctor ratio reveals the ways in which the healthcare delivery system is organized.

The values shown in Table 6.9 deserve a brief comment. The diachronic analysis does not reserve any particular surprises. If we consider all twenty-seven countries, in 2019 the ratio was, on average, 3.2 nurses for each doctor. In the year 2000, again considering all twenty-seven countries, the ratio was always 3.2. In short, we can conclude that, on average, the numerical relationship between nurses and doctors has remained constant over the last two decades. In all countries, during the period 2000–2019, both the number of practicing doctors and that of practicing nurses grew in absolute terms. In just over half of the countries, the number of doctors grew faster than nurses, however, in other countries the opposite was true.

---

[2] For some countries, in the absence of data relating to "practicing nurses," the value relating to "professionally active" nurses is used.

176 HOSPITALS, DOCTORS AND NURSES

Table 6.9 *The nurse-to-doctor ratio*

	2000	2019
Australia	4.0	3.2
Austria	1.4	1.3
Belgium	3.2	3.6
Canada	4.4	3.6
Czech Republic	2.3	2.0
Denmark	3.2	2.4
Finland	4.3	4.4
France	2.2	3.4
Germany	3.1	3.1
Greece	0.6°	0.6°
Hungary	2.0	2.0
Ireland	5.9°	3.8
Israel	1.6	1.6
Italy	1.5	1.4
Japan	4.4	4.7
Korea	2.3	3.0
Netherlands	3.3	3.0
New Zealand	4.3	3.1
Norway	3.6	3.6
Poland	2.2	2.1
Portugal	1.4°	1.3°
Spain	1.1	1.5
Sweden	3.2	2.6
Switzerland	3.3	4.1
Turkey	0.8	1.2
United Kingdom	4.1	2.6
United States	4.4	4.6

Note: ° The ratio is calculated in relation to doctors "licensed to practice."
Source: OECD (2020)

The comparison of the different national systems, in relation to the most recent year available, is more interesting. In fact, what has already been highlighted above is confirmed, namely, that in the twenty-seven countries considered, the distribution of doctors and nurses is far from uniform. There are countries in which at least four nurses practice for each practicing doctor. This is the case in Japan (4.7 nurses per doctor), the United States (4.6), Finland (4.4) and Switzerland (4.1). On the other hand, there are countries where the ratio between nurses and doctors is much lower. This is the case in Turkey (1.2), Austria (1.3), Italy (1.4) and Spain (1.5). As before, the values of Greece and Portugal are not comparable with those of other countries since the ratio is calculated by taking into account the doctors who are "licensed to practice."

Analyzing the ratio of nurses to doctors allows us to make a quick reference to the important topic of "task shifting" (WHO, 2008; Maier and Aiken, 2016; EU, 2019). With this expression we are generally referring to a redistribution of skills between different professional figures (EU, 2019). Specifically, by task shifting we mean the assumption by nurses of clinical tasks that in the past were the exclusive responsibility of doctors (Maier, 2015; Laurant et al., 2018). The most relevant clinical activities that can be delegated – even only partially, or under certain conditions – to professional nurses concern the diagnosis of diseases, the prescription of drugs and therapies, the referral of patients to specialists and the order and interpretation of diagnostic tests (Delamaire and Lafortune, 2010; Maier and Aiken, 2016). In some countries, task shifting concerns a broad spectrum of skills; in other countries, the recruitment of new skills by nurses is more limited (Maier et al., 2018). In some national contexts, task shifting is officially recognized and encouraged, while in other countries it is practiced in the absence of formal recognition (Maier, 2015).

Chapter 8 will deal with the so-called health politics, and the conflicts between the various stakeholders who are mobilizing to influence strategic choices in the health field. At this time, task shifting is, in many countries, a subject of strong division and open conflict between the representative organizations of doctors and those representing the nursing profession. In many national contexts, doctors are reluctant to give up part of their prerogatives, and see the transfer of skills to nurses (or to other professionals, such as pharmacists or midwives) as a possible threat to their prestige and professional power (Delamaire and Lafortune, 2010; EU, 2019). On the other hand, the nursing associations point out that the educational and training path of nurses is now much longer and more demanding than it was in the past. Therefore, nurses (especially advanced practice nurses) claim the recognition of greater skills, especially in care settings such as local and home care. A high degree of task shifting – this is the position of the nurses' spokespersons – would allow the legitimate completion of the professionalization process of nurse practitioners (a process that, in many countries, is blocked or otherwise incomplete, due to the doctors' vetoes). However, above all, it would make the provision of healthcare more effective. Task shifting is considered a possible solution to a multiplicity of problems. It can reduce doctors' workload; it can favor access to care in remote areas (mountain and rural); it can reduce the overall costs of the system (nurses earn usually less than doctors); and it can increase the resilience and flexibility of the healthcare delivery system (Delamaire and Lafortune, 2010; Laurant et al., 2018; EU, 2019). Therefore, these are the positions in the field in terms of task shifting. The stakes are evidently high, and it is not surprising that the issue of the definition of nursing skills is a topic of heated debate in many countries.

According to a comparative study conducted a few years ago (Maier and Aiken, 2016), the OECD countries show, at least with reference to primary care, a different degree of task shifting between doctors and nurses. There are cases – including Australia, Canada, Finland, Ireland, New Zealand, United Kingdom and United States – where the official delegation of functions to nurses is very extensive. On the contrary, there are countries, (among them Greece, Turkey, but also Austria, Czech Republic, France, Germany, Norway, Poland and Switzerland), where doctors are reluctant to give up part of their prerogatives, and where the formally attributed competences to the nursing profession are decidedly more limited.

7 Healthcare Reforms over the Last Thirty Years

7.1 REFORMING HEALTHCARE SYSTEMS: BETWEEN LEGACY AND POLICY TRANSFER

In the previous chapters, the health systems of the twenty-seven countries covered in this study were compared and cataloged on the basis of a multiplicity of organizational dimensions. However, the picture painted so far risks to appear static, as if health systems were inert constructs that remain stable over time. But obviously this is not the case; health systems are constantly evolving, they are mobile targets. They sometimes change through radical and sudden reforms, although more frequently they change slowly and incrementally (Wilsford, 1994; Klein, 1995; Oliver and Mossialos, 2005; Béland, 2010; Tuohy, 2018).

Truly radical reforms and pathbreaking – that is, involving the replacement of one organizational model with another – are rare events. In fact, each national system has its own imprinting, which tends to be preserved and strengthened over time. The reformist initiatives adopted in individual countries hardly contradict this imprint. More than a change of the model, usually the reforms – even those considered more ambitious and far-reaching – promote a change within the model adopted previously. The options from which national policy makers can choose are, therefore, conditioned by the historical path followed and by the choices made in the past (Wilsford, 1994; Hacker, 1998; Oliver and Mossialos, 2005). In terms of funding, only a few of the twenty-seven countries considered here have changed their funding model over the last three decades, with the exception of Eastern European countries (involved in an epochal process of democratic transition). The countries equipped with a universalist system generally did not question it. Among the SHI countries, only a couple have transitioned to a mandatory residence insurance model. Even regarding the provision of care, again excluding the countries of Eastern Europe, no country has gone from a highly integrated to a highly separated system, or vice versa. In short, countries tend to maintain their own financing and delivery model.

On the other hand, however, it is equally true that between countries – at least among those in the OECD area – a continuous exchange of ideas and suggestions takes place. Ideas travel from one country to another, and governments tend to propose solutions that have already been tested elsewhere; the reform measures adopted in one country often turn out to be a reworking of solutions already implemented abroad. In this regard, we are speaking of "policy transfer" processes (Dolowitz and Marsh, 1996, 2000), that is, the circulation of ideas, objectives and policy tools from some forerunner countries (called "early adopters") to others (the so-called emulators) that draw teaching and inspiration from the experience of the former.

The purpose of this chapter is to reflect on the main trajectories of change that have characterized the health systems of OECD countries in the last three decades, from the fall of the Berlin Wall to the present day. For this purpose, it is possible to identify five major "reform themes" (Saltman and Figueras, 1998), or "reform trends" (Saltman et al., 2012), which traveled transversally through countries generating processes of emulation and policy transfer. The five major reform themes are as follows: (1) stimulation of greater competition; (2) promotion of integration (both in terms of financing and provision); (3) decentralization; (4) strengthening the rights of the patient; (5) extension of insurance coverage. For most of these five themes it is possible to identify a reform that has acted as a forerunner, which other countries have subsequently been inspired by and followed.

I urge the reader to pay attention to one aspect. The individual "reform themes" have usually been implemented differently depending on the organizational model adopted. While sharing a common goal, the NHS countries have usually made use of solutions and policy tools that are different from those that have circulated in the SHI countries.

7.2 PRO-COMPETITION REFORMS

A first, important, reformist strand is represented by the attempts of many national governments to introduce market-style mechanisms and greater competition in their healthcare systems (van de Ven, 1996; Saltman and Figueras, 1998; Docteur and Oxley, 2003; Toth, 2010a). This reform theme was evidently fueled by neoliberal ideas and the precepts of New Public Management, that were very popular in the late 1980s and early 1990s (Jacobs, 1998; McGregor, 2001; Simonet, 2011; Scott-Samuel et al., 2014).

The goal of introducing greater elements of competition has been implemented in two different versions, depending on the organizational model adopted in the individual countries. In NHS countries, competition between providers has been encouraged especially through the creation of "internal markets." In SHI countries, where competition between providers already existed, competition between sickness funds was stimulated.

7.2.1 The Purchaser-Provider Split and the "Internal Markets"

The first strategy followed by many countries that have a NHS was to promote more competition among healthcare providers.

Leading the way in this direction was the United Kingdom, starting with the NHS and Community Care Act of 1990. The reform approved by the Conservative government of Margaret Thatcher intended to stimulate competition between public providers through the creation of an "internal market" (Enthoven, 1985). A necessary condition for this objective was the split between purchasing structures and structures providing health services (Ham, 2009). The District Health Authorities (DHAs) would act as purchasing agencies. Based on the number of citizens residing in a district, the DHAs were assigned a budget with which to purchase all the necessary services for their clients. The second category of purchasers was made up of doctors who were fundholders (Ham, 2009; Tuohy, 2018). General practitioners were given the opportunity to associate and receive a budget with which to purchase some services on behalf of their patients. The provision of secondary care would be handled by the hospitals, which in many cases were transformed into autonomous trusts. The hospitals were put in competition with each other to win supply contracts. The rationale behind the reform was to spur competition among public providers, introducing incentives for their productivity (Klein, 2013). Nothing really changed for NHS users since providers could not be selected by the individual patient, but by district authorities and general practitioners. Therefore, there was no enhancement of citizens' freedom of choice.

At an international level, the Thatcher reform immediately aroused great fascination, and the logic of the internal market found admirers in many countries. Among these, the country that most faithfully followed the British example was New Zealand, with the reform approved in 1993 by the National Party government led by Bolger. The 1993 New Zealand reform aimed at the separation of purchasers and providers and the creation of an internal market (Goodyear-Smith and Ashton, 2019). Public hospitals were to serve as the principal providers and were transformed into autonomous enterprises (Ashton et al., 2005). The function of purchasing, on the other hand, was entrusted to four regional healthcare authorities that, each in their own jurisdictions, would have to negotiate with public and private healthcare providers, in addition to a Public Health Commission contracting for public health services (Goodyear-Smith and Ashton, 2019).

The ideas that inspired the Thatcher reform also reached Italy, where, even in the Italian NHS, the 1992–1993 reform introduced the essential elements of the internal market (France et al., 2005). The local health units were transformed into public enterprises with legal personality and ample autonomy. The larger hospitals were separated from the local health authorities and transformed into autonomous hospitals. Private suppliers were made equal to public suppliers as long as they met certain quality standards and accepted the rates set by the regions. Citizens were free to choose from all accredited, public and private providers (Toth, 2015b).

In Spain and Sweden, the novelties bouncing from the United Kingdom were only partially adopted. In Spain, contractual mechanisms between purchasing structures and providers were introduced throughout the country starting in 1993. However, the internal market model has only been fully tested in some autonomous communities (Cabiedes and Guillén, 2001). Also in Sweden the split between providers and purchasers proceeded with different speed and methods according to the county (Blomqvist, 2004; Anell et al., 2012).

In Portugal, there have been several attempts to apply the principles of New Public Management to the health system (Nunes and Ferreira, 2019). A first attempt was made in 1997 with the introduction of the purchaser-provider split (Oliveira and Pinto, 2005). However, this reform was only partially implemented. A second attempt was made in 2002, with the adoption of the contractual model and the corporatization of public hospitals (Nunes and Ferreira, 2019).

7.2.2 Competition between Insurers

While in several NHS countries the intent was to promote competition among providers, in some SHI countries the goal of reform efforts was, instead, to stimulate greater competition among the sickness funds.

The leader in this direction was the Netherlands. Starting in 1992, the Dutch who were compulsorily enrolled in the SHI (that is, two-thirds of the population) were allowed to choose the sickness fund with which to insure each year. Previously, the funds could only accept members in the region to which they belong; thus, they lost the characteristic of local monopolists and entered into competition with other funds operating throughout the country (Helderman et al., 2005).

Like the Thatcher reform, the Dutch reform soon attracted proselytes. A reform that was very similar to the Dutch reform was, in fact, launched a few months later in Germany. The 1993 Health Care Structure Act, approved by the fourth Kohl government, guaranteed the majority of German workers the freedom to choose which sickness fund to subscribe to. Previously, this freedom was very limited and concerned only some categories (Wörz and Busse, 2005). In order to discourage insurers from discrimination on the basis of risk, sickness funds were required to accept all subscribers (Giaimo, 2016).

Among the SHI countries that wanted to promote competition between sickness funds, the Czech Republic should also be mentioned. In the early 1990s, the Czech health system underwent a process of profound transformation. The previous socialist model was replaced by a system of SHI, which allowed members the freedom to choose both the hospital in which to be treated and the sickness fund to which to register (Alexa et al., 2015; Nemec et al., 2015).

7.3 LET US INTEGRATE! REFORMS IN FAVOR OF INTEGRATION

An important reform issue that has emerged in recent decades concerns the drive toward greater organizational integration (Saltman et al., 2012). Here too, in a similar way to what has been seen for pro-competitive reforms, a distinction can be made between the countries that have made the financing system more integrated (by unifying the sickness funds), and those that have, instead, tried to make the service provision system more integrated.

7.3.1 The Integration of Sickness Funds

Let us start with the SHI countries that wanted to reduce the fragmentation regarding the insurers by promoting the merger of multiple sickness funds.

The Korea Republic paved the way in 1999, when the Korean parliament approved a reform of the funding system that required all sickness funds to merge into a single national insurance scheme (Kwon and Reich, 2005). Previously, more than 350 health insurance societies operated in Korea, which workers belonged to, based on profession or place of residence (Kwon and Reich, 2005; Kwon et al., 2015). The introduction of national health insurance, therefore, led to the adoption of a single-payer model, with uniform contribution rates and the same benefit package (Kwon et al., 2015).

Even in Poland, a law passed in 2004 required that the sickness funds, which were established only a few years earlier, be replaced by a single insurance institution. Previously, the Polish system of SHI was organized into sixteen sickness funds on a territorial basis, plus a separate fund for law enforcement, military and state rail members (Polak et al., 2019). Therefore, since the 2004 reform, a single National Health Fund (*Narodowy Fundusz Zdrowia*, NFZ) operates in Poland, as a monopsonistic purchaser (Sowada et al., 2019).

Similar to the Korean and Polish reforms, another was adopted in Turkey in 2006. As a consequence of this reform, three of the major SHI schemes were merged into a single sickness fund, the General Health Insurance Scheme (GHIS). The three schemes that previously operated (SSK, Bağ-Kur and GERF) had different administrative structures with varying benefit packages and regulations (Tatar et al., 2011). The new general insurance scheme began operating in 2008 with an aim to provide equal benefits to all its clients. In 2010, it also incorporated the mandatory scheme reserved for active civil servants. The unification was completed in 2012 when the targeted program in favor of those who were less well-off (the so-called green card) was transferred to the single fund (Ökem and Çakar, 2015). The unified GHIS today includes both those who were previously covered under the four transferred social security schemes and everyone joining the SHI system for the first time (Tatar et al., 2011).

Also in Greece, in 2011, the sickness funds were unified under the National Organization for the Provision of Healthcare

Services (EOPYY). Following this reform, the four major SHI funds, (that covered salaried employees in the private sector, farmers, the self-employed and civil servants), merged into EOPYY, which would act as a single purchaser of health services for all their clients, guaranteeing them a uniform benefit package (Economou et al., 2017).

7.3.2 *The Integration of the Provision System*

We saw in Chapter 4 how – regarding the provision of healthcare – national systems are placed in different positions along the integration-separation continuum. The reforms in favor of competition, as described above, especially those of a neoliberal matrix adopted during the first half of the nineties, aimed at making the systems more separated. This was accomplished by splitting purchaser and provider functions, separating hospital facilities from territorial services, granting greater freedom of choice and sometimes opening up competition between public and private suppliers.

However, in many countries, shortly after implementation began, enthusiasm for neoliberal, market-oriented experiments began to fade, and the criticisms toward competitive and contract-like mechanisms grew (Toth, 2010a). In particular, since the mid-nineties, many national governments preferred to set aside explicit reference to competition and the separated model, to instead insist on public planning and coordination between the various components of the health system. Depending on the country, this meant a preference for hierarchical rather than contractual relationships; greater regulatory and planning tasks by public agencies; integration of primary and secondary care; the introduction of gatekeeping mechanisms; and incentives for family doctors to work in a group practice. Reforms that included measures such as those listed above evidently intended to make delivery systems more integrated than they previously were.

It is good to immediately clarify that in almost all the countries analyzed in this work, over the last three decades some measures have been tested and introduced that aimed at making the provision system more integrated. It would be impossible to do a census and mention them all. So, we will limit our discussion to a few cases, by way of example.

A relevant case of pro-integration reform consists in the measures adopted in France in the second half of the 1990s, first by the government of the Gaullist Juppé and then by that of the socialist Jospin. These governments were based on the common assumption that the French health system suffered from excessive fragmentation. Patients enjoyed too much freedom, which often resulted in the request for redundant services. Coordination between the various providers was lacking, and the connection between primary and specialist care was loose. Starting from this diagnosis, the measures proposed by the Juppé and Jospin governments operated in different directions (Rochaix and Wilsford, 2005). In 1996, the regional agencies that were responsible for hospital planning were established. Since then, hospitals have had to undergo more stringent accreditation procedures and are required to coordinate with neighboring structures in order to avoid overlapping (Steffen, 2010). These agencies were later (from 2009) incorporated into the regional health agencies. The latter were called upon to integrate not only hospitals but also primary care and social medicine (Nay et al., 2016). With the aim of increasing the quality and uniformity of care provided, an agency for health accreditation and evaluation was established at national level (later replaced by the High Authority for Health) with the task of drafting guidelines and standards with which all providers are required to comply. Another novelty consisted in the introduction of a permanent patient file in which doctors would have to write down all the relevant information for the diagnosis and treatment of a particular patient, with an evident intent to promote continuity of care, avoiding unnecessary or contradictory visits and prescriptions (Rochaix and Wilsford, 2005). Finally, in 1998 the experimentation began, which a 2004 law extended to the entire adult population, namely, with *médecins traitants*, which are doctors (both general practitioners or specialists) who perform "gatekeeping"[1] functions (Steffen, 2010). The reforms adopted in France in the second half of the 1990s, therefore, went in the direction of reducing the fragmentation of the delivery system and integrating further the different primary and secondary care providers. These initiatives were subsequently consolidated, and flanked by new tools that also aimed at making the system more integrated. Among these are the multi-professional health houses (*maisons de santé*, established in 2007), and the territorial health professional communities (established in 2016).

The innovations introduced in France by the Juppé and Jospin governments also aroused curiosity abroad, especially in SHI countries. Among these is Germany: The reforms launched in the early 2000s by the Schröder government took up some of the measures contained in the Juppé plan, including the incentives to adopt, on a voluntary basis, a gatekeeping model (Reibling and Wendt, 2012); measures were also envisaged, such as integrated care contracts, aimed at promoting the coordination of care at the local level (Giaimo, 2016; Kifmann, 2017). The French example was also followed by Belgium (Gerkens and Merkur, 2010): A 1999 law established a patient file similar to that adopted in France, and gatekeeping incentives were introduced.

Reforms aimed at making provision systems more integrated have been adopted not only in SHI countries, but also in separate universalist ones, such as, Australia and Canada.

In Australia, various reform measures adopted in recent years have aimed at promoting greater integration of both primary and hospital care (Hall, 2010; Duckett, 2018). Starting in 2015, the Primary Health Networks (PHNs) were established for the purpose of making the primary care network more integrated. About thirty PHNs are currently operative in Australia. As concerns specialist care, in 2011 the Local Hospital Networks (LHNs) were established. These

---

[1] Following the 2004 law, patients can still access medical specialists directly, but they are reimbursed at a lower rate if they lack a referral.

networks are separate statutory authorities, (each with its own Council, appointed by the State Minister), to which state governments delegate the management and financing of public hospitals (Hall, 2010). At present, about 140 LHNs are operative throughout the Australian territory. Also in Canada, the main objective whereby the Regional Health Authorities (RHAs) were established was to strengthen the integration of providers and stimulate the continuity of care (Marchildon, 2013).

7.4 GOING LOCAL: THE THEME OF DECENTRALIZATION

A reform issue that has received great attention over the last few decades is that of decentralization (Saltman et al., 2007; Costa-Font and Greer, 2013). At least on paper, the main advantage of decentralization should be to bring decision-makers closer to citizens. This is the essence of the argument, a decentralized system should be able to adapt and respond more effectively to the needs of individual local communities (Saltman and Bankauskaite, 2006; Treisman, 2007). However, it is also true that a high level of decentralization risks fragmenting the system, generating not only higher costs but, above all, differences in treatment for those who reside in different areas of the country (Saltman et al., 2007; Treisman, 2007).

Reflecting on what should be the right balance between decentralization and centralization is controversial, both at a political level and at the level of academic debate (Saltman et al., 2007; Adolph et al., 2012; Costa-Font and Greer, 2013). The comparison is also confused by the fact that different meanings are attributed to the term "decentralization" (Saltman and Bankauskaite, 2006; Costa-Font and Greer, 2013). Therefore, let us avoid possible misunderstandings. Here decentralization is understood to be the transfer of competences in healthcare organization from a higher to a lower level of government and, in particular, from the national level to subnational levels (Mills, 1990). Depending on the country, the recipients of the transfer of authority can be regions, provinces, counties or municipalities. In federal systems, the transfer can take place from the national level to that of the individual states. Therefore, decentralization can take many forms, which vary in relation to the nature of the competences that are transferred to the levels of government involved, and to the regulatory and financial constraints to which the various actors must comply (Adolph et al., 2012; Costa-Font and Greer, 2013). Decentralization methods obviously depend on the constitutional architecture of the individual countries as well as on the prevailing healthcare organization model (Mills, 1990).

Wanting to make a distinction between the different forms of decentralization, the processes of "deconcentration" could be kept distinct from those of "devolution" (Rondinelli et al., 1983; Mills, 1990). This distinction seems to follow the approach between "administrative" decentralization and "political" decentralization (Saltman and Bankauskaite, 2006; Treisman, 2007). Although there is no unanimous consensus regarding these labels, there is talk of "deconcentration" (or administrative decentralization) in cases in which the transfer of health responsibilities has nonelective peripheral organs as recipients, usually with competences only in the health sector, (such as, for example, regional health agencies whose leaders are appointed by the national government). On the other hand, there is a process of "devolution" (or political decentralization) when the transfer of powers concerns local entities with independent popular legitimacy (such as municipalities, or democratically elected intermediate levels of government). In the case of devolution, local governments are general-purpose, that is, they have competences in a variety of policy sectors, not only in the healthcare sector (Adolph et al., 2012).

The relationship between centralization and decentralization lends itself to being conceived as a continuum rather than as a rigid dichotomy (Mills, 1990). In reality, there are no totally centralized and no completely decentralized health systems. Individual national cases always fall into some intermediate position between the two opposite poles. So let us see which countries, in recent decades, intended to change their position along this continuum. Not all governments

7.4 GOING LOCAL. THE THEME OF DECENTRALIZATION 191

have moved in the same direction. It will soon be seen how some countries have intended to make their health systems more decentralized, while others have taken the opposite path.

7.4.1 Reforms in Favor of Decentralization

Compared to the other lines of reform, in the matter of decentralization it is more difficult to identify a country that has acted as a precursor and model of reference. This is also due to the fact that many national health systems have always been highly decentralized. This is the case in federal countries (such as Australia, Canada, but also the United States), and in the Nordic countries (in which local governments have traditionally had important responsibility in health matters). It is clear that an already largely decentralized system does not need further pressure toward decentralization.

The Spanish and Italian cases are good examples of health reforms aimed at transferring relevant competences from a central to a regional level. In Spain, the devolution process was gradual, spread over more than two decades. A peculiarity of the Spanish case is that the transfer of responsibilities in the field of healthcare was negotiated on a case-by-case basis between the national government and the regional governments, and proceeded asymmetrically and spaced out over time (Jiménez-Rubio and García-Gómez, 2017). In the first phase, from 1981 to 1994, full competences in the health field were transferred to only the so-called seven historical regions (including Catalonia, Andalusia and Valencia). In 2002, health responsibilities were also transferred to the remaining ten autonomous communities.

In Italy, the regionalization process, (as a result of which health has become the main competence attributed to regional governments), was initiated with the 1992–1993 reform, and was subsequently consolidated through the 2001 constitutional reform (Tediosi et al., 2009; Toth, 2014).

Even in the United Kingdom, the more general devolution process has had important repercussions on the organization of the

National Health Service. In 1999, the devolved governments of Scotland, Wales and Northern Ireland were given the powers to organize (and budgets to finance) health services in their jurisdictions, while the UK government has remained responsible for managing the health system in England. During the first years following the devolution, healthcare services in the four UK nations have already been differentiating themselves in terms of strategic objectives, organizational structure and performance achieved (Ham, 2009; Bevan, 2014).

In Hungary, a reform passed in 1990 transferred ownership of most primary care facilities, clinics and hospitals from the central government to local governments. As a consequence of this transfer, local authorities have become the main healthcare providers in the Hungarian health system (Gaál et al., 2011).

A more recent case of devolution occurred in the Czech Republic following a comprehensive reform of the public administration approved in 2002. Ownership of many emergency units, long-term care structures, primary care facilities and of approximately half of the hospitals in the Czech Republic was transferred from the state to fourteen newly formed, self-governing regions (Alexa et al., 2015). Some regions, taking advantage of the autonomy granted to them, also decided to change the legal status of some hospitals, transforming them into joint stock companies.

Through the reforms just mentioned, greater powers in the health field have been transferred from the national government to democratically elected subnational levels. Therefore, in all these countries there has been a process of health "devolution." In other national contexts, the reforms have, instead, triggered a process of "deconcentration," as the transfer concerned decentralized bodies controlled by the central government. This is the case in Portugal, where five regional health administrations were established in 1993, whose directors were appointed by the Minister of Health. Regional agencies have also been established in France and Canada over the past three decades. In Canada, the majority of provinces established

Regional Health Authorities between the end of the 1980s and the mid-1990s. The boards of the RHAs are appointed by provincial ministries (Marchildon, 2013). In France, regional hospital agencies were first established in 1996, and then, in 2009, regional health agencies (*Agences régionales de la santé*, ARS); and the directors of the latter were appointed by the Ministry of Health (Chevreul et al., 2015; Nay et al., 2016). However, it should be noted that both Canadian and French regional agencies do not really aim to decentralize the system, but rather to encourage integration between providers.

7.4.2 *Pro-centralization Reforms*

In the early 2000s, the push toward greater decentralization in healthcare seems to have lost, at least in part, its vigor, and some national governments have adopted reforms that go in the opposite direction, namely, that of greater centralization (Saltman, 2008).

Leading the way on the road to centralization was Norway. In 2002 the management of all Norwegian public hospitals was taken away from the county councils, which had previously owned and operated them, and it was assigned to the national government. The latter then divided the hospital network into five newly created regional health authorities (now four), which are organized as state enterprises and whose directors are appointed in Oslo (Saltman, 2008; Brekke and Straume, 2017).

Also in Ireland, the establishment of the Health Service Executive (HSE) represented a process of centralization. The HSE was established with the Health Act of 2004, replacing the previous regional health boards. The heads of the latter were mainly made up of elected representatives nominated by the counties and by components made up of professional bodies (McDaid et al., 2009). The HSE is a national government agency, whose directors are appointed by the Ministry of Health.

In terms of decentralization and centralization, New Zealand is a case to be studied, because from the early 1990s it has experienced different organizational arrangements as a consequence of a frenetic succession of reforms in both directions (Gauld, 2012; Goodyear-Smith and Ashton, 2019). Prior to 1991, New Zealand healthcare was organized into fourteen democratically elected area health boards. The Bolger government, (a center-right coalition led by the National Party), decided to dismiss these boards, replacing them first with commissioners, and then in 1993 with four Regional Health Authorities, appointed by the government. However, the Regional Health Authorities did not last long. In 1997 they were dismantled and their functions were centralized in a single Health Funding Authority (HFA). But even this arrangement lasted for only a few years. In 2000, as a consequence of the return to government of a Labor-led coalition (headed by Prime Minister Clark), the HFA was abolished, and replaced by about twenty District Health Boards (DHBs). The DHBs are funded by the Ministry of Health, and their boards have up to eleven members, the majority of whom are locally elected and the remainder appointed by the Minister of Health.

7.5 STRENGTHENING PATIENTS' RIGHTS

An important reformist "strand" has given itself the objective of strengthening patients' rights (Saltman and Figueras, 1998; Docteur and Oxley, 2003). Over the past three decades, most OECD countries have, in fact, approved laws or charters aimed at recognizing and protecting these rights (Coulter, 2011).

When dealing with the fundamental rights of the patient, reference is usually made to a "core-package" of guarantees that includes (Rider and Makela, 2003; Nys and Goffin, 2011): the right to be treated with dignity; the right to privacy; the patients' right to receive all information relating to the treatments they must undergo, (the information must include the risks and side effects associated with the treatment, as well as any alternatives); the right to express their consent to the processing; the right to access their medical records; the right to complaint and compensation. Depending on the country, in addition to the core-package, additional guarantees may be granted to the patient, including the freedom to choose the provider, the right to a second opinion, the guarantee of a maximum waiting time, participation in decisions regarding the healthcare system, the institution of a patient ombudsman (Fallberg, 2000; Rider and Makela, 2003; Nys and Goffin, 2011).

One of the first countries to move in the direction of strengthening the rights of healthcare users was the United Kingdom, with the approval of the Patient's Charter in 1991. This Charter had the merit of putting on paper some general duties that the NHS undertook to fulfill toward its clients. It was an important step, also from a cultural and symbolic point of view, which had the intention of creating an "awareness," and setting certain standards that NHS facilities and staff would be required to abide by (Coulter, 2011). However, this approach had its limits since the rights set out in the Charter were not legally challengeable.

This is the reason why many national governments subsequently preferred to strengthen the rights of patients by taking a different path: The approval of a special law in which the patient's rights were made explicit, making them legally enforceable and appealable before a court. The Netherlands embodied this approach, with the approval of the Medical Treatment Contract Act in 1994. Finland was also among the first European countries to enact legislation to protect patients' rights in 1992. However, this provision covered only some of the rights included in the "core package" described previously.

For European governments, a further push toward recognizing the fundamental rights of patients – as well as the British and Dutch examples – came from the Amsterdam Declaration of 1994.[2] Thus it was that, especially in the second half of the 1990s and the early 2000s, many countries proceeded to legislate on patients' rights.

Following the Dutch approach, countries that adopted a specific law protecting patient rights include (Hart, 2004; Nys and Goffin, 2011) the previously mentioned Finland (1992), Israel (1996), Greece

---

[2] *WHO Declaration on the Promotion of Patients' Rights in Europe* (1994).

(1997), Hungary (1997), Denmark (1998), Turkey (1998), Norway (1999), Belgium (2002), France (2002), Spain (2002) and a few years later, Poland (2008). Around the same time, the following countries adopted a Patients' Charter: Ireland (1995), Portugal (1997) and Austria (2001). In addition to the British approach (non-legally binding charter), and the Dutch approach (single law introducing enforceable individual entitlements), it is possible to identify a third approach, the so-called split legislation (Hart, 2004). Countries that are in this category – including, for example, Germany, Italy and Sweden – in which, despite the absence of a single specific law protecting the rights of the patient, the latter are equally protected because they are covered by different pieces of legislation (Nys and Goffin, 2011).

7.5.1 *Freedom to Choose the Provider*

Among patients' rights that can be recognized, one of the most appreciated is the possibility to freely choose the healthcare provider. As also seen in Chapter 4, in all the countries analyzed in this book the choice of the family doctor is now guaranteed. The freedom to choose the hospital – as well as the individual professional within the chosen structure – varies from country to country. If we turn back the hands of time and go back to the late 1980s, the picture looked very different. In some countries, especially in those with a public health service, choosing the family doctor was not allowed, moreover, individuals were automatically enrolled in the primary care center closest to their home. In many countries, the patient was not allowed to choose the hospital in which to be admitted. The facility was the closest geographically or the one chosen by the family doctor.

Therefore, in the early 1990s, many governments decided to give their citizens greater freedom of choice regarding the provider. One of the countries that first took this path was Sweden. The center-right Bildt government, in office from 1991 to 1994, encouraged various measures aimed at promoting the pluralism of providers and guaranteeing users more opportunities of choice (Blomqvist, 2004). The opening of private medical practices was encouraged. In 1993 the primary care reform was launched, under which citizens were allowed to choose their family doctor. Previously there was no such possibility and they were assigned by the authorities to the nearest public health center. In 1991, county councils were invited to guarantee patients the freedom to choose their hospital (Vrangbaek et al., 2012).

During the 1990s, other countries, including Spain, Denmark and Norway, moved to expand patients' freedom of choice. In Spain, the freedom to choose a general practitioner was granted in 1993, and that of the medical specialist in 1996 (Reibling and Wendt, 2012). In Denmark the possibility to choose hospital for treatment was granted in 1993, and extended in 2002, so that the Danes can choose between all public hospitals in the country, including a selection of private facilities (Olejaz et al., 2012). In Norway, a 1999 law guarantees freedom of choice among all public hospitals. This choice was also then extended to private (affiliated) structures in 2004 (Ringard et al., 2013).

The path followed by the United Kingdom is indicative. Starting in 2001, at the beginning of the second mandate, the Blair government insisted, in particular, on the issues regarding patients' freedom of choice and the quality of providers. Starting in 2006, NHS patients who have a referral for an examination by a specialist were granted the opportunity to choose from a shortlist of at least four alternative providers. From 2008 on, British patients were allowed to choose from any provider that met the Healthcare Commission's standards and that charged NHS rates (Klein, 2013). In order to facilitate patients' choice, the Blair government implemented a system of performance rating for NHS providers. Indeed, the assumption was that it was not sufficient to give patients the freedom to choose, if they did not have the means to judge which providers were better than others. By opting for a typical "naming and shaming" strategy (Helderman et al., 2012; Bevan, 2014), in the early 2000s a system was set up for the periodic evaluation of all the healthcare facilities within the country, giving citizens the possibility to compare the performance of the different providers. From 2001 to 2005, the assessments of the different healthcare facilities were expressed using a scale from zero to three stars, as in tourist guides (Klein, 2013; Bevan, 2014). Assessment was entrusted to an independent agency, the Healthcare Commission (later transformed into the Care Quality Commission). The star rating was later replaced by other performance rating methods, but even today, British patients can easily consult a comparative assessment of providers on the Care Quality Commission website.

7.5.2 The Waiting-Time Guarantee

Timeliness of care is to a great extent related to the issue of patient rights. Among the rights of the patient, some governments have, in fact, also included the right to receive the care needed in a reasonably short time. On the other hand, long waiting lists are a sore point for many healthcare systems, especially in countries with a universalist system (Siciliani et al., 2013; Viberg et al., 2013).

Among the various strategies that can be adopted to reduce waiting lists (Siciliani and Hurst, 2005; Siciliani et al., 2013), several national governments have decided to tackle the problem by setting maximum times within which citizens are entitled to receive the treatment prescribed for them. Northern European countries, in particular Sweden (Fallberg, 2000), led the way in the "waiting-time guarantee" strategy.

In 1992, the Swedish government (led by Carl Bildt) established that to receive a series of specialized "elective" (i.e., non-emergency) surgery treatments, one should not wait more than three months. If the wait exceeds this limit, the patient would have the right to contact public facilities in other counties or even private facilities. In the latter case, the costs incurred by the patient would then be charged to the county of residence. This first experiment in 1992 involved only a dozen treatments and was abandoned after a few years (Hanning and Spångberg, 2000). The same principle of the waiting-time guarantee was re-proposed a few years later, in 2005, when the social democratic government led by Persson introduced the formula "0-7-90-90." This formula indicates: zero waiting time to have the first contact with the healthcare system; a maximum wait of seven days to be seen by a general practitioner; a maximum of ninety days waiting time for consultation with a specialist; and an interval of no more than ninety days between the diagnosis and the start of therapeutic treatment or surgery (Anell et al., 2012).

Following the Swedish example, the strategy of introducing a guarantee regarding maximum waiting times has attracted converts in many other countries. In Denmark, for example, a 1993 law set a maximum time of three months within which public structures were required to provide certain specialized services (Vrangbaek and Christiansen, 2005). This maximum limit was subsequently lowered at first to two months and then to only one month (Olejaz et al., 2012). In Denmark, as well as in Norway, an interesting novel method was introduced. If the wait exceeded the maximum guaranteed limit, patients were allowed to go to foreign hospitals, at the expense of the public service (Siciliani and Hurst, 2005).

In England, from the year 2000, the instrument of maximum waiting times was declined in a somewhat different way. In countries such as Sweden or Denmark, as we have seen, a maximum time is set, and, if the limit is not respected, patients are allowed to avail of alternative providers' services free of charge. The British government, on the other hand, preferred to set "waiting time targets." The public hospitals that were not able to meet these targets would be penalized (Propper et al., 2010).

Legislative or governmental provisions introducing maximum waiting times were subsequently introduced – by the Swedish formula of patient guarantees, or by the English formula of performance targets – in other countries besides those mentioned, including: Finland, the Netherlands, New Zealand, Ireland, Italy, Portugal and Spain (Siciliani et al., 2013; Viberg et al., 2013).

7.6 GOING UNIVERSAL: EXTENDING HEALTH COVERAGE

Another interesting line of reform concerns the strategies adopted by national governments to more broadly extend health coverage (consequently reducing the number of the uninsured) and to make it more uniform (Docteur and Oxley, 2003). As seen in Chapter 3, some of the twenty-seven countries analyzed in this book do not guarantee insurance coverage for the entire population. The presence, within a country, of categories without adequate health coverage obviously poses a problem of social equity, which can easily become a topic of heated political debate. Also in Chapter 3, it was found that over the last few decades the number of noninsured individuals has been decreasing on the average. This means that reforms have been undertaken in some countries to make the system universal or at least to extend compulsory health coverage.

The main reform initiatives[3] that were aimed at extending compulsory insurance coverage were those adopted in Israel and Switzerland in 1994, in France in 1999, in the Netherlands in 2006, in Germany in 2007 and in the United States in 2010. We will briefly present these six reforms in chronological order. The reader is invited to pay close attention to a particularly relevant aspect. The extension of health coverage can take place in two ways: by replacing the financing system, thus passing from one model to another, or by "fixing" the existing model by putting a patch on it. It is something similar to what happens in a tailor's shop. You can make a dress from scratch, or you can readjust the old one, adding an adornment or a patch. Some countries have changed their funding model as seen in Israel, Switzerland and the Netherlands. Other countries, without replacing the model adopted previously, have simply added a piece to it. This is the strategy that is followed in France, in the United States with the Obama reform and to a large extent also in Germany.

---

[3] In addition to the six reforms mentioned, there are others that can be traced back to this "reform line," having had the intention of expanding the insurance coverage of the population. In Turkey, for example, a targeted program (called a "green card") was introduced in 1992 for low-income people; this program has significantly reduced the number of the uninsured. Another example is the 2016 legislation which in Greece restored the universality, at least on paper, of the public health service.

7.6 GOING UNIVERSAL: EXTENDING HEALTH COVERAGE 201

7.6.1 Israel 1994

In the history of Israeli healthcare, a turning point arrived in 1988 with the government appointment of a commission of inquiry into the functioning and efficiency of the health care system (Rosen et al., 2015). This commission was chaired by Benjamin Netanyahu. Up to that point, about 95 percent of the Israeli population was insured, even though enrollment within the four competing sickness funds was on a voluntary basis (Chinitz, 1995). Being uninsured was largely a problem of poor ultra-Orthodox Jews and some Israeli Arabs (Clarfield et al., 2017).

Following the indications provided by the Netanyahu Commission, in 1994 the Knesset, the Israeli parliament, approved the National Health Insurance Law after an intense political struggle (Chinitz, 1995). The latter came into force in 1995, ensuring a standard benefits package for the entire population. In fact, the reform provides that all Israelis are covered by a national insurance plan, and that they can choose between four competing nonprofit health plans, as described in Chapter 5.

7.6.2 Switzerland 1994

Up to the mid-1990s, Switzerland had a voluntary insurance system. Following the example of what had been experienced in other countries of continental Europe, in Switzerland there had also been a long discussion about whether or not to establish a national compulsory insurance scheme. Over the years, several bills were presented and debated in parliament, but none of them were ever definitively approved (Immergut, 1992). At the beginning of the 1990s the proposal for a national health insurance plan returned to the agenda since there was, in fact, the desire to not only keep the ever-increasing costs of the health system in check but to also promote greater equity among citizens. These pressures led the Swiss parliament to approve, after a bitter confrontation, the law establishing compulsory health insurance (1994). This provision was subjected to a referendum and once it had popular approval, the reform came into effect in 1996.

As mentioned in Chapter 1, the 1994 Health Insurance Law established a system of mandatory residence insurance, supported by a strict regulation of insurers and public subsidies for the benefit of low-income individuals.

7.6.3 *France 1999*

A reform that has left a lasting mark on the French health system is represented by the *Couverture Maladie Universelle* (CMU), approved by the Jospin government in 1999 and implemented from the following year. This reform guaranteed basic coverage to all legal residents in France, so those who were previously not covered were now included (Barroy et al., 2014). The law establishing the CMU was not limited to this. Again, in order to protect the weaker sections of the population, it also indicated that the State provide not only the basic package but also a form of complementary insurance free of charge to those who are less well-off (Nay et al., 2016).

7.6.4 *The Netherlands 2006*

In the last three decades, the Dutch healthcare system has experienced various reform initiatives (Kroneman et al., 2016). The most important reform is the one implemented in 2006, which was approved by the second Balkenende government. The 2006 reform was largely inspired by the recommendations contained in the 1987 Dekker Report[4] (Maarse et al., 2016), and has introduced a

---

[4] In 1986 the Dutch government appointed an independent commission, led by Wisse Dekker (former president of Philips), with the task of imagining a comprehensive reform of the healthcare system, which would make the latter more efficient and more fair (Tuohy, 2018). The Dekker Commission published its final report in 1987. The Dekker report provided for the introduction of a universal insurance scheme that was supposed to cover both the basic package and "exceptional" risks. The sickness funds and private insurance companies would be in competition with each other. The insurers would receive financing from a central fund on a capitation basis, adjusted according to the risk of the patients actually taken care of.

unified mandatory insurance scheme and provided for a regulated competition system, which would promote the efficiency of the system and increase citizens' freedom of choice.

Before the reform was approved, approximately 2 percent of the Dutch population lacked health coverage (van de Ven and Schut, 2008). The problem was not only the prevalence of coverage but also the difference in treatment of the various insurance schemes (Tuohy, 2018). Following the 2006 reform, the rules to which insurers have to comply were made uniform, and all Dutch residents are obliged to purchase an insurance policy covering a standard, basic benefits package.

7.6.5 Germany 2007

Over the past three decades Germany, as argued above, has transformed its traditional mandatory SHI scheme into a system that today has many elements that are similar to the mandatory residence insurance model. This transformation mainly took place following the 2007 reform (The Act to Strengthen Competition in SHI), promoted by the Grosse Koalition government led by Angela Merkel. Before that, a part of the German population (mainly the self-employed) was excluded from the compulsory system of the SHI, and could decide whether or not to insure privately.

The 2007 reform, which was the subject of heated political debate and met with dissent from various interest groups (Giaimo, 2016), comprises a wide range of measures that have significantly modified the way the German healthcare system is regulated and financed. The most relevant change is the introduction of a universal insurance obligation. Starting in 2009, the obligation to take out insurance is no longer limited to some professional categories, but includes all German residents. Non-SHI subscribers are required to have a private healthcare insurance policy. Private insurers are obliged to offer their policyholders a basic tariff to cover a benefit basket similar to the one guaranteed by the SHI (Busse and Blümel, 2014).

7.6.6 *United States 2010*

The main objectives of the Affordable Care Act, approved in March 2010, were to make the health insurance market fairer, to reduce the cost of policies, and above all, to decrease the number of the uninsured (Jacobs and Skocpol, 2010). With regard to the latter objective, it cannot be denied that the reform has had an effect at least in the short term. In 2009, the year before the reform was approved, the uninsured in the United States were around 49 million (or 16 percent of the population), while their number fell to 26.1 million (8 percent) in 2019 (US Census Bureau, 2020).

The increase in the percentage of policyholders was achieved mainly in two ways: (1) by increasing the number of beneficiaries of the public Medicaid program and (2) by providing less affluent individuals with subsidies (in the form of premium tax credits) aimed at purchasing a private policy, to be obtained mainly through the "health insurance marketplaces."

The 2010 reform, as everyone knows, was strongly desired by President Obama, as the qualifying goal of his first term in the White House, and was immediately the subject of a heated political diatribe (Tuohy, 2018).

7.7 REFORM THEMES AND POLITICAL COLOR

At the end of this overview of the major reform issues in the healthcare sector, we can highlight a further aspect, on which we have not particularly focused so far, that is, the ideological assumptions underlying the individual reform streams and their "political color." Reforms, which naturally apply to all policy sectors, not just healthcare, are usually conditioned by the historical period and the ideological orientation of the governments that promote them. Waves of reform are often influenced by passing fads. It frequently happens that a reform aimed at a specific objective is followed, after a short time, by a counter-reform in the opposite direction (Toth, 2010a). It is, therefore, natural to ask whether or not the reform initiatives attributable to the five reform themes have a particular political color.

Let us start with the reforms that were intended to promote greater competition, either at the provider level (with purchaser-provider split and internal markets) or at the level of insurers. From point of view of timing, pro-competition reforms were concentrated, above all, in the first half of the 1990s, when the appeal of the neoliberal paradigm was stronger. Looking at the ideological orientation of the governments proposing these reforms, we note that the majority of them were center-right (Conservatives or Christian Democrats). The Thatcher government, which promoted the 1990 British reform, was conservative, as was the Bolger government, which passed the 1993 reform bill in New Zealand. The Bildt government in Sweden was also conservative (in the early 1990s, when some counties adopted the purchaser-provider split model), as well as the Portuguese government that promoted the reform of 2002 and the Czechoslovakian government in 1991. Christian-Democratic leadership was found in the Netherlands Lubbers government (at the time of the 1992 reform), and also in Germany with the Kohl government (at the time of the 1993 *Strukturreform*). Finally, the two Italian governments had a Christian Democratic majority under which the 1992–1993 reform was approved in two successive steps. On the other hand, the Portuguese government (with Guterres as prime minister) in 1997 was socialist. Apart from some inevitable exceptions, the theme of pro-competition reforms, therefore, seems to have been fed by a particular ideological humus, characterized by the influence of neoliberal ideas and New Public Management, and by the presence of conservative forces in the government.

The picture appears different if we focus on pro-integration reforms. The latter are spread over a longer period of time, and do not seem particularly ideologically connoted. In fact, they have been adopted indifferently by right-wing and by left-wing governments. The Korean government in 1999, the Turkish government in 2006 (led by Erdogan), the German government in 2011 (led by Angela

Merkel), the French government in 1996 (Juppé) and the Australian government in 2015 (Abbott) were under conservative or Christian-democratic leadership. However, the Polish government in 2004, the French government in 1999 (led by Jospin), the German government in the early 2000s (Schroeder) and the Australian government in 2011 (Gillard) were under social-democratic or Labor leadership. Therefore, it could be assumed that the goal of greater integration is a "transversal" or "bipartisan" theme.

The push in favor of healthcare "decentralization" seems to have been a topic in vogue especially during the 1990s. Already, in the early 2000s, the rhetoric of "going local" has faded, so much so as to suggest a possible, generalized turnaround (Saltman, 1998; Saltman et al., 2007). Like the theme of integration, that of decentralization does not seem to have a clear ideological color. Reforms aimed at devolution or deconcentration have been adopted indifferently by right-wing governments (Hungary in 1990, Italy in 1992–1993, France in 1996 and 2009), and left-wing governments (Portugal in 1993, the United Kingdom in 1999, the Czech Republic in 2002). In Spain, as is well known, the issue of devolution is particularly controversial and occupies a central place in the political debate. Over the years, devolution in healthcare has enjoyed the approval of both of the governments led by the socialist Gonzalez and those led by the popular Aznar. The two reforms we mentioned as examples of re-centralization (Norway and Ireland) were both launched by governments that can be labeled as center-right. The cases analyzed are evidently too few to draw general indications. However, it could be suggested that decentralization is a transversal theme, while perhaps centralization could be a theme that is more akin to Conservative governments.

Let us move on to reforms aimed at strengthening patient rights. The majority of these reforms were concentrated in a short time span, between the mid-1990s and 2002. In just six to seven years, at least a dozen countries have adopted legislation with similar content in patient rights. Some fifteen countries have previously been mentioned that have adopted similar reforms. In more than two out of three cases, the reform law (or the introduction of a Patient Charter) was passed under a center-right government. We can, therefore, hypothesize that the issue of the recognition of patients' rights is a topic that tends to be more dear to right-wing parties than to those on the left.

Finally, consider the fifth reform theme, which concerns the extension of insurance coverage. We have previously focused on six big reforms aimed at extending health coverage. These measures were adopted at different times. From a formal point of view, four of these reforms are to be attributed to left-wing governments, one is to be attributed to a center-right government, in the remaining case the government (the first Merkel government) was a grand coalition of Christian Democrats and Social Democrats. However, it should be noted that – with the exception of the Obama reform, strongly supported by the Democrats despite the stiff opposition of the Republicans – such reforms have usually been the result of a bipartisan agreement or collaboration.

The associations that we have found, or also only hypothesized, between the content of the reforms and the color of the proposing governments, all things considered, appear plausible even from a conceptual point of view. Let us assume, for a moment, that the categories of right-wing and left-wing are still useful for interpreting politics, and that, as argued by Norberto Bobbio (1996), the essence of the right is an emphasis on individual freedom, while the left gives priority to social equality. Therefore, by applying these categories to the health field, it appears reasonable that the political forces of the right are more sensitive to issues such as competition, freedom of choice and the individual rights of the patient. Just as it is plausible that leftist governments attach greater importance to public regulation, uniformity of treatment and the broadened extension of insurance coverage.

The topic just raised, the relationship between politics and choices in health matters, appears suggestive and stimulating, however, it requires further study in order to not be trivialized. The next chapter will, therefore, be devoted to this.

8   Health Politics

8.1   THE PERSPECTIVE OF HEALTH POLITICS

The healthcare organization models illustrated in the previous chapters do not constitute neutral solutions, neither from a value point of view nor from an economic or political point of view. Each model of financing and delivery of healthcare services evidently embodies specific values and interests. Each model of governance of the health system embodies a particular vision of the role of the State and the private sector, of the border between individual and collective responsibility, of the right degree of freedom to be recognized by the citizen and of the idea of social equity.

As discussed in Chapter 1, some models (such as the direct market or VHI) allow users maximum freedom of choice, while freedom of choice in others (for example, NHS) is much more limited. In some models, public intervention is reduced (in VHI systems the State can, for example, limit itself to a bland regulation of the insurance market), while in others, the role of the State is predominant (in the NHS, the public actor not only finances, but directly provides healthcare to the entire population). Depending on the model, the role attributed to the private sector changes. Universalist systems, especially the NHS, end up fatally reducing the opportunities for action by private actors (insurance companies, private hospitals, etc.), while systems such as VHI or compulsory residence insurance, instead, leave ample room for private initiatives, regarding both financing and provision. Some systems tolerate – it should perhaps be said that they intentionally favor – discrepancies in the treatment of citizens, trusting in the benefits of competition between insurers and providers. Instead, other systems aim to treat all residents uniformly, even at the cost of sacrificing competition and freedom of choice. Some financing systems (those that are universalist) involve a massive redistribution of income between more and less well-off citizens. In other models, the redistributive effects are much more modest (as in VHI), if not even nil (as in the direct market or with MSAs).

Not only the financing and provision models adopted in individual countries but also the reforms undertaken in recent decades, as seen in Chapter 7, reflect different values and ideological orientations. Reforms aimed at stimulating competition, increasing freedom of choice and strengthening patient rights have been most frequently advanced by center-right governments (Christian Democrats and Conservatives). Likewise, reforms aimed at integrating the delivery system, strengthening public regulation, ensuring uniformity of treatment have been supported, above all, by left-wing governments (Labor, Social Democrats and Socialists).

In short, the point that we want to emphasize here is the following: The policy objectives to be achieved and the policy tools that are selected to pursue these objectives are not merely technical decisions, free from political, social and economic considerations. Opting for one healthcare model over another cannot be considered a politically neutral choice. Quite the contrary. In individual national contexts, the choice regarding which model of healthcare to adopt usually splits public opinion and political forces. In fact, every organizational structure benefits some individuals at the expense of others. Interest groups, left and right wing parties and health professionals regard the problem from differing points of view, promoting solutions that are antithetical.

If what has just been said is acceptable – namely that the strategic choices regarding the financing and organization of health services are always the result of a political confrontation – then there is an interesting prospect of analysis that we can call "health politics" (Toth, 2020c). Adopting this perspective means starting from the assumption that health policies emerge from an arena (Lowi, 1964) in which multiple actors, the bearers of different visions and interests, confront one another in an attempt to make their demands prevail. The policy mixes that are adopted, therefore, reflect the balances of force between the players in the field, the alliances (sometimes durable, sometimes ephemeral) between the interest groups, the mood of public opinion and the positions of the individual political forces. In other words, focusing on health politics means unveiling the "political game" that determines healthcare decisions (as well as nondecisions).

In order to reconstruct this game, we will follow the advice of certain authors (Heclo, 1994; Hall, 1997), and we will investigate the issue of health politics by unpacking it into three fundamental components: ideas, interests and institutions (Quadagno, 2010; Marmor and Wendt, 2011; Klein and Marmor, 2012). These three components have been called the "three I's" (Palier and Surel, 2005).

This chapter is organized as follows. In Section 8.2, we will resume and complete the presentation of the different financing models that began in the first two chapters. This will make it possible to identify a typical evolutionary path, and to trace the trajectories through which the individual national systems have evolved over time. In Section 8.3 we ask ourselves the question that inspires the entire chapter, and which we will try to answer in the following sections, namely, why do OECD countries adopt different healthcare models? In an attempt to answer this question, we will review some of the main explanations already advanced in the literature. Some of them emphasize the importance of ideas, that is, of ideal principles, of national cultures, of political rhetoric, of the ideological orientation of governments (Section 8.4). In the following section, the emphasis will instead be on "interests." Within the health arena, multiple groups clash, the bearers of opposing interests; these groups use the resources at their disposal to influence – to their own advantage – the choices of policy makers. Health policies are then the result of power struggles. Finally, Section 8.6 focuses on political institutions, underlining their importance in prefiguring and determining policy outcomes (not only in the healthcare field but also in other sectors).

In Section 8.7, we gather the pieces of the mosaic by integrating the "three I's" and suggesting an overall interpretation in response to the "why question" formulated in Section 8.3.

8.2 THE IMPORTANCE OF THE HISTORICAL PATH

In Chapter 1, seven financing models were presented, beginning with the market and voluntary insurance, to then illustrate the targeted programs and the Bismarckian model of SHI. Then it was the turn of universalist schemes and mandatory residence insurance. Last, medical savings accounts were mentioned. The order in which the financing models have just been mentioned reflects not only a logical criterion but also, at least in part, the timing with which these models have historically established themselves on the international scene.

As has already been proposed (Immergut, 1992), one can conceive an "ideotypical pattern of development" of health systems, articulated in three successive stages.

The first stage corresponds to the diffusion, alongside the simple market, of forms of voluntary insurance. These forms arose either by entrepreneurial initiative (private insurance companies for profit) or with purposes of solidarity (nonprofit mutual organizations), with the aim to redistribute risks within certain social groups. In some countries, the State intervened to regulate such forms of VHI, offering some sort of economic incentive to those who decide to take part. As Alber (1982) points out, government programs of this kind – which involve public subsidies for the subscription of voluntary insurance – have long represented the privileged way in which European states have responded to the ever-increasing demand for social security. At the end of the nineteenth century, public subsidies for private insurance had long been foreseen in Great Britain, and spread to Sweden (1891), Denmark (1892), Belgium (1894), France (1898) and other countries. In some countries, the principle of voluntary health insurance has been "underpinned" by the establishment of some typically "targeted" programs, designed to protect certain categories considered particularly at risk, mainly the poor.

The second stage of the evolutionary path leads to social health insurance. As mentioned previously, the first country to adopt such a system was Germany, starting with the Bismarckian legislation of 1883. Since then, in terms of compulsory health insurance, the German model has become the reference model with which other countries had to compare. As in Germany, as well as in many other countries, the obligation to take out health insurance was initially aimed only at the categories of workers deemed most fragile. Over the years, however, this obligation was extended to (1) an ever-greater number of occupational groups; (2) not just to individual subscribers but also to their respective dependants; and (3) not only to active workers but also to pensioners. Following the logic of a progressive extension of insurance coverage, many countries have come to include the vast majority of the population in mandatory social insurance schemes (Normand and Busse, 2002). As with voluntary insurance, in many countries the social insurance model has also been flanked by targeted programs, which are financed by tax revenues and intended to provide assistance to certain categories that otherwise would not have been covered by compulsory sickness funds.

The third stage of the development path is represented by the affirmation of the universalist principle. Although in some countries its institution had already been proposed before, it was only at the end of the 1930s that this model made its appearance on the international scene. Moreover, this financing mechanism is often accompanied by a public service delivery system. The composition of these two elements generates, as explained in the previous chapters, the typical model of the "national health service." The first country to adopt the universalist model was New Zealand, in 1938. Despite the birthright of New Zealand, however, the reference point for all the other universalist systems that subsequently arose was, since its establishment in 1946, the British National Health Service (NHS). Not surprisingly, the NHS is also called the "Beveridge model," from the name of the English economist William Beveridge: He was called to chair the parliamentary commission which in 1942 recommended the establishment of the NHS in the United Kingdom.

In order not to confuse the reader, it is good to insert a clarification at this point. In Chapter 1, we presented seven financing models. In this chapter, we are forced to simplify the picture a little by reducing the number of possible models. Therefore, we will proceed to discuss some mergers. First of all, we will keep the VHI model together with that of the simple market because in all voluntary insurance systems the direct purchase of services is always allowed by paying out-of-pocket. As has been pointed out, targeted programs are always, by definition, ancillary solutions, which aim to compensate for the coverage limitations fatally generated by voluntary insurance or SHI systems. For the purposes of this chapter, "targeted" programs can be regarded, more than autonomous systems, as being "corrective," which in some countries are introduced in addition to the basic models of voluntary insurance or SHI. The mandatory residence insurance model will be kept separate, at first, from both the SHI and the universalist models (see Table 8.1). Subsequently, the compulsory residence insurance will be assimilated to the SHI. Beyond the differences, both models share the primarily "regulatory" role attributed to the State in that the public actor merely imposes an obligation on citizens, but does not personally finance healthcare (as is the case in the universalist model). Finally, we come to MSAs, which in this chapter are not covered because none of the OECD countries adopts this model as their main funding system (see Chapter 2).

In light of the amalgamations and simplifications proposed above, we can conceive of a typical evolutionary path divided into three phases: (1) voluntary insurance; (2) social health insurance (or mandatory residence insurance); and (3) the universalist model (including both separate and integrated versions).

If we conceive of the voluntary insurance phase as the starting point for all countries, there are two crucial steps: the first is from voluntary insurance to SHI and the second is from SHI to the adoption

Table 8.1 *Introduction of major healthcare compulsory programs*

	First laws establishing mandatory social health insurance (year and groups to which it originally applied)	Law establishing a universalist scheme	Law establishing mandatory residence insurance
Australia	–	1974	
Austria	**1888** (blue-collar workers)	–	
Belgium	**1944** (salaried employees)	–	
Canada	–	**1966**	
Czech Republic	**1888** (blue-collar workers)	**1952**˙	
Denmark	–	**1971**	
France	**1930** (low-income workers)	–	
Finland	–	**1963**	
Germany	**1883** (low-income blue-collar workers)	–	**2007**
Greece	**1934** (urban salaried employees)	**1983**	
Hungary	**1891** (blue-collar workers)	**1972–1975**˙	
Ireland	**1911** (low-income workers)	**1970**	
Israel	–		**1994**
Italy	**1943** (private sector salaried employees)	**1978**	
Japan	**1922** (low-income blue-collar workers)	–	
Korea	**1977** (employees in large companies)	–	

Netherlands	**1941** (low-income workers)	–	**2006**
New Zealand	–	**1938**	
Norway	**1909** (low-income salaried employees)	**1956**	
Poland	**1920** (low-income salaried employees)	**1972**[*]	
Portugal	**1946** (blue-collar workers)	**1979**	
Spain	**1942** (blue-collar workers)	**1986**	
Sweden	–	**1953**	
Switzerland	–	–	**1994**
Turkey	**1945** (private sector and blue collar public sector employees)	–	
United Kingdom	**1911** (low-income workers)	**1946**	
United States	–	–	

Note: [*] The countries of Eastern Europe, during the communist regime, adopted a centralized state-run system, known as the "Semashko model."

Source: Based on data in Flora (1986); Immergut (1992); Cutler and Johnson (2004); Toth (2013)

216 HEALTH POLITICS

of a universalist scheme. Table 8.1 shows, country by country, the dates for which the first mandatory SHI law and that which established a universalist scheme (financed through tax revenues) were respectively approved. The last column of Table 8.1 shows the year of the first establishment of a mandatory residence insurance system.

8.2.1 The Evolutionary Trajectories of Individual Countries

Turning now to examine the evolutionary trajectories followed by the various countries, some common paths can be identified.

The first path involves the adoption of a social health insurance scheme, without the subsequent approach to either the universalist model or that of mandatory residence insurance. Six out of twenty-seven countries followed this path: Austria, Belgium, France, Japan, the Republic of Korea and Turkey.

A second evolutionary path is characterized by the adoption of the universalist model after experimenting with a mandatory SHI system. This is the path followed by seven of the twenty-seven countries considered: Greece, Ireland, Italy, Norway, Portugal, Spain and the United Kingdom.

A third evolutionary path is that followed by countries that have passed directly from voluntary private insurance to the universalist model, without ever having adopted a Bismarckian system of SHI. Six countries have followed this trajectory: Australia, Canada, Denmark, Finland, New Zealand and Sweden.

A particular path was followed by the three countries of Eastern Europe (the Czech Republic, Hungary and Poland). These three countries first introduced an SHI system, then transitioned, under the communist regime, to a centralized state-run model, (called the Semashko model, named after the first People's Commissar for Health who reorganized the healthcare system in the Soviet Union), to then return – with the transition to democracy – to a model of SHI.

Four countries have established a form of mandatory residence insurance system. Two of them (Germany and the Netherlands) arrived at this by reforming their previous SHI systems. The other two (Israel and Switzerland) came to mandatory residence insurance from a voluntary insurance system.

Excluded from the paths identified above is the United States, which has never launched a compulsory scheme, neither SHI, nor universalist, nor mandatory residence insurance.

The data reported in Table 8.1 can be read row by row, but it is also suitable for reading by column. In this way, three distinct historical phases stand out clearly. The first runs from the Bismarckian legislation of 1883 to 1946. This is the era in which forms of SHI are introduced for the first time. The second phase is the one in which universalist schemes are established, which is from 1946 to the 1980s. Apart from a couple of trespasses (the Korean and New Zealand cases), there is no overlap between the two phases. As mentioned in Chapter 5, mandatory residence insurance is a more recent model than the others, which was adopted from the early 1990s onward. Each organizational model has, therefore, characterized an era. The Bismarckian model dominated until the end of the Second World War. The universalist model characterized the period that immediately followed, up to the fall of the Berlin Wall. In the 1990s, countries that have changed their model, with the exception of Eastern European countries, have adopted a mandatory residence insurance model.

8.3 THE "WHY" QUESTION

In the light of the considerable differences which are evident between the different models of healthcare organization, questions instantly arise over why the economically more developed countries have followed different paths. After we dwelt in the previous chapters on how the various systems are organized, by analyzing their similarities and differences, it is now time to ask why. Why do some countries have an SHI system, others have mandatory residence insurance, others have a separated universalist system and still others a NHS? And why are there countries, such as the United States, that do not adopt any of the previous models?

This is obviously the question that torments all health policy scholars, and it is also the one we intend to address in this chapter. The "why" question can also be formulated in the following way. If it is true – as we have hypothesized in the previous section – that the historical evolution of health systems can be represented through a tripartite sequence (voluntary insurance, SHI, universalist scheme), why have some countries stopped at the first stage (VHI), others at the second stage (SHI) and others have gone further and reached the third stage (universalist scheme)?

The "why" question has given rise to the most varied answers. Some scholars have identified the cause of the differences between health systems in the prevalent political culture of each nation (Jacobs, 1993; Blank et al., 2018). A different explanation is the one proposed by Navarro (1989), which leads the choice of a specific health model back to the strength of the working class. Where in the past the working class has been more organized, the foundations have been laid for the adoption of a NHS; on the contrary, in countries where the labor movement and trade unions have traditionally been weaker – such as in the United States – we still have health systems that are more open to the private sector. As will be seen below, various authors trace strategic choices in the health field to partisanship and the ideological orientation of national governments.

A further explanation applies the well-known theory of "path dependence" to the healthcare sector (David, 1985; Pierson, 2000). This theory assumes that once a system is established, it tends to consolidate over time, becoming difficult to modify. In other words, the strategies adopted in the past strongly condition and constrain subsequent choices. Like all public policies, health policies are largely path dependant (Wilsford, 1994; Oliver and Mossialos, 2005). A certain financing or provision model, once fully operational, tends to become legitimate in the eyes of public opinion and to create advantages for certain categories of actors, who will, therefore, have an interest in maintaining the status quo (Pierson, 2011). Any attempt to radically change the system will, therefore, encounter strong resistance. The perspective of path dependence, although it concentrates mainly on the inertial nature of policies, however, does not deny that there can be changes of even great importance. However, the latter can only occur in exceptional conditions, of profound discontinuity. The moments of discontinuity that allow radical changes of strategy with respect to the past are called "critical junctures" (Collier and Collier, 1991; Wilsford, 1994; Hacker, 2002). The differences between the health models adopted in the various countries can, therefore, be interpreted on the basis of the choices that national governments have made in certain historical passages. The decisions made at such crucial moments ended up binding future strategies, precluding alternative options and making the choices already made irreversible (or in any case difficult to reverse). The current structure of a single national system can then only be understood by tracing its evolutionary path.

Among the many possible explanations, some conceive the process of formulating health policies as an arena (Lowi, 1964) in which actors, such as governments, health professionals, trade unions, employers, political parties, insurance companies and so on, compete. The past outcomes of these clashes were influenced not only by the strength of the actors (and the alliances they were able to build) but also by the rules of the game and the institutional constraints, which distinguish each national system.

In this chapter, we will try to investigate the possible answers to the "why" question more thoroughly, trying to take into account the different dimensions of "healthcare politics," that is, the ideas, interests and political institutions.

It is correct to point out to the reader that the "why" question that has just been formulated, as well as the possible answers that have been associated with it, are inspired by research questions and theoretical hypotheses that have been circulating for several years and are the subject of debate in this line of studies. In many cases, these hypotheses have been elaborated by beginning from the interpretation of the US anomaly, and have then been extended – sometimes stretched – to include other national cases. The ambition of this work is to arrive at interpretations that can be convincing with reference not only to the American case, but to all twenty-seven countries that are considered in this book.

8.4 IDEAS: THE IMPORTANCE OF VALUES AND IDEOLOGICAL ORIENTATION

Some of the answers to the "why" question that have been formulated in the previous section focus on the values rooted in individual countries and, more generally, on an "ideational" factor. Highlighting the importance of ideas means to emphasize the way problems are framed, the assumptions that guide the selection of alternative solutions and the rhetoric through which certain policy options are legitimized (or discredited).

8.4.1 National Culture

A first interpretation places the emphasis on the type of culture prevalent in each individual national context. Along the lines of some seminal studies on the welfare state (Flora and Alber, 1981; Castles, 1982; Esping-Andersen, 1990), the "culturalist" explanation assumes that a strong liberal tradition inhibits state intervention in the health field, making the adoption of compulsory social insurance less likely and even less of a universalist scheme.

Developing this thesis, Blank et al. (2018) proposes to divide countries into three classes based on the dominant political culture: individualistic, egalitarian and communitarian. If this tripartition has been interpreted correctly, "individualistic" culture is based on the assumption that taking care of one's health is essentially an individual responsibility. Therefore, the government must not intervene in the healthcare field and must not limit individual freedom (by imposing insurance or other obligations). On the other hand, the "egalitarian" culture is based on the principle that the State must intervene directly to guarantee the same rights and equal treatment for all citizens since the uniformity of treatment prevails over individual freedom. "Communitarian culture" is, to some extent, in an intermediate position with respect to the previous two. The strategic level is constituted, neither by the State nor by the individual, but by "intermediate bodies." Healthcare management must not be public (as in egalitarian cultures) nor delegated to the market (as in individualistic cultures), but must be entrusted to social partners, professional associations, mutual organizations and local communities. The State must therefore refrain from being directly involved in the financing and provision of health services. Instead, it must limit itself to regulating the system in order to ensure its fairness and solidarity.

According to Blank et al. (2018), countries that are characterized by a "communitarian culture" (such as, Germany or Japan) should show many affinities with the principle of social health insurance. In fact, this system leaves ample space for private actors, mutual organizations and social partners, while the government is mainly entrusted with regulatory tasks. Nations in which an "egalitarian" culture prevails – such as the United Kingdom, New Zealand or Sweden – should, instead, have a greater propensity toward the universalist model (particularly in a version of the National Health Service) or a markedly public system capable of guaranteeing, at least on paper, the same rights to all citizens. Finally, there are countries that are characterized by an "individualistic" culture (such as the United States, Australia or Singapore), in which the majority of the population should look favorably on a system that favors voluntary private insurance and that preserves the freedom of individual citizens by reducing public intervention to a minimum.

This culturalist explanation seems to fit well with the American case. The uniqueness of this country is, in fact, attributed by many to its particular political culture, strongly tinged with individualism and anti-statism. As has been thoroughly argued, the majority of the American population is not willing to give up their freedom of choice; conceives healthcare more as an individual than a collective good; is convinced that the management of healthcare must be taken care of by individuals and not by the State (Starr, 1982; Jacobs, 1993;

Quadagno, 2005). The culturalist thesis is certainly suggestive, even if it has the defect of being difficult to demonstrate empirically (Steinmo and Watts, 1995; Blake and Adolino, 2001). It is not easy to operationalize the concept of national culture and measure the degree of individualism or of egalitarianism of a given national community. The attribution of individual countries to the three categories of culture, therefore, risks becoming questionable.

8.4.2 The Ideological Orientation of Governments

A second question that we intend to investigate is whether there exists a link between the healthcare models adopted in different national contexts and the ideological orientation of the governments which have instituted them. This theme is already present to a large degree in the debate over the development of the welfare state in Western countries (Castles, 1982; Myles and Quadagno, 2002). The argument made by certain authors, which remains controversial, is that leftist parties have played a decisive role in the development and extension of the welfare state, in contrast to conservative parties, which have more often slowed its expansion (Esping-Andersen, 1985; Huber and Stephens, 2001). The topic of partisanship and the ideological factor was also investigated with reference to the strategies adopted in the healthcare field (Navarro et al., 2006; Jordan, 2011; Montanari and Nelson, 2013; Mackenbach and McKee, 2015; Falkenbach et al., 2019).

The argument regarding partisanship rests on the observation that, within individual countries, the debate regarding how much to spend on healthcare and on which organizational model to adopt has often proven to be highly ideologized (Immergut, 1992; Navarro and Shi, 2001; Montanari and Nelson, 2013), in that conservative political forces tended to look suspiciously at excessive State interference, supporting forms of social health insurance. Unions and left-wing parties have, instead, taken sides in favor of a broader public intervention and the creation of a NHS (or in any case a universalist scheme).

Dwelling on the more or less decisive role of the socialist or social democratic parties allows us to give an explanation of the US case as well. Some authors, including Navarro (1989) and Maioni (1997), argue that the main reason why the United States still lacks national health insurance today is to be found, in this country, in the absence of a large authentically social democratic party. Compared to the European social democratic parties, the American Democrats have always been a more composite team with more moderate positions,[1] which has not traditionally had organic relations with the trade unions and which has never joined the Socialist International (which the large socialist, labor and social democratic parties that we find in many other OECD countries have joined).

To assess how much the ideological orientation affects the strategic choices made in healthcare matters, we can look at the legislative measures where, in the various countries, the SHI and the universalist models were introduced for the first time.

8.4.3 Social Health Insurance and Conservative Governments

The legislative measures with which national governments first instituted forms of social health insurance, (at least for some professional categories), almost all fall, as we have seen previously, between the 1880s and the end of the Second World War. The first country to emulate the Bismarckian model was Austria (1888), the last one was Portugal in 1946 and, much later, the Republic of Korea in 1977.

Looking at the timing with which the SHI model has spread, it has not failed to underline the importance of the demonstrative effect that Bismarckian social legislation has been able to exert on the

---

[1] The fact that the American Democrats are not a social democratic party in the classical sense does not mean that they have not fought for more public intervention in healthcare. The opposite is true. The issue of healthcare reform has been, on several occasions, a workhorse of this party: Even before the Obama reform, all the main attempts to establish national healthcare insurance in the United States bear the signature of democratic presidents, from Franklin D. Roosevelt to Truman, from Lyndon Johnson to Clinton (Peterson, 1993; Oberlander, 2003).

governments of neighboring countries (Cutler and Johnson, 2004). German influence spread in various ways. Some governments have simply been impressed with the German social protection scheme, among these is the British government. It is said that Lloyd George became convinced of the need to introduce a compulsory insurance scheme, (the relative law was then approved in 1911), just after returning from an official visit to Germany (Hennock, 1987). France introduced the first forms of compulsory insurance after the First World War, extending the scheme already in force in Alsace and Lorraine (regions that belonged to Germany before the Peace Treaty of Versailles) to the entire national territory. Other countries, such as the Netherlands and Belgium, have confirmed the SHI system after evaluating its benefits during the German occupation.

Let us consider the ideological orientation of the governments that have adopted SHI schemes for the first time in their own country. The whole appears to be well-matched (see Table 8.2).

We find Conservative governments that are not democratically elected (the Bismarck government in Second Reich Germany, the Taaffe government in the Austro-Hungarian Empire); liberal or Conservative governments (France, Hungary, Norway, Poland, the United Kingdom); military governments (Japan); authoritarian regimes (Italy, Korea, Portugal, Spain, Turkey); post-war (Belgium) or post-dictatorship (Greece) governments of national unity. In the Netherlands the first compulsory insurance scheme (1941) was imposed by the German occupation forces. Therefore, generally speaking, it was mainly conservative or nondemocratic governments that introduced SHI schemes.

One plausible explanation is that these governments, this holds true particularly for countries with executives who are not responsible to the parliament, have used social legislation as a strategy to make up for their legitimacy deficits. As Flora and Alber (1981) explain, national elites often use social security policies as a means of exchange, in order to ensure the consensus of the working classes and, at the same time, defuse some of the principal claims of

8.4 IDEAS 225

Table 8.2 *First laws introducing social health insurance*

	Year	Government in charge
Austria	1888	Taaffe (Conservatives; not elected by Parliament)
Belgium	1944	Pierlot (Christian Democrats; government of national unity)
Czech Republic	1888	The Czech lands were still part of the Austro-Hungarian Empire
France	1930	Tardieu (Conservatives)
Germany	1883	Bismarck (Conservatives; not elected by Parliament)
Greece	1934	Tsaldaris (Conservatives: government of national unity)
Hungary	1891	Szapáry (Liberal Party)
Ireland	1911	Ireland was still part of the United Kingdom
Italy	1943	Mussolini (authoritarian)
Japan	1922	Tomosaburo (military)
Korea	1977	Park Chung-Hee (Conservatives; authoritarian regime)
Netherlands	1941	German occupying forces
Norway	1909	Knudsen (Liberals)
Poland	1920	Skulski (Conservatives)
Portugal	1946	Salazar (authoritarian)
Spain	1942	Franco (authoritarian)
Turkey	1945	Saraçoğlu (authoritarian one-party regime)
United Kingdom	1911	Asquith (Liberals)

the workers' movements. The Bismarck government is emblematic: It was pointed out that the social legislation for which this government went down in history was motivated not only by the desire to protect the working classes but also to regain political legitimacy and preserve social order. After the anti-socialist laws in 1878 (for which several leaders of the Social Democratic Party were arrested, socialist organizations and meetings were banned and workers' newspapers were suppressed), Bismarck needed to win back the favor

226 HEALTH POLITICS

of the working classes, so, the granting of social rights to industrial workers seemed the best way to regain consensus (Cutler and Johnson, 2004).

8.4.4 Universalist Schemes and Leftist Governments

The period between the end of the Second World War and the 1980s was, instead, characterized by the use of the universalist model. The first countries to establish a universalist scheme were New Zealand (1938) and the United Kingdom (1946). Between the 1950s and the early 1970s, it was then the turn of the Nordic countries (Sweden, Norway, Finland and Denmark), as well as Canada, Ireland and Australia. Around the same time, the Eastern European countries (the Czech Republic, Hungary and Poland) adopted a universalist system run by the State, by following the Soviet example. Finally, between the end of the 1970s and the mid-1980s, it was the Southern Europe countries' turn.

If we look at the color of the governments that have introduced universalist schemes (Table 8.3), the scenario appears very different compared to the previous period, as eleven out of sixteen governments are left or center-left governments (including the communist regimes of the three Eastern European countries). In Canada and Italy, the introduction of a universalist system was the result of an agreement that could be defined as "bipartisan." In Canada, the healthcare reform of 1966 resulted from an agreement between liberals and social democrats, (the liberals did not have a parliamentary majority and social democratic support was essential for the survival of the Pearson government). The Italian 1978 healthcare reform was approved by a government of national solidarity, a single-party Christian Democratic minority government with "external support" from the Communist party; the Communists made the health reform a necessary condition for their support (Toth, 2015b). In only three countries (Denmark, Finland and Ireland), were there laws establishing the universalist scheme that were passed when center-right governments were in office.

Table 8.3 *Laws introducing a universalist scheme*

	Year	Government in charge
Australia	1974	Whitlam (Labour)
Canada	1966	Pearson (Liberal minority government supported by Social-Democrats)
Czech Republic	1952	Zápotocky (Communist regime)
Denmark	1971	Baunsgaard (Centre-right coalition)
Finland	1963	Karjalaincn (Liberal-Conservative Agrarian Party)
Greece	1983	Papandreou (Socialist Party)
Hungary	1972–1975	Fock (Communist regime)
Ireland	1970	Lynch (Fianna Fáil)
Italy	1978	Andreotti (Christian democratic minority government supported by the Communist Party)
New Zealand	1938	Savage (Labour)
Norway	1956	Gerhardsen (Labour)
Poland	1972	Jaroszewicz (Communist regime)
Portugal	1979	Pintassilgo (caretaker government led by Socialists)
Spain	1986	Gonzalez (Socialist Party)
Sweden	1953	Erlander (Social Democrats)
United Kingdom	1946	Attlee (Labour)

One should also note that, in certain cases, it was the first socialist government in the history of the country that approved the founding legislation for a universalist scheme. This was true for the Savane government in New Zealand, for the Gonzalez government in Spain and for the Papandreou government in Greece. The Attlee government in the United Kingdom was the first Labor government to enjoy a parliamentary majority. While the Whitlam government in Australia marked Labor's return to power after twenty-three years. This serves to underline how the introduction of universalist schemes often coincide with moments of discontinuity in the political life of the country, and how many leftist governments have considered the adoption of the universalist model as rallying call that is characteristic of their work.

With no pretensions to stipulating laws of a general nature, the data reported above authorize us to believe – or at least to hypothesize – that the major choices in the healthcare field have often been influenced by the ideological orientation of the governments in office. A large majority of laws instituting a system of SHI have been taken on by conservative or nondemocratic governments; while those instituting a universalist scheme have been, in most cases, the work of left-wing governments. This obviously does not mean that universal single-payer public systems have been instituted in all countries that have left-wing parties in the government. In France and Germany, for example, Socialists and Social Democrats have governed for long periods of time without ever supporting the creation of a NHS. Nor can one affirm that all right-wing parties have systematically opposed the universalist model. In some countries, the institution of this model was the fruit of bipartisan accord. In others, once introduced, the universal single-payer public system has ended up gaining a vast consensus and Conservative governments have refrained from proposing its dismantlement.

Hypothesizing an affinity between SHI and Conservative governments on one hand, and between universalist model and leftist governments on the other, appears quite plausible even on a logical level. As previously noted, the SHI model envisions reduced public intervention and at the same time ensures greater freedom of choice by patients for the provider. Therefore, this seems to be more congenial to right-wing parties (whether Conservatives or Christian Democrats). Conversely, the universalist model, and in particular, the NHS, envisages a much more extensive intervention on the part of the State and proposes equality of treatment for all citizens, even at the cost of less individual freedom of choice. It should not be surprising that a system with these characteristics is more often invoked by left-wing parties.

8.5 INTERESTS: PRESSURE GROUPS AND THE CLASH BETWEEN DOCTORS AND THE STATE

In the previous section we focused on values, cultural assumptions, the ideological factor and conceiving health politics mainly as a "clash of ideas." But in addition to ideas, material interests also count. Health policies, in fact, reflect conflicts, agreements and power relations between governments and the most influential interest groups. The healthcare sector has enormous commercial interests; it has significant effects on employment; it significantly affects the quality of citizens' lives and family spending; and it is often used as a vehicle for obtaining social and political consensus. It is, therefore, inevitable that stakeholders and interest groups are mobilized around both the large and small choices within the healthcare sector.

8.5.1 Interest Groups in Healthcare

Different categories of interests can be represented in the healthcare arena (Tuohy and Glied, 2011; Buse et al., 2012; Weissert and Weissert, 2019): healthcare professionals (doctors, nurses, dentists and all allied health professions), insurers (for-profit insurance companies, sickness funds, voluntary nonprofit mutual organizations), owners of hospitals, pharmaceutical companies, other manufacturers and suppliers (such as medical equipment manufacturers, companies specializing in hospital construction and companies providing IT systems), as well as associations for the protection of patients with certain pathologies, business associations and unions, lobbying groups for patients' rights. And the list could go on, because there are many who have some interest, or some "stakes" in the healthcare field.

Depending on the relationships they have with policy makers, interest groups can be perceived as insiders or outsiders (Grant, 1989; Maloney et al., 1994; Page, 1999; Buse et al., 2012). Insider groups are regularly consulted by the government since they are considered to be more legitimate and representative. These groups boast closer contact with policy makers (health ministers, members of parliamentary committees, etc.), and so they generally prefer direct lobbying.[2] In many OECD countries, associations representing the healthcare professions (especially doctors) are typically insider groups. Therefore, they are officially consulted for all issues that may affect them.

On the other hand, outsider groups are those that legislators do not recognize as privileged interlocutors, therefore, they are usually excluded from consultations and have more sporadic relations with the government and parliamentarians. Being largely excluded from the most important decision-making venues, outsider groups – by choice or necessity – rely more on indirect lobbying, focusing on protest demonstrations and raising public awareness.

Within the insider groups, a further distinction can be made between high-profile and low-profile groups (Grant, 1989). The former are those who seek high public visibility and that often appear in the mass media. Low-profile groups, on the other hand, are those who shy away from excessive media exposure and prefer to operate in a more hidden way. In many cases, the choice between a "high" or a "low" profile derives from the nature of the group and the respective membership. It is plausible that a group that is in competition with others, and that is looking for new members, gives greater visibility to its activities, also to demonstrate to public opinion that it is a vital and enterprising group. Other groups do not have this need, and prefer lobbying without very much publicity. In many countries medical unions, or patient associations attempt to be high profile. Conversely, lobbies representing the pharmaceutical companies and the hospital owners more frequently adopt a low profile.

---

[2] By direct lobbying we mean communications with members or employees of a legislative body, or with any other government official who may participate in formulating the legislation. By indirect lobbying, on the other hand, we mean public initiatives (public demonstrations, communication campaigns, strikes and other forms of protest) aimed at raising public awareness on certain issues and showing the ability to mobilize individual groups. These forms of mobilization are to be considered indirect as they aim to put pressure on legislators not through a direct approach, but through the conditioning of public opinion.

8.5.2 The Obama Reform and Interest Groups

The Obama reform, approved in 2010, clearly highlights how choices in the healthcare field are conditioned by the strategies and positions of the interest groups and by the relationships they have with policy makers.

Over the course of the last century, many attempts to radically reform the American health system failed, crushed by fierce opposition from some influential interest groups, including the American Medical Association (AMA), insurance companies and the US Chamber of Commerce (Starr, 1982; Steinmo and Watts, 1995; Giaimo, 2002; Oberlander, 2003; Quadagno, 2005; Morone, 2010).

Building on past failures, during 2009 Obama and his staff then sought to win over to their side some of the organized groups who were potentially hostile to the healthcare reform advocated by the presidency (Miller, 2010; Oberlander, 2010; Weissert and Weissert, 2019). The representatives of the professional and business groups deemed to be most influential were invited, one at a time, to the White House. At the end of the negotiations, Obama and his staff reached separate agreements with important lobbies (Jacobs and Skocpol, 2010; Miller, 2010), including the following: the union of pharmaceutical companies (PhRMA), which later proved to be very generous in financing the campaign in support of the reform; the American Hospital Association; the main medical associations (the AMA and the American College of Physicians); the association representing the main insurance companies (AHIP, America's Health Insurance Plans), which in the spring of 2009 publicly declared its support for the reform proposal. The generalist unions also supported the pro-reform coalition. Both the AARP (American Association of Retired Persons) and AFL-CIO (the largest trade union federation in the United States) gave their public endorsement to the Obama reform, followed by the other major trade unions in the country. The president obtained the commitment of his interlocutors to support the health reform plan under discussion in Congress. In return, the aforementioned interest groups snatched some substantial compensation and the reassurance that the elements they disliked would be removed from the bill (Jacobs and Skocpol, 2010; Weissert and Weissert, 2019).

A turning point in some ways epochal was the position held by AMA, long considered one of the most influential lobbies in the country (Campion, 1984; Morone, 1990). In the past, this association had always fiercely opposed any attempt to introduce national insurance, contributing decisively to burying many reform proposals (Starr, 1982; Campion, 1984; Skocpol, 1993; Marmor, 2000; Oberlander, 2003).

The Obama administration's strategy of co-opting potentially hostile groups and reaching separate agreements with them paid off. This strategy had the effect of realigning coalitions traditionally for and against reform (Jacobs and Skocpol, 2010), with the migration of some groups from one side to another. The coalition in support of the reform benefited from this, and it turned out to be broader and more aggressive than in the past. To achieve this, Obama and his staff showed political pragmatism (Oberlander, 2010), showing that they were open to compromise for solutions, toward both interest groups and individual members of Congress.[3]

8.5.3   The Standoff between Doctors and the Government

As the case of the Obama reform highlights, the choices made in the field of healthcare can be traced back to the balance of power between government and interest groups (Alford, 1975; Wilsford,

---

[3] In addition to negotiations with interest groups, there were those with individual parliamentarians. The reform project had to pass multiple votes, first in committee and then in the chamber, both in the House and in the Senate. In anticipation of each of these votes, the group leaders of the Democratic Party had to put together the necessary votes. In this laborious work of weaving the majority, President Obama and his staff provided fundamental help. As reported by the newspapers, Obama telephoned a large number of parliamentarians, personally courting those deemed crucial. In addition to the president's moral suasion, some substantial compensation was also put on the plate to convince the more riotous parliamentarians (for the benefit of the states for which these members of Congress were representatives).

1995; Marmor, 2000; Quadagno, 2004). Among interest groups, the one which has traditionally been the most combative and influential in the healthcare sector is that made up of doctors (Starr, 1982; Freddi and Björkman, 1989; Wilsford, 1991; Moran, 1999; Giaimo, 2002). To underline the great influence held by doctors in past decades, expressions have been coined such as "medical dominance" (Freidson, 1970) or "medical sovereignty" (Starr, 1982). But where does the opposition between governments and the medical profession come from?

At the cost of simplifying the issue, the confrontation between medical professionals and the State may be summarized in the following terms. On one hand, the State aims to limit the autonomy of physicians and to restrain their earnings. Consequently, governments should prefer a NHS in which healthcare professionals are salaried public employees. On the other hand, doctors fight for their own professional autonomy and for gaining a more favorable method of remuneration. Physicians usually prefer to maintain the status of independent professionals, perceiving any attempt to "nationalize" the healthcare system as a threat (Immergut, 1992; Hacker, 1998). Therefore, among the various systems of organization of healthcare services, the NHS model is the least appreciated by doctors. Described in this way, the actors' preferences perhaps appear a little simplistic. It is a fact, however, that medical associations have organized large protests in almost all countries where a NHS has been introduced (Immergut, 1992; Laugesen and Rice, 2003).

In this regard, the experience of the United Kingdom is emblematic. The United Kingdom, as we already know, was the first European country to adopt a NHS; the founding law was passed in parliament in 1946 and the National Health Service officially began operating two years later. The period between the approval of the reform and its operational start was marked by an exhausting negotiation between the government and representatives of the British Medical Association (BMA). The standoff was no-holds-barred, and the medical specialists, after prolonged protests, even threatened to boycott the nascent public health service. The situation was unlocked only in extremis, just before the operational start of the NHS, when the British government yielded to some requests from the counterpart. Family doctors were allowed to remain freelancers under an agreement with the National Health Service. In addition to permission to practice privately outside their working hours, the medical specialists were granted a very generous salary. The joke with which Minister Bevan commented on the conclusion of the negotiation was this: *"I stuffed their mouths with gold"* (Bevan and Robinson, 2005). The conditions that the doctors tore up at that point were no longer questioned during the following decades (Klein, 2013).

What was just described certainly does not represent an isolated case. Negotiations completely similar to that initiated by the British government and the BMA took place in many other countries, including Canada, Ireland, Italy, New Zealand (Tuohy, 1999; Laugesen and Rice, 2003; Toth, 2015b; Goodyear-Smith and Ashton, 2019; Wren and Connolly, 2019). Episodes such as this show how tense relations between government and medical representatives have been in the vicinity of an overall reform of the healthcare system. In order to ensure the doctors' collaboration, governments have often had to accept solutions that involve compromise. Concessions to the medical staff typically concerned the employment relationship, the method of remuneration and the right to private practice.

If it is true that doctors and the government give rise to a test of strength in order to predict the outcome of the confrontation, then in each individual national context it is necessary to compare the power held by the two counterparties. This is what David Wilsford (1991) believes, whose hypothesis can be summarized as follows: In countries in which the government has proved to be stronger than doctors, there will probably be a NHS or, in any case, a healthcare system with a strong public presence. On the other hand, where doctors have created a strong pressure group in the presence of a weak government, there will be a healthcare system that is more open to the private sector (VHI or SHI). To assess how much power the government has over interest groups, the architecture of the political system and the institutional constraints that characterize each individual national case must be considered. This is what we will attempt to do in the next section.

8.6 INSTITUTIONS: THE IMPORTANCE OF POLITICAL INSTITUTIONAL RULES

To reconstruct health politics, it is not enough to consider ideas and interests (which are also important), but the third "I" should also be included in the analysis: institutions, understood as political institutions.

To investigate this last dimension, there is a vast body of literature which may be of use. Numerous esteemed studies have highlighted the importance of institutional rules and their impact on policy making (Steinmo et al., 1992; Weaver and Rockman, 1993). The power that a government wields in its clashes with other actors depends in great part on the institutional context in which it is situated. And when we talk about the institutional context we are referring not only to formalized rules but also to the unwritten practices that have developed around them. Turning to the analysis of healthcare policies, we can assume that the outcome of the confrontation between the government and various interest groups that are active in the healthcare arena (insurance companies, trade unions, the pharmaceutical industry, businesses, hospital owners, doctors and other health professions, etc.) is strongly influenced by institutional rules and, in particular, by the measure with which political power is concentrated or dispersed (Immergut, 1992; Steinmo and Watts, 1995; Maioni, 1997; Blake and Adolino, 2001; Giaimo, 2002; Mackenbach and McKee, 2015).

Steinmo and Watts (1995), for example, maintain that the United States does not have national healthcare insurance, not so much because successive governments have not wanted it, but rather because American institutions are designed in such a manner as to discourage comprehensive and radical reforms in the social field. The system of checks and balances foreseen by the American constitution confers limited autonomy to the executive branch, exposing it to the veto power of pressure groups opposed to reform. Ellen Immergut (1992) develops an argument that is similar to this in many respects, referring to three European countries. In the early 1990s, when *Health Politics* was published, Sweden had a NHS, France had a typical SHI scheme and a voluntary insurance system still existed in Switzerland. The different choices of healthcare models are explained in relation to the degree of autonomy enjoyed by the executive branch in the respective countries. In Sweden, Immergut argues, the government had full autonomy, while interest groups have had little veto power. Under these conditions, setting up a NHS has been easier than elsewhere. On the contrary, the Swiss government enjoys a more reduced autonomy, which gives greater power to interest groups (which have, in fact, greatly postponed the approval of a compulsory insurance scheme). The French, at an institutional design level, would constitute an intermediate case with respect to the other two countries, and so this explains the presence of a SHI scheme.

What the authors mentioned above and others maintain, to a great extent, is that in those countries in which political power is concentrated[4] in the hands of the executive branch, it is more likely that the will of the government will prevail over that of interest groups (translated for the healthcare field: The government has a better chance of implementing a universalist model, and in particular a NHS). Vice versa, in those systems where power is dispersed among multiple actors, the executive is weaker and interest groups find it easier to block its initiatives. Therefore, in the field of healthcare, this means that interest groups have a greater chance of blocking the approval of a system that they disapprove of (and thus no NHS).

---

[4] Dealing with dispersion and concentration of political power, the reference is to two well-known theories in the field of comparative politics: the first is the distinction between majoritarian and consensual democracy models proposed by Arendt Lijphart (1999), while the second is the veto players theory developed by George Tsebelis (1995, 2002).

Some studies (Blake and Adolino, 2001; Toth, 2013) tried to test this hypothesis in reference not only to the United States and the three European cases selected by Immergut but also to a large number of OECD countries. These studies seem to confirm that – in general, despite some unavoidable exceptions – over the decades the adoption of a universalist scheme has been more probable in those countries where political power is more concentrated. Conversely, in countries where political power is dispersed among multiple veto players, the probability of maintaining the preexisting SHI or VHI system may have been higher. It should be noted that this association is valid only for democratic regimes, and is convincing especially in reference to the period between the end of the Second World War and the fall of the Berlin Wall (since then, the distinctive traits of some Western democracies have been confused).

8.7 CONCLUSIONS: PUTTING TOGETHER THE PIECES OF HEALTH POLITICS

Let us try to sum up what we have seen in this chapter and in the previous one. Since the perspective of health politics is made up of several elements, all the pieces of the mosaic may now be put together.

Health policies – like many other policy areas – are characterized by inertia (Wilsford, 1994; Maioni, 1997; Hacker, 1998). Once a certain model of health organization is adopted in a country, it tends to consolidate and perpetuate itself over time. In fact, every financing and delivery system for health services tends to acquire legitimacy in the eyes of health professionals and citizens, and favors certain categories of actors (insurers, providers, users and public bureaucracies) who have an interest in preserving it. In accordance with the path dependence theory, previously mentioned, there are policy choices that, once adopted, it becomes difficult, if not impossible, to go back and undertake alternative strategies (Pierson, 2000).

Therefore, major reforms in the health sector, such as the transition from one financing model to another, are rare events in the history of a country, which can only occur under particularly favorable conditions that are also called "policy windows" or "windows of opportunity" (Kingdon, 1984; Tuohy, 1999; Zahariadis, 2003). Kingdon (1984) argues that for an issue to find a place in the public policy agenda, the coupling of three streams is required, which are problems, policy proposals and politics.

Previously there were examples of major health reforms that occurred in conjunction with quite exceptional moments in the country's political history, such as, a change of regime, the establishment of political forces that had never governed before or a landslide election victory. In countries such as Greece, Portugal and Spain, for example, the adoption of a NHS occurred during the transition from an authoritarian regime to democracy. In countries such as the United Kingdom and New Zealand, the NHS was established by the first Labor government in the country's history. In the German case, a major reform of the centennial SHI system was enacted immediately after the Reunification. Most of the countries of Eastern Europe, immediately after the fall of the Berlin Wall, with the transition from a socialist regime to democracy, radically reformed their model of healthcare organization. And the list of examples could go on.

For a radical reform to be enacted, opening a policy window is not enough. Windows of opportunity open infrequently, often unexpectedly, and do not stay open long (Kingdon, 1984). Those who have an interest in pushing forward a reform proposal must then be ready to take advantage of the favorable opportunities that present themselves. Like surfers waiting for a good wave (Kingdon, 1984; Toth, 2015b), even the "policy entrepreneurs," those who take action to carry out a reform, must know how to seize the moment.

As noted in the previous sections, the windows of opportunity that have opened up over the decades have been used differently by right-wing and left-wing governments. As a general pattern of behavior, Conservative governments have more easily attempted to establish (and then consolidate) a SHI system. Left-wing executive branches have often struggled to adopt the universalist model, and in particular a NHS.

In choosing a strategy to follow, the various political forces will have certainly calculated the impact of social and electoral consensus. In other words, when deciding whether or not to support a given reform, ideas regarding how much a healthcare model is considered to be legitimate and interests in the field have certainly held a significant weight, while each model favors some subjects, at the expense of others. Supporters of opposing ideas and interests, however, risk balancing and neutralizing each other.

In the long run, the political institutions that characterize individual countries seem to have made a difference. In countries where there are fewer veto points, a universalist scheme is more likely to have been adopted over the decades. On the contrary, countries in which there are more veto points are more frequently characterized by a VHI, a SHI or a compulsory residence insurance system. Highlighting the importance of political institutions means to simply affirm that completing all stages of the standard developmental sequence, (from VHI to the universalist model), has been somewhat easier and quicker in those political systems that have fewer veto players. Indeed, in majoritarian systems, the opportunity to give a radical imprint to policies presents itself more frequently than in consensual systems where occasions for the passage of radical reforms are much rarer, and where changes tend to be subject to collective negotiations and incremental in nature (Giaimo, 2002; Tuohy, 2018).

Conclusions

We have finally come to the end of this long overview of the various ways in which healthcare is financed and provided in twenty-seven OECD countries. In the context of conclusions, it is worthwhile to recapitulate some of the main points that emerged in the previous chapters.

NOT JUST BISMARCK AGAINST BEVERIDGE: GOING BEYOND THE STANDARD CLASSIFICATION

Wanting to compare and classify national health systems, there are many scholars who apply the classic contrast between the Bismarck model and the Beveridge model. In this way, healthcare systems end up being grouped into three categories: (1) Social Health Insurance systems (Bismarck); (2) the countries in which a National Health Service (Beveridge) operates; and (3) systems which, being neither Beveridge nor Bismarck, rely on voluntary insurance. The breakdown of health systems according to these three models can be considered the "standard tripartite classification" (Freeman and Frisina, 2010), which has been used in many scientific papers and research reports.

As noted in previous chapters, the juxtaposition between SHI and NHS countries still has meaning. But the three models of the standard classification (voluntary health insurance, SHI, NHS) do not exhaust the variety of organizational structures and the multiple combinations found in reality. For this reason, a more articulated classification has been adopted in this book, which takes into account both the dimension of financing and that of the provision of healthcare.

In terms of financing, others are added to the three categories of the standard classification: targeted programs (which cover a fundamental "remedial" function in many nonuniversalist systems), mandatory residence insurance (which starts from assumptions and produces very different effects from those of the traditional Bismarckian model) and the Medical Savings Accounts (which do not operate according to the insurance logic of risk sharing). Not to mention the direct market, which is a model that is often neglected in the classifications (perhaps because it is taken for granted), although it plays an important role (absorbing a significant share of healthcare expenditure) in almost all OECD countries. In the opinion of the author, reasoning on the basis of seven "primary" financing models, instead of on just three, allows us to better focus on the peculiarities of the individual national systems, grasping the different logics with which they are designed.

ALL HEALTH SYSTEMS ARE HYBRID

There are multiple organizational variants of the "primary" models, which – as in construction games – can be assembled together in different compositions. We have indeed confirmed that all national healthcare systems are hybrid and composite. No country, among those analyzed, uses a single financing model. There are those who mix three, some four, some five simultaneously. To describe the hybrid nature of health systems, the image of the cocktail was previously evoked. Depending on the country, financing models are combined with each other in different proportions and ways. Each country has its own recipe, its own peculiar formula, with which it mixes the different ingredients. If we had used only the three categories of the standard tripartite classification, the recipes would have been incomplete. We would have omitted some fundamental ingredients, which instead, contribute to differentiate the various national cocktails, giving them their own distinctive flavor.

Thinking in terms of hybrid systems, and comparing the twenty-seven countries, we have seen how each national system is segmented and articulated, internally, into subsystems that operate according to different logics and models. The segmentation can be obtained either by dividing healthcare into different packages or by dividing the population into subgroups (holders of different forms of coverage). All countries analyzed in this book have some kind of segmentation. No country guarantees all healthcare to the entire population through the exact same organizational methods.

THE UNINSURED: A PROBLEM NOT ONLY IN THE UNITED STATES

The analysis of data relating to health expenditure in OECD countries did not reserve any particular surprises. The level of healthcare spending does not seem to depend so much on the financing model adopted in individual countries, but rather on per capita income. In fact, the data reported confirm – both from a comparative and a diachronic perspective – that healthcare expenditure typically grows faster than GDP.

The data concerning the insurance coverage of the population are less obvious. The problem of the "uninsured," that is, of individuals without any form of primary health insurance, is usually associated with only the United States. However, the data reported in Chapter 3 show that many other OECD countries do not formally provide healthcare coverage to the entire population. Considering all OECD countries (therefore, not only the twenty-seven countries analyzed in this book), the uninsured total almost forty-seven million, corresponding to 3.6 percent of the population. Within EU countries, there are more than seven million uninsured (or 1.4 percent of EU residents). Evidently, the problem is serious, and so, there is a need for greater efforts on the part of national and supra-national policy makers to face and resolve this. Yet, outside the United States, and particularly within the European Union, the issue does not seem to attract particular attention, either in the media or in the scientific literature.

INTEGRATED AND SEPARATED PROVISION SYSTEMS

Often, healthcare systems are classified only on the basis of how they are financed. Or, if we also want to include the provision dimension, a distinction is made between public and private suppliers. In Chapter 4, a different path was taken. In fact, an attempt has been made to classify the national systems of healthcare delivery on the basis of their degree of organizational separation/integration. For this purpose, two opposing models have been outlined: the integrated and the separated models.

The twenty-seven countries considered in this research project are roughly evenly distributed along the entire separation/integration axis. The majority of SHI systems have characteristics that are closer to the separate model, while the majority of universalist countries are more oriented toward the integrated model. However, the association between the financing model and the provision model is by no means automatic.

FOUR FAMILIES AND SOME OUTLIERS

Despite the specificities of each individual national case, it is possible, by cross-referencing financing models with provision models, to outline four families of health systems, that is, two of larger dimensions (about ten countries per family) and two of smaller dimensions. Some countries straddle two different models, while others are not attributable to any of the four families.

The two larger families follow the traditional contrast between the NHS and SHI. The Bismarck and Beveridge models are not "dinosaurs" (van der Zee and Kroneman, 2007), they still exist. However, it is true that both families today constitute rather heterogeneous groupings, in that within each family, there are significant differences between one country and another. SHI countries diverge from each other on the basis of multiple dimensions. On an organizational level, the most relevant distinction seems to be that between the single-payer and multi-payer versions. On the outcomes front, it should be emphasized that some SHI countries guarantee – thanks to the adoption of targeted programs – universal coverage of the population, while others leave a minority of the population uninsured. The NHS countries are distinguished, above all, on the basis of the level of decentralization and publicness of their health system. The NHS of the Nordic countries has different traits from that found in the Southern European countries.

About a quarter of the countries analyzed in this book cannot be labeled as either SHI or NHS. Australia and Canada are separated universalist systems. The Netherlands, Switzerland and, to some extent, also Germany embodies the mandatory residence insurance model. We preferred to consider Greece, Israel and United States separately and consider them as outliers, and in any case, as being atypical when compared to the others.

FIVE GREAT REFORM THEMES

In Chapter 7, we ventured into an exercise that was anything but trivial, that is, to try to condense the countless reform initiatives that have been launched in recent decades into a few, large, common themes. Although others can certainly be identified (such as, the continuing need to contain costs, the strengthening of primary care or the impact of ICT on healthcare delivery), our attention has focused on five "strands" of reform, namely, (1) reforms aimed at stimulating competition; (2) the search for greater integration; (3) decentralization; (4) strengthening the rights of the patient; and (5) the extension of insurance coverage.

The impression one gets from the analysis of the cross-country diffusion of these reform issues is that healthcare reforms follow trends, some temporary, others more lasting. Continuous processes of emulation and policy transfer are developing between countries. Looking at the picture as a whole (thus including all twenty-seven countries, over a period of three decades), many reform initiatives seem to recall the motion of the pendulum. A reform in one direction is often followed by another in the opposite direction. Individual health systems can be located on some axes: the public-private (or state-market) axis; the center-periphery axis; the integration-separation axis. Along these axes, the individual countries frequently move, oscillate between one pole and another, in search of the best balance, the best trade-off.

The oscillation of reforms often reflects the alternation of governments of different orientations.

HEALTH POLITICS

In the final chapter of this book, we could not avoid asking ourselves the "why" question: Why do the twenty-seven countries considered here adopt different organizational models to govern the healthcare sector? Each model of governance of the healthcare system reflects a different interpretation of the role to be attributed to the State, the margin of freedom to be granted to the individual, the division between public and private responsibilities as well as the idea of equity and social solidarity. Adopting one model instead of another makes a lot of difference. Each organizational structure has different repercussions on patients, providers, insurers, public managers and all other stakeholders.

The strategic choices made in the healthcare field, and the reasons for which a particular model is selected, can be interpreted by referring to "health politics." Both the organizational structures implemented and the reforms undertaken over the decades can actually be conceived as the result of a "political game." This game is influenced by ideas, interests and political institutions (the three I's). On the ideas front, we have seen how organizational models, as well as some reform objectives, may have a clear political leaning. Their adoption can then be explained by the ideological orientation of the proposing governments. No less important is the role of the interests at stake. In fact, health policies derive, to a large extent, from the outcome of frictions, agreements and power relations between the various stakeholders and interest groups. The most influential groups – including, in many countries, the medical profession – have been able to guide the choices of policy makers toward the solutions they prefer. Finally, we come to the institutions. Health politics, like all games, follows rules, which change from country to country. The outcome of the confrontation between different ideas and conflicting interests is strongly structured and influenced by the structure of the political institutions operating in each individual country. In countries where political power is more concentrated in the hands of the executive, over the decades it has tended to be easier to undertake radical reforms and adopt a universalist model.

References

Aas, I. M. (1995). Incentives and financing methods. *Health Policy*, 34(3), 205–220.

Abiiro, G. A. & de Allegri, M. (2015). Universal health coverage from multiple perspectives: a synthesis of conceptual literature and global debate. *BMC International Health and Human Rights*, 15(1), 17–23.

Adams, T. (2010). Gender and feminization in health care professions. *Sociology Compass*, 4(7), 454–465.

Adolph, C., Greer, S. & Fonseca, E. M. (2012). Allocation of authority in European health policy. *Social Science & Medicine*, 75(9), 1595–1603.

Alber, J. (1982). *Vom Armenhaus zum Wohlfahrtsstaat: Analysen zur Entwicklung der Sozialversicherung in Westeuropa*. Frankfurt: Campus Verlag.

Alders, P. & Schut, F. T. (2019). The 2015 long-term care reform in the Netherlands: getting the financial incentives right? *Health Policy*, 123(3), 312–316.

Alexa, J., Rečka, L., Votápková, J., van Ginneken, E., Spranger, A. & Wittenbecher, F. (2015). Czech Republic: health system review. *Health Systems in Transition*, 17(1), 1–165.

Alford, R. (1975). *Health Care Politics: Ideological and Interest Group Barriers to Reform*. Chicago: University of Chicago Press.

Amelung, V., Stein, V., Goodwin, N., Balicer, R., Nolte, E. & Suter, E., eds. (2017). *Handbook Integrated Care*. Cham: Springer.

Andersen, R. M., Rice, T. H. & Kominski, G. F., eds. (2011). *Changing the US Health Care System: Key Issues in Health Services Policy and Management*. San Francisco: Jossey-Bass.

Anell, A., Glenngård, A. H. & Merkur, S. (2012). Sweden: health system review. *Health Systems in Transition*, 14(5), 1–159.

Arrow, K. J. (1963). Uncertainty and the welfare economics of medical care. *The American Economic Review*, 53(5), 941–973.

Arts, W. & Gelissen, J. (2002). Three worlds of welfare capitalism or more? A state-of-the-art report. *Journal of European Social Policy*, 12(2), 137–158.

Ashton, T., Mays, N. & Devlin, N. (2005). Continuity through change: the rhetoric and reality of health reform in New Zealand. *Social Science & Medicine*, 61(2), 253–262.

Bachner, F., Bobek, J., Habimana, K., et al. (2018). Austria: health system review. *Health Systems in Transition*, 20(3), 1–256.

248 REFERENCES

Baeten, R., Spasova, S., Vanhercke, B. & Coster, S. (2018). *Inequalities in Access to Healthcare: A Study of National Policies.* Brussels: European Social Policy Network.

Barnum, H., Kutzin, J. & Saxenian, H. (1995). Incentives and provider payment methods. *The International Journal of Health Planning and Management,* 10(1), 23–45.

Barr, M. D. (2001). Medical savings accounts in Singapore: a critical inquiry. *Journal of Health Politics, Policy and Law,* 26(4), 709–726.

Barroy, H., Or, Z., Kumar, A. & Bernstein, D. (2014). *Sustaining Universal Health Coverage in France: a Perpetual Challenge.* Washington, DC: The World Bank.

Bazzoli, G. J., Shortell, S. M., Dubbs, N., Chan, C. & Kralovec, P. (1999). A taxonomy of health networks and systems: bringing order out of chaos. *Health Services Research,* 33(6), 1683–1717.

Béland, D. (2010). Policy change in health care research. *Journal of Health Politics, Policy and Law,* 35(4), 615–641.

Bennett, C. & Howlett, M. (1992). The lessons of learning: reconciling theories of policy learning and policy change. *Policy Sciences,* 25(3), 275–294.

Berenson, R. A., Upadhyay, D., Delbanco, S. F. & Murray, R. (2016). *Payment Methods: How They Work.* Washington, DC: Urban Institute.

Bernal-Delgado, E., García-Armesto, S., Oliva, J. et al. (2018). Spain: health system review. *Health Systems in Transition,* 20(2), 1–179.

Bevan, G. (2014). *The Impacts of Asymmetric Devolution on Health Care in the Four Countries of the UK.* London: Health Foundation.

Bevan, G. & Robinson, R. (2005). The interplay between economic and political logics: path dependency in health care in England. *Journal of Health Politics, Policy and Law,* 30(1–2), 53–78.

Biller-Andorno, N. & Zeltner, T. (2015). Individual responsibility and community solidarity – the Swiss health care system. *The New England Journal of Medicine,* 373(23), 2193–2197.

Blake, C. & Adolino, J. (2001). The enactment of national health insurance: a Boolean analysis of twenty advanced industrial countries. *Journal of Health Politics, Policy and Law,* 26(4), 679–708.

Blank, R. H., Burau, V. & Kuhlmann, E. (2018). *Comparative Health Policy.* Basingstoke: Palgrave Macmillan.

Bleakley, A. (2014). Gender matters in medical education. In A. Bleakley, ed., *Patient-Centred Medicine in Transition.* Cham: Springer, pp. 111–126.

Blomqvist, A. (2011). Public-sector health care financing. In S. Glied & P. C. Smith, eds., *The Oxford Handbook of Health Economics.* Oxford: Oxford University Press, pp. 257–284.

REFERENCES 249

Blomqvist, P. (2004). The choice revolution: privatization of Swedish welfare services in the 1990s. *Social Policy & Administration*, 38(2), 139–155.

Blumenthal, D. (2006). Employer-sponsored health insurance in the United States: origins and implications. *New England Journal of Medicine*, 355(1), 82–88.

Bobbio, N. (1996). *Left and Right: The Significance of a Political Distinction*. Chicago: University of Chicago Press.

Boerma, T., Eozenou, P., Evans, D., Evans, T., Kieny, M. P. & Wagstaff, A. (2014). Monitoring progress towards universal health coverage at country and global levels. *PLoS Medicine*, 11(9), 1–8.

Boerma, W. (2006). Coordination and integration in European primary care. In R. Saltman, A. Rico & W. Boerma, eds., *Primary Care in the Driver's Seat? Organizational Reform in European Primary Care*. Maidenhead: Open University Press, pp. 3–21.

Böhm, K., Schmid, A., Götze, R., Landwehr, C. & Rothgang, H. (2013). Five types of OECD healthcare systems: empirical results of a deductive classification. *Health Policy*, 113(3), 258–269.

Boon, H., Verhoef, M., O'Hara, D. & Findlay, B. (2004). From parallel practice to integrative health care: a conceptual framework. *BMC Health Services Research*, 4, 15–19.

Brekke, K. R. & Straume, O. R. (2017). Competition policy for health care provision in Norway. *Health Policy*, 121(2), 134–140.

Burau, V. & Blank, R. H. (2006). Comparing health policy: an assessment of typologies of health systems. *Journal of Comparative Policy Analysis*, 8(1), 63–76.

Burns, L. & Pauly, M. (2002). Integrated delivery networks: a detour on the road to integrated health care? *Health Affairs*, 21(4), 128–143.

Buse, K., Mays, N. & Walt, G. (2012). *Making Health Policy*. Maidenhead: Open University Press.

Busse, R. & Blümel, M. (2014). Germany: health system review. *Health Systems in Transition*, 16(2), 1–296.

Busse, R., Saltman, R. B. & Dubois, H. (2004). Organization and financing of social health insurance systems: current status and recent policy developments. In R. B. Saltman, R. Busse & J. Figueras, eds., *Social Health Insurance Systems in Western Europe*. Maidenhead: Open University Press, pp. 33–80.

Busse, R., Blümel, M., Knieps, F. & Bärnighausen, T. (2017). Statutory health insurance in Germany: a health system shaped by 135 year of solidarity, self-governance, and competition. *The Lancet*, 390, 882–897.

Cabiedes, L. & Guillén, A. (2001). Adopting and adapting managed competition: health care reform in Southern Europe. *Social Science & Medicine*, 52(8), 1205–1217.

250 REFERENCES

Calnan, M., Hutten, J. & Tiljak, H. (2006). The challenge of coordination: the role of primary care professionals in promoting integration across the interface. In R. Saltman, A. Rico & W. Boerma, eds., *Primary Care in the Driver's Seat? Organizational Reform in European Primary Care*. Maidenhead: Open University Press, pp. 85–104.

Campion, F. (1984). *The AMA and US Health Policy since 1940*. Chicago: University of Chicago Press.

Castles, F., ed. (1982). *The Impact of Parties*. London: Sage.

Cheng, T. C., Joyce, C. M. & Scott, A. (2013). An empirical analysis of public and private medical practice in Australia. *Health Policy*, 111(1), 43–51.

Chevreul, K., Berg Brigham, K., Durand-Zaleski, I. & Hernández-Quevedo, C. (2015). France: health system review. *Health Systems in Transition*, 17(3), 1–218.

Chinitz, D. (1995). Israel's health policy breakthrough: the politics of reform and the reform of politics. *Journal of Health Politics, Policy and Law*, 20(4), 909–932.

Choné, P. (2017). Competition policy for health care provision in France. *Health Policy*, 121(2), 111–118.

Christiansen, T. & Vrangbæk, K. (2018). Hospital centralization and performance in Denmark-Ten years on. *Health Policy*, 122(4), 321–328.

Christianson, J. & Conrad, D. (2011). Provider payment and incentives. In S. Glied and P. C. Smith, eds., *The Oxford Handbook of Health Economics*. Oxford: Oxford University Press, pp. 624–648.

Clarfield, A. M., Manor, O., Nun, G. B., et al. (2017). Health and health care in Israel: an introduction. *The Lancet*, 389, 2503–2513.

CMS (2019). *National Health Expenditure Accounts*. Baltimore: Centers for Medicare and Medicaid Services.

Collier, R. & Collier, D. (1991). *Shaping the Political Arena. Critical Junctures, the Labor Movement, and Regime Dynamics in Latin America*. Princeton: Princeton University Press.

Collins, S., Bhupal, H. & Doty, M. (2019). *Health Insurance Coverage Eight Years after the ACA: Fewer Uninsured Americans and Shorter Coverage Gaps, but More Underinsured*. New York: Commonwealth Fund.

Connelly, L. B., Paolucci, F., Butler, J. & Collins, P. (2010). Risk equalisation and voluntary health insurance markets: the case of Australia. *Health Policy*, 98(1), 3–14.

Connolly, S. & Wren, M. A. (2017). Unmet healthcare needs in Ireland: analysis using the EU-SILC survey. *Health Policy*, 121(4), 434–441.

Conrad, D. & Shortell, S. (1996). Integrated health systems: promise and performance. *Frontiers of Health Services Management*, 13(1), 3–40.

Costa-Font, J. & Greer, S. L., eds. (2013). *Federalism and Decentralisation in European Health and Social Care*. Basingstoke: Palgrave Macmillan.

Cotlear, D., Nagpal, S., Smith, O., Tandon, A. & Cortez, R. (2015). *Going Universal: How 24 Developing Countries Are Implementing Universal Health Coverage Reforms from the Bottom Up*. Washington: The World Bank.

Coulter, A. (2011). *Engaging Patients in Healthcare*. New York: McGraw-Hill.

Culyer, A. J. (1989). Cost containment in Europe. *Health Care Financing Review*, annual supplement, 21–32.

Cutler, D. & Johnson, R. (2004). The birth and growth of the social insurance state: explaining old age and medical insurance across countries. *Public Choice*, 120(1–2), 87–121.

Cylus, J., Richardson, E., Findley, L., Longley, M., O'Neill, C. & Steel, D. (2015). United Kingdom: health system review. *Health Systems in Transition*, 17(5), 1–125.

Damiani, G., Silvestrini, G., Federico, B., et al. (2013). A systematic review on the effectiveness of group versus single-handed practice. *Health Policy*, 113(1–2), 180–187.

David, P. A. (1985). Clio and the economics of QWERTY. *American Economic Review*, 75(2), 332–337.

De Pietro, C., Camenzind, P., Sturny, I., et al. (2015). Switzerland: health system review. *Health Systems in Transition*, 17(4), 1–288.

Delamaire, M. L. & Lafortune, G. (2010). *Nurses in Advanced Roles: A Description and Evaluation of Experiences in 12 Developed Countries*. OECD Health Working Papers No. 54. Paris: OECD.

Delnoij, D., van Merode, G., Paulus, A. & Groenewegen, P. (2000). Does general practitioner gatekeeping curb health care expenditure? *Journal of Health Services Research & Policy*, 5(1), 22–26.

Delnoij, D., Klazinga, N. & Glasgow, K. (2002). Integrated care in an international perspective. *International Journal of Integrated Care*, 2(1), 1–4.

Dmytraczenko, T. & Almeida, G. (2015). *Toward Universal Health Coverage and Equity in Latin America and the Caribbean*. Washington: The World Bank.

Docteur, E. & Oxley, H. (2003). *Health-Care Systems: Lessons from the Reform Experience*. OECD Economics Department Working Papers No. 374. Paris: OECD.

Doern, G. B. & Phidd, R. W. (1983). *Canadian Public Policy: Ideas, Structure, Process*. Toronto: Methuen.

252 REFERENCES

Dolowitz, D. & Marsh, D. (1996). Who learn what from whom: a review of the policy transfer literature. *Political Studies*, 44(2), 343–357.

Dolowitz, D. & Marsh, D. (2000). Learning from abroad: the role of policy transfer in contemporary policy-making. *Governance*, 13(1), 5–23.

Duckett, S. (2018). Expanding the breadth of Medicare: learning from Australia. *Health Economics, Policy and Law*, 13(3–4), 344–368.

Economou, C., Kaitelidou, D., Karanikolos, M. & Maresso, A. (2017). Greece: health system review. *Health Systems in Transition*, 19(5), 1–192.

Enthoven, A. C. (1985). *Reflections on the Management of the National Health Service*. London: Nuffield Provincial Hospital Trust.

Esping-Andersen, G. (1985). *Politics against Markets: The Social Democratic Road to Power*. Princeton: Princeton University Press.

Esping-Andersen, G. (1990). *The Three Worlds of Welfare Capitalism*. Cambridge: Polity Press.

Esping-Andersen, G. (1999). *Social Foundations of Postindustrial Economies*. Oxford: Oxford University Press.

EU (2019). *Task Shifting and Health System Design*. Luxembourg: Publications Office of the European Union.

European Commission (2017). *State of Health in the EU. Companion Report 2017*. Luxembourg: Publications Office of the European Union.

Eurostat (2020). *Healthcare Statistics*. Luxembourg: Eurostat. https://ec.europa.eu/eurostat/web/health/overview.

Evans, J., Baker, R., Berta, W. & Barnsley, J. (2013). The evolution of integrated health care strategies. *Advances in Health Care Management*, 15, 125–161.

Evans, R. G. (1981). Incomplete vertical integration: the distinctive structure of the health care industry. In J. van der Gaag and M. Perlman, eds., *Health, Economics, and Health Economics*. Amsterdam: North Holland, pp. 329–354.

Evans, R. G. (1987). Going for gold: the redistributive agenda behind market-based health care reform. *Journal of Health, Politics, Policy and Law*, 22(2), 427–465.

Evans, R. G. (2000). Canada. *Journal of Health Politics, Policy and Law*, 25(5), 889–897.

Falkenbach, M., Bekker, M. & Greer, S. L. (2019). Do parties make a difference? A review of partisan effects on health and the welfare state. *European Journal of Public Health*, 30(4), 673–682.

Fallberg, L. H. (2000). Patients' rights in the Nordic countries. *European Journal of Health Law*, 7(2), 123–144.

Fierlbeck, K. (2011). *Health Care in Canada*. Toronto: University of Toronto Press.

Flood, C. M. & Haugan, A. (2010). Is Canada odd? A comparison of European and Canadian approaches to choice and regulation of the public/private divide in health care. *Health Economics, Policy and Law*, 5(3), 319–341.

Flora, P., ed. (1986). *Growth to Limits. The European Welfare States since World War II*. Berlin: De Gruyter.

Flora, P. & Alber, J. (1981). Modernization, democratization and the development of welfare states in Western Europe. In P. Flora and A. Heidenheimer, eds., *The Development of Welfare States in Europe and America*. New Brunswick: Transaction Books, pp. 37–47.

FRA (2012). *The Situation of Roma in 11 EU Member States. Survey Results at a Glance*. Luxembourg: European Union Agency for Fundamental Rights – Publications Office of the European Union.

France, G., Taroni, F. & Donatini, A. (2005). The Italian health-care system. *Health Economics*, 14(S1), 187–202.

Freddi, G. & Björkman, J., eds. (1989). *Controlling Medical Professionals. The Comparative Politics of Health Governance*. London: Sage.

Freeman, R. (2000). *The Politics of Health in Europe*. Manchester: Manchester University Press.

Freeman, R. & Frisina, L. (2010). Health care systems and the problem of classification. *Journal of Comparative Policy Analysis*, 12(1–2), 163–178.

Freidson, E. (1970). *Professional Dominance*. New York: Atherton.

Frenk, J. & Donabedian, A. (1987). State intervention in medical care: types, trends and variables. *Health Policy and Planning*, 2(1), 17–31.

Frogner, B. K., Hussey, P. S. & Anderson, G. F. (2011). Health systems in industrialized countries. In S. Glied and P. C. Smith, eds., *The Oxford Handbook of Health Economics*. Oxford: Oxford University Press, pp. 8–30.

Fujisawa, R. & Lafortune, G. (2008). *The Remuneration of General Practitioners and Specialists in 14 OECD Countries: What Are the Factors Influencing Variations across Countries?* OECD Health Working Papers No. 41. Paris: OECD.

Gaál, P., Szigeti, S., Csere, M., Gaskins, M. & Panteli, D. (2011). Hungary: health system review. *Health Systems in Transition*, 13(5), 1–266.

Gannot, R., Chinitz, D. & Rosenbaum, S. (2018). What should health insurance cover? A comparison of Israeli and US approaches to benefit design under national health reform. *Health Economics, Policy and Law*, 13(2), 189–208.

Garrido, M. V., Zentner, A. & Busse, R. (2011). The effects of gatekeeping: a systematic review of the literature. *Scandinavian Journal of Primary Health Care*, 29(1), 28–38.

254 REFERENCES

Gauld, R. (2012). New Zealand's post-2008 health system reforms: toward re-centralization of organizational arrangements. *Health Policy*, 106(2), 110–113.

Gerdtham, U. G. & Jönsson, B. (2000). International comparisons of health expenditure: theory, data and econometric analysis. In A. J. Culyer and J. P Newhouse, eds., *Handbook of Health Economics*. Amsterdam: Elsevier, vol. 1, pp. 11–53.

Gerkens, S. & Merkur, S. (2010). Belgium: health system review. *Health Systems in Transition*, 12(5), 1–266.

Geva-May, I. & Maslove, A. (2000). What prompts health care policy change? On political power contest and reform of health care systems (the case of Canada and Israel). *Journal of Health Politics, Policy and Law*, 25(4), 717–741.

Giaimo, S. (2002). *Markets and Medicine. The Politics of Health Care in Britain, Germany and the United States*. Ann Arbor: University of Michigan Press.

Giaimo, S. (2016). *Reforming Health Care in the United States, Germany, and South Africa*. Basingstoke: Palgrave Macmillan.

Gillies, R., Shortell, S., Anderson, D., Mitchell, J. & Morgan, K. (1993). Conceptualizing and measuring integration: findings from the Health Systems Integration Study. *Hospital & Health Services Administration*, 38(4), 467–486.

Gönenç, R., Hofmarcher, M. & Wörgötter, A. (2011). *Reforming Austria's Highly Regarded but Costly Health System*. OECD Economics Department Working Papers, No. 895. Paris: OECD.

Goodwin, N., Stein, V. & Amelung, V. (2017). What is integrated care? In V. Amelung, V. Stein, N. Goodwin, R. Balicer, E. Nolte and E. Suter, eds., *Handbook Integrated Care*. Cham: Springer, pp. 3–23.

Goodyear-Smith, F. & Ashton, T. (2019). New Zealand system: universalism struggles with persisting inequities. *The Lancet*, 394, 432–442.

Goujard, A. (2018). *France: Improving the Efficiency of the Healthcare System*. OECD Economics Department Working Papers, No. 1455. Paris: OECD.

Grant, W. (1989). *Pressure Groups, Politics and Democracy in Britain*. London: Philip Allan.

Gray, G. (1998). Access to medical care under strain: new pressures in Canada and Australia. *Journal of Health Politics, Policy and Law*, 23(6), 905–947.

Greß, S., Groenewegen, P., Kerssens, J., Braun, B. & Wasem, J. (2002). Free choice of sickness funds in regulated competition: evidence from Germany and The Netherlands. *Health Policy*, 60(3), 235–254.

Greß, S., Delnoij, D. & Groenewegen, P. (2006). Managing primary care behavior through payment systems and financial incentives. In R. Saltman, A. Rico and W. Boerma, eds., *Primary Care in the Driver's Seat? Organizational Reform in European Primary Care*. Maidenhead: Open University Press, pp. 184–200.

Grigorakis, N., Floros, C., Tsangari, H. & Tsoukatos, E. (2016). Out of pocket payments and social health insurance for private hospital care: evidence from Greece. *Health Policy*, 120(8), 948–959.

Hacker, J. S. (1998). The historical logic of National Health Insurance: structure and sequence in the development of British, Canadian, and U.S. medical policy. *Studies in American Political Development*, 12(2), 57–130.

Hacker, J. S. (2002). *The Divided Welfare State*. Cambridge: Cambridge University Press.

Hagen, T. & Kaarbøe, O. (2006). The Norwegian hospital reform of 2002: central government takes over ownership of public hospitals. *Health Policy*, 76(3), 320–333.

Hall, J. (1999). Incremental change in the Australian Health Care System. *Health Affairs*, 18(3), 95–110.

Hall, J. (2010). Health-care reform in Australia: advancing or side-stepping? *Health Economics*, 19(11), 1259–1263.

Hall, P. A. (1993). Policy paradigms, social learning, and the state: the case of economic policy making in Britain. *Comparative Politics*, 25(3), 275–296.

Hall, P. A. (1997). The role of interests, institutions, and ideas in the comparative political economy of the industrialized nations. In M. I. Lichbach and A. Zuckerman, eds., *Comparative Politics: Rationality, Culture, and Structure*. Cambridge: Cambridge University Press, pp. 174–207.

Halm, E. A., Causino, N. & Blumenthal, D. (1997). Is gatekeeping better than traditional care? A survey of physicians' attitudes. *The Journal of the American Medical Association*, 278(26), 1677–1681.

Ham, C. (2009). *Health Policy in Britain*, 6th ed. Basingstoke: Palgrave Macmillan.

Hanning, M. & Spångberg, U. W. (2000). Maximum waiting time–a threat to clinical freedom?: implementation of a policy to reduce waiting times. *Health Policy*, 52(1), 15–32.

Hart, D. (2004). Patients' rights and patients' participation individual and collective involvement: partnership and participation in health law. *European Journal of Health Law*, 11(1), 17–28.

Hartman, M., Martin, A. B., Benson, J. & Catlin, A. (2020). National health care spending in 2018: growth driven by accelerations in Medicare and private insurance spending. *Health Affairs*, 39(1), 8–17.

Heclo, H. (1994). Ideas, interests, and institutions. In L. C. Dodd and C. Jillson, eds., *The Dynamics of American Politics. Approaches and Interpretations*. Boulder: Westview Press, pp. 366–392.

REFERENCES

Helderman, J. K., Schut, F., van der Grinten, T. & van de Ven, W. (2005). Market-oriented health care reforms and policy learning in the Netherlands. *Journal of Health Politics, Policy and Law*, 30(1–2), 189–209.

Helderman, J. K., Bevan, G. & France, G. (2012). The rise of the regulatory state in health care: a comparative analysis of the Netherlands, England and Italy. *Health Economics, Policy and Law*, 7(1), 103–124.

Hennock, E. (1987). *British Social Reform and German Precedents*. Oxford: Clarendon Press.

Hsiao, W. C. (1995). Medical savings accounts: lessons from Singapore. *Health Affairs*, 14(2), 260–266.

Huber, E. & Stephens, J. (2001). *Development and Crisis of the Welfare State*. Chicago: University of Chicago Press.

Hurst, J. W. (1991). Reforming health care in seven European nations. *Health Affairs*, 10(3), 7–21.

Hussey, P. & Anderson, G. F. (2003). A comparison of single- and multi-payer health insurance systems and options for reform. *Health Policy*, 66(3), 215–228.

Immergut, E. (1992). *Health Politics. Interests and Institutions in Western Europe*. New York: Cambridge University Press.

Jacobs, A. (1998). Seeing difference: market health reforms in Europe. *Journal of Health Politics, Policy and Law*, 23(1), 1–33.

Jacobs, L. (1993). *The Health of Nations. Public Opinion and Making of American and British Health Policy*. Ithaca: Cornell University Press.

Jacobs, L. & Skocpol, T. (2010). *Health Care Reform and American Politics: What Everyone Needs to Know*. New York: Oxford University Press.

Jiménez-Rubio, D. & García-Gómez, P. (2017). Decentralization of health care systems and health outcomes: evidence from a natural experiment. *Social Science & Medicine*, 188, 69–81.

Johnson, J., Stoskopf, C. & Shi, L. eds. (2018). Comparative Health Systems. A Global Perspective, Burlington, MA, Jones & Bartlett Learning.

Johnston, B. M., Burke, S., Barry, S., Normand, C., Fhallúin, M. N. & Thomas, S. (2019). Private health expenditure in Ireland: assessing the affordability of private financing of health care. *Health Policy*, 123(10), 963–969.

Jones, D. K., Bradley, K. & Oberlander, J. (2014). Pascal's wager: health insurance exchanges, Obamacare, and the Republican dilemma. *Journal of Health Politics, Policy and Law*, 39(1), 97–137.

Jordan, J. (2011). Health care politics in the age of retrenchment. *Journal of Social Policy*, 40(1), 113–134.

Kaiser Family Foundation (2019). *Employer Health Benefits. 2019 Annual Survey*. San Francisco: Henry J. Kaiser Family Foundation.

Karanikolos, M., Mladovsky, P., Cylus, J., et al. (2013). Financial crisis, austerity, and health in Europe. *The Lancet*, 381, 1323–1331.

Kasza, G. (2002). The illusion of welfare "regimes." *Journal of Social Policy*, 31(2), 271–287.

Kato, D., Ryu, H., Matsumoto, T., et al. (2019). Building primary care in Japan: literature review. *Journal of General and Family Medicine*, 20(5), 170–179.

Kentikelenis, A. (2015). Bailouts, austerity and the erosion of health coverage in Southern Europe and Ireland. *The European Journal of Public Health*, 25(3), 365–366.

Keskimäki, I., Tynkkynen, L. K., Reissell, E., et al. (2019). Finland: health system review. *Health Systems in Transition*, 21(2), 1–166.

Kifmann, M. (2017). Competition policy for health care provision in Germany. *Health Policy*, 121(2), 119–125.

Kilminster, S., Downes, J., Gough, B., Murdoch-Eaton, D. & Roberts, T. (2007). Women in medicine – is there a problem? A literature review of the changing gender composition, structures and occupational cultures in medicine. *Medical Education*, 41(1), 39–49.

Kingdon, J. W. (1984). *Agendas, Alternatives, and Public Policies*. Boston: Little, Brown & Co.

Klein, R. (1995). Big Bang health care reform: does it work?: the case of Britain's 1991 National Health Service Reforms. *The Milbank Quarterly*, 73(3), 299–337.

Klein, R. (2013). *The New Politics of NHS*, 7th ed. Boca Raton: CRC Press.

Klein, R. & Marmor, T. (2012). Politics and policy analysis: fundamentals. In T. Marmor and R. Klein, eds., *Politics, Health, Health Care*. Yale: Yale University Press, pp. 1–21.

Kodner, D. (2009). All together now: a conceptual exploration of integrated care. *Healthcare Quarterly*, 13(special issue), 6–15.

Kodner, D. & Spreeuwenberg, C. (2002). Integrated care: meaning, logic, applications, and implications – a discussion paper. *International Journal of Integrated Care*, 2(14), 1–6.

Korpi, W. & Palme, J. (1998). The paradox of redistribution and strategies of equality: welfare state institutions, inequality, and poverty in western countries. *American Sociological Review*, 63(5),661–687.

Kringos, D., Boerma, W., Hutchinsonand, A. & Saltman, R. (2015). *Building Primary Care in a Changing Europe*. Copenhagen: WHO Regional Office for Europe.

Kroneman, M., Maarse, H. & van der Zee, J. (2006). Direct access in primary care and patient satisfaction. *Health Policy*, 76(1), 72–79.

Kroneman, M., Boerma, W., van den Berg, M., Groenewegen, P., de Jong, J. & van Ginneken, E. (2016). The Netherlands: health system review. *Health Systems in Transition*, 18(2), 1–239.

Kutzin, J. (1998). The appropriate role for patient cost sharing. In R. Saltman, J. Figueras and C. Sakellarides, eds., *Critical Challenges for Health Care Reform in Europe*. Buckingham-Philadelphia: Open University Press, pp. 78–112.

Kutzin, J. (2001). A descriptive framework for country-level analysis of health care financing arrangements. *Health Policy*, 56(3), 171–204.

Kutzin, J. (2013). Health financing for universal coverage and health system performance: concepts and implications for policy. *Bulletin of the World Health Organization*, 91(8), 602–611.

Kwon, S. & Reich, M. R. (2005). The changing process and politics of health policy in Korea. *Journal of Health Politics, Policy and Law*, 30(6), 1003–1026.

Kwon, S., Lee, T. J. & Kim, C. Y. (2015). Republic of Korea health system review. *Health Systems in Transition*, 5(4), Manila: WHO Regional Office for the Western Pacific.

Lafortune, G., Schoenstein, M. & Moreira, L. (2016). Trends in health labour markets and policy priorities to address workforce issues. In *Health Workforce Policies in OECD Countries. Right Jobs, Right Skills, Right Places*. Paris: OECD Publishing, pp. 37–62.

Lagomarsino, G., Garabrant, A., Adyas, A., Muga, R. & Otoo, N. (2012). Moving towards universal health coverage. Health insurance reforms in nine developing countries in Africa and Asia. *The Lancet*, 380, 933–943.

Langenbrunner, J. C. & Wiley, M. M. (2002). Hospital payment mechanisms: theory and practice in transition countries. In M. McKee and J. Healy, eds., *Hospitals in a Changing Europe*. Buckingham: Open University Press, pp. 150–176.

Laugesen, M. & Rice, T. (2003). Is the doctor in? The evolving role of organized medicine in health policy. *Journal of Health Politics, Policy and Law*, 28(2–3), 289–316.

Laurant, M., van der Biezen, M., Wijers, N., Watananirun, K., Kontopantelis, E. & van Vught, A. (2018). Nurses as substitutes for doctors in primary care. *Cochrane Database of Systematic Reviews*, 7(7), CD001271. doi: 10.1002/14651858.CD001271.pub3.

Lee, S. L, Chun, C. B., Lee, Y. G. & Seo, N. K. (2008). The National Health Insurance system as one type of new typology: the case of South Korea and Taiwan. *Health Policy*, 85(1), 105–113.

Lee, S. Y., Kim, C. W., Seo, N. K. & Lee, S. E. (2017). Analyzing the historical development and transition of the Korean health care system. *Osong Public Health and Research Perspectives*, 8(4), 247–254.

Lijphart, A. (1999). *Patterns of Democracy. Government Forms and Performance in Thirty-Six Countries*. New Haven: Yale University Press.

Lowi, T. (1964). American business, public policy, case-studies, and political theory. *World Politics*, 16(4), 677–715.

Lyttkens, C. H., Christiansen, T., Häkkinen, U., Kaarboe, O., Sutton, M. & Welander, A. (2016). The core of the Nordic health care system is not empty. *Nordic Journal of Health Economics*, 4(1), 7–27.

Maarse, H. (2006). The privatization of health care in Europe: an eight-country analysis. *Journal of Health Politics, Policy and Law*, 31(5), 981–1014.

Maarse, H., Jeurissen, P. & Ruwaard, D. (2016). Results of the market-oriented reform in the Netherlands: a review. *Health Economics, Policy and Law*, 11(2), 161–178.

Mackenbach, J. P. & McKee, M. (2015). Government, politics and health policy: a quantitative analysis of 30 European countries. *Health Policy*, 119(10), 1298–1308.

Magnussen, J., Vrangbaek, K. & Saltman, R., eds. (2009). *Nordic Health Care Systems: Recent Reforms and Current Policy Challenges*. Maidenhead: McGraw-Hill.

Maier, C. (2015). The role of governance in implementing task-shifting from physicians to nurses in advanced roles in Europe, U.S., Canada, New Zealand and Australia. *Health Policy*, 119(12), 1627–1635.

Maier, C. & Aiken, L. (2016). Task shifting from physicians to nurses in primary care in 39 countries: a cross-country comparative study. *The European Journal of Public Health*, 26(6), 927–934.

Maier, C., Köppen, J. & Busse, R. (2018). Task shifting between physicians and nurses in acute care hospitals: cross-sectional study in nine countries. *Human resources for health*, 16(1), 24.

Maioni, A. (1997). Parting at the crossroads. The development of health insurance in Canada and the United States, 1940–1965. *Comparative Politics*, 29(4), 411–431.

Maloney, W., Jordan, G. & McLaughlin, A. (1994). Interest groups and public policy: the insider/outsider model revisited. *Journal of Public Policy*, 14(1), 17–38.

Marchildon, G. (2013). Canada: health system review. *Health Systems in Transition*, 15(1), 1–179.

Marchildon, G. (2019). Health system in Canada. In A. Levy, S. Goring, C. Gatsonis, B. Sobolev, E. van Ginneken and R. Busse, eds., *Health Services Evaluation*. New York. Springer, pp. 769–777.

Marmor, T. (2000). *The Politics of Medicare*. New York: De Gruyter.

Marmor, T. & Oberlander, J. (2011). The patchwork: health reform, American style. *Social Science & Medicine*, 72(2), 125–128.

Marmor, T. & Wendt, C. (2011). Introduction. In T. Marmor and C. Wendt, eds., *Reforming Healthcare Systems. Volume I. Ideas, Interests and Institutions.* Cheltenham: Edward Elgar, pp. xiii–xxxvii.

Martin, D. P., Diehr, P., Price, K. F. & Richardson, W. C. (1989). Effect on a gatekeeper plan on health services use and charges: a randomized trial. *American Journal of Public Health*, 79(12), 1628–1632.

Martin, D., Miller, A. P., Quesnel-Vallée, A., Caron, N. R., Vissandjée, B. & Marchildon, G. P. (2018). Canada's universal health-care system: achieving its potential. *The Lancet*, 391, 1718–1735.

Mathes, T., Pieper, D., Mosch, C. G., Jaschinski, T. & Eikermann, M. (2014). Payment methods for hospitals. *Cochrane Database of Systematic Reviews*, (6), Art. No. CD011156.

Matsuda, R. (2016). Public/private health care delivery in Japan: and some gaps in "universal" coverage. *Global Social Welfare*, 3(3), 201–212.

McDaid, D., Wiley, M., Maresso, A. & Mossialos, E. (2009). Ireland: health system review. *Health Systems in Transition*, 11(4), 1–268.

McGregor, S. (2001). Neoliberalism and health care. *International Journal of Consumer Studies*, 25(2), 82–89.

Merçay, C., Dumont, J. C. & Lafortune, G. (2016). Trends and policies affecting the international migration of doctors and nurses to OECD countries. In *Health Workforce Policies in OECD Countries. Right Jobs, Right Skills, Right Places.* Paris: OECD Publishing, pp.103–128.

Miller, T. (2010). Health reform: only a cease-fire in a political hundred years' war. *Health Affairs*, 29(6), 1101–1105.

Mills, A. (1990). Decentralization concepts and issues: a review. In A. Mills, J. P. Vaughan, D. L. Smith and I. Tabibzadeh, eds., *Health System Decentralization: Concepts, Issues and Country Experience.* Geneva: World Health Organization, pp. 10–42.

Montanari, I. & Nelson, K. (2013). Health care determinants in comparative perspective: the role of partisan politics for health care provision. *International Journal of Comparative Sociology*, 54(5–6), 445–466.

Moran, M. (1999). *Governing the Health Care State.* Manchester: Manchester University Press.

Moreira, L. & Lafortune, G. (2016). Education and training for doctors and nurses: what's happening with numerus clausus policies? In *Health Workforce Policies in OECD Countries. Right Jobs, Right Skills, Right Places.* Paris: OECD Publishing, pp. 63–102.

Moreno, J. D. (1990). *Paying the Doctor: Health Policy and Reimbursement.* Westport: Auburn House.

Morgan, D. & Astolfi, R. (2015). Financial impact of the GFC: health care spending across the OECD. *Health Economics, Policy and Law*, 10(1), 7–19.

Morone, J. (1990). *The Democratic Wish*. New York: BasicBooks.

Morone, J. (2010). Presidents and health reform: from Franklin D. Roosevelt to Barack Obama. *Health Affairs*, 29(6), 1096–1100.

Mossialos, E. & Dixon, A. (2002). Funding health care: an introduction. In E. Mossialos, A. Dixon, J. Figueras and J. Kutzin, eds., *Funding Health Care: Options for Europe*. Buckingham, Open University Press, pp. 1–30.

Mossialos, E. & Le Grand, J., eds. (1999). *Health Care and Cost Containment in the European Union*. Aldershot: Ashgate.

Mossialos, E. & Thomson, S. (2002). Voluntary health insurance in the European Union. In E. Mossialos, A. Dixon, J. Figueras and J. Kutzin, eds., *Funding Health Care: Options for Europe*. Buckingham-Philadelphia: Open University Press, pp. 128–160.

Mossialos, E. & Thomson, S. (2004). *Voluntary Health Insurance in the European Union*. Copenhagen: World Health Organization.

Mossialos, E., Allin, S. & Davaki, K. (2005). Analysing the Greek health system: a tale of fragmentation and inertia. *Health Economics*, 14(S1), 151–168.

Mossialos, E., Djordjevic, A., Osborn, R. & Sarnak, D. (2017). *International Profiles of Health Care Systems*. New York: The Commonwealth Fund.

Myles, J. & Quadagno, J. (2002). Political theories of the welfare state. *Social Service Review*, 76(1), 34–57.

Navarro, V. (1989). Why some countries have national health insurance, others have national health services, and the United States has neither. *International Journal of Health Services*, 19(3), 383–404.

Navarro, V. & Shi, L. (2001). The political context of social inequalities and health. *Social Science & Medicine*, 52(3), 481–491.

Navarro, V., Muntaner, C., Borrell, C., et al. (2006). Politics and health outcomes. *The Lancet*, 368, 1033–1037.

Nay, O., Béjean, S., Benamouzig, D., Bergeron, H., Castel, P. & Ventelou, B. (2016). Achieving universal health coverage in France: policy reforms and the challenge of inequalities. *The Lancet*, 387, 2236–2249.

Nemec, J., Pavlík, M., Malý, I. & Kotherová, Z. (2015). Health policy in the Czech Republic: general character and selected interesting aspects. *Central European Journal of Public Policy*, 9(1), pp. 102–113.

Newhouse, J. P. (1977). Medical-care expenditure: a cross-national survey. *The Journal of Human Resources*, 12(1), 115–125.

Normand, C. & Busse, R. (2002). Social health insurance financing. In E. Mossialos, A. Dixon, J. Figueras and J. Kutzin, eds., *Funding Health Care: Options for Europe*. Buckingham-Philadelphia: Open University Press, pp. 59–79.

Nunes, A. M. & Ferreira, D. C. (2019). The health care reform in Portugal: outcomes from both the New Public Management and the economic crisis. *The International Journal of Health Planning and Management*, 34(1), 196–215.

Nys, H. & Goffin, T. (2011). Mapping national practices and strategies relating to patients' rights. In M. Wismar, W. Palm, J. Figueras, K. Ernst and E. van Ginneken, eds., *Cross-Border Health Care in the European Union*. Copenhagen: WHO Regional Office for Europe, pp. 159–216.

O'Connell, T., Rasanathan, K. & Chopra, M. (2014). What does universal health coverage mean? *The Lancet*, 383, 277–279.

Oberlander, J. (2003). *The Political Life of Medicare*. Chicago: The University of Chicago Press.

Oberlander, J. (2010). Long time coming: why health reform finally passed. *Health Affairs*, 29(6), 1112–1116.

OECD (1987). *Financing and Delivering Health Care: A Comparative Analysis of OECD Countries*. Paris: Organisation for Economic Cooperation and Development.

OECD (1994). *The Reform of Health Care Systems. A Review of Seventeen OECD Countries*. Paris: Organisation for Economic Cooperation and Development.

OECD (2002). *OECD Health Data 2002. A Comparative Analysis of 30 Countries*. Paris: Organisation for Economic Cooperation and Development.

OECD (2004). *Proposal for a Taxonomy of Health Insurance*. Paris: Organisation for Economic Cooperation and Development.

OECD (2016a). *Health Systems Characteristics Survey*. Paris: Organisation for Economic Cooperation and Development. www.oecd.org/els/health-systems/characteristics.htm.

OECD (2016b). *Better Ways to Pay for Health Care*. Paris: OECD Publishing.

OECD (2016c). *Health Workforce Policies in OECD Countries. Right Jobs, Right Skills, Right Places*. Paris: OECD Publishing.

OECD (2018). *Health at a Glance: Europe 2018*. Paris: OECD Publishing.

OECD (2019a). *France: Country Health Profile 2019*. Paris: OECD Publishing.

OECD (2019b). *Germany: Country Health Profile 2019*. Paris: OECD Publishing.

OECD (2019c). *Ireland: Country Health Profile 2019*. Paris: OECD Publishing.

OECD (2019d). *Greece: Country Health Profile 2019*. Paris: OECD Publishing.

OECD (2019e). *Health at a Glance 2019: OECD Indicators*. Paris: OECD Publishing.

OECD (2019f). *Recent Trends in International Migration of Doctors, Nurses and Medical Students*. Paris: OECD Publishing.

OECD (2020). *OECD Health Statistics.* Paris: OECD Publishing.

Ökem, Z. G. & Çakar, M. (2015). What have health care reforms achieved in Turkey? An appraisal of the "Health Transformation Programme." *Health Policy,* 119(9), pp. 1153–1163.

Okma, K. & Crivelli, L. (2013). Swiss and Dutch consumer-driven health care: ideal model or reality? *Health Policy,* 109(2), 105–112.

Okma, K. & Marmor, T. (2015). The United States. In K. Fierlbeck and H. A. Palley, eds., *Comparative Health Care Federalism.* Farnham: Ashgate, pp. 139–148.

Olejaz, M., Juul Nielsen, A., Rudkjøbing, A., Okkels Birk, H., Krasnik, A. & Hernández-Quevedo, C. (2012). Denmark: health system review. *Health Systems in Transition,* 14(2), 1–192.

Oliveira, M. D. & Pinto, C. G. (2005). Health care reform in Portugal: an evaluation of the NHS experience. *Health Economics,* 14(S1), 203–220.

Oliver, A. & Mossialos, E. (2005). European health systems reforms: looking backward to see forward? *Journal of Health Politics. Policy and Law,* 30(1–2), 7–28.

Ono, T., Lafortune, G. & Schoenstein, M., (2013). *Health Workforce Planning in OECD Countries: A Review of 26 Projection Models from 18 Countries.* OECD Health Working Papers No. 62. Paris: OECD.

Österle, A. (2013). Austria: a health care system between continuity and gradual changes. In E. Pavolini and A. M. Guillén, eds., *Health Care Systems in Europe under Austerity.* Basingstoke: Palgrave Macmillan, pp. 147–168.

Page, E. C. (1999). The insider/outsider distinction: an empirical investigation. *British Journal of Politics and International Relations,* 1(2), 205–214.

Palier, B. & Surel, Y. (2005). Les «trois I» et l'analyse de l'État en action. *Revue française de science politique,* 55(1), 7–32.

Paolucci, F. (2010). *Health Care Financing and Insurance: Options for Design.* Heidelberg: Springer.

Paris, V., Hewlett, E., Auraaen, A., Alexa, J. & Simon, L. (2016). *Health Care Coverage in OECD Countries in 2012.* OECD Health Working Papers. Paris: OECD.

Pauly, M. V. (1968). The economics of moral hazard: comment. *The American Economic Review,* 58(3), 531–537.

Pauly, M. V. (1984). Is cream-skimming a problem for the competitive medical market? *Journal of Health Economics,* 3(1), 87–95.

Pedersen, K. M., Andersen, J. S. & Søndergaard, J. (2012). General practice and primary health care in Denmark. *The Journal of the American Board of Family Medicine,* 25(S1), 34–38.

264 REFERENCES

Peterson, M. A. (1993). Political influence in the 1990s: from iron triangles to policy networks. *Journal of Health Politics, Policy and Law*, 18(2), 395–438.

Petmesidou, M. & Guillén, A. M. (2008). "Southern-style" national health services? Recent reforms and trends in Spain and Greece. *Social Policy & Administration*, 42(2), 106–124.

Pierson, P. (2000). Increasing returns, path dependence, and the study of politics. *American Political Science Review*, 94(2), 251–267.

Pierson, P. (2011). *Politics in Time: History, Institutions, and Social Analysis*. Princeton: Princeton University Press.

Polak, P., Świątkiewicz-Mośny, M. & Wagner, A. (2019). Much Ado about nothing? The responsiveness of the healthcare system in Poland through patients' eyes. *Health Policy*, 123(12), 1259–1266.

Preker, A., Jakab, M. & Schneider, M. (2002). Health financing reforms in central and eastern Europe and the former Soviet Union. In E. Mossialos, A. Dixon, J. Figueras and J. Kutzin, eds., *Funding Health Care: Options for Europe*. Buckingham: Open University Press, pp. 80–108.

Propper, C., Sutton, M., Whitnall, C. & Windmeijer, F. (2010). Incentives and targets in hospital care: evidence from a natural experiment. *Journal of Public Economics*, 94(3–4), 318–335.

Quadagno, J. (2004). Why United States has no national health insurance: stakeholder mobilization against the welfare state, 1945–1996. *Journal of Health and Social Behavior*, 45(extra issue), 25–44.

Quadagno, J. (2005). *One Nation Uninsured. Why the US Has No National Health Insurance*. Oxford: Oxford University Press.

Quadagno, J. (2010). Institutions, interest groups, and ideology: an agenda for the sociology of health care reform. *Journal of Health and Social Behavior*, 51(2), 125–136.

Rechel, B. & McKee, M. (2009). Health reform in Central and Eastern Europe and the former Soviet Union. *The Lancet*, 374, 1186–1195.

Reeves, A., McKee, M. & Stuckler, D. (2015). The attack on universal health coverage in Europe: recession, austerity and unmet needs. *The European Journal of Public Health*, 25(3), 364–365.

Reibling, N. & Wendt, C. (2012). Gatekeeping and provider choice in OECD healthcare systems. *Current Sociology*, 60(4), 489–505.

Reich, M., Gordon, D. & Edwards, R. (1973). A theory of labor market segmentation. *The American Economic Review*, 63(2), 359–365.

Rice, T., Rosenau, P., Unruh, L., Barnes, A., Saltman, R. & van Ginneken, E. (2013). United States of America: health system review. *Health Systems in Transition*, 15(3), 1–431.

REFERENCES 265

Rico, A., Saltman, R. B. & Boerma, W. (2003). Organizational restructuring in European Health Systems: the role of primary care. *Social Policy & Administration*, 37(6), 592–608.

Rider, M. E. & Makela, C. J. (2003). A comparative analysis of patients' rights: an international perspective. *International Journal of Consumer Studies*, 27(4), 302–315.

Ringard, Å., Sagan, A., Sperre Saunes, I. & Lindahl, AK. (2013). Norway: health system review. *Health Systems in Transition*, 15(8), 1–162.

Robinson, J. (2001). Theory and practice in the design of physician payment incentives. *The Milbank Quarterly*, 79(2), 149–177.

Robinson, J. (2005). Health savings accounts. The ownership society in health care. *The New England Journal of Medicine*, 353(12), 1199–1202.

Robinson, J. & Casalino, L. (1996). Vertical integration and organizational networks in health care. *Health Affairs*, 15(1), 7–22.

Robinson, R. (2002). User charges for health care. In E. Mossialos, A. Dixon, J. Figueras and J. Kutzin, eds., *Funding Health Care: Options for Europe*. Buckingham-Philadelphia: Open University Press, pp. 161–183.

Rochaix, L. & Wilsford, D. (2005). State autonomy, policy paralysis: paradoxes of institutions and culture in the French health care system. *Journal of Health Politics, Policy and Law*, 30(1–2), 97–120.

Rodwin, V. G. (2018). The French health care system. *World Hospitals and Health Services*, 54(1), 49–55.

Roemer, M. I. (1960). Health departments and medical care – a world scanning. *American Journal of Public Health*, 50(2), 154–160.

Rondinelli, D. A., Nellis, J. R. & Cheema, G. S. (1983). *Decentralization in Developing Countries*. Washington, DC: The World Bank.

Rosen, B. (2018). Expanding Canadian Medicare to include a national pharmaceutical benefit while controlling expenditures: possible lessons from Israel. *Health Economics, Policy and Law*, 13(3–4), 323–343.

Rosen, B., Waitzberg, R. & S. Merkur, S. (2015). Israel: health system review. *Health Systems in Transition*, 17(6), 1–212.

Rothgang, H., Cacace, M., Grimmeisen, S. & Wendt, C. (2005). The changing role of the state in healthcare systems. *European Review*, 13(S1), 187–212.

Rothgang, H., Cacace, M., Frisina, L., Grimmeisen, S., Schmid, A. & Wendt, C. (2010). *The State and Healthcare. Comparing OECD Countries*. Basingstoke: Palgrave Macmillan.

Sagan, A., Panteli, D. Borkowski, W. et al. (2011). Poland: health system review. *Health Systems in Transition*, 13(8), 1–193.

Sakamoto, H., Rahman, M., Nomura, et al. (2018). Japan health system review. *Health Systems in Transition*, 8(1), New Delhi: World Health Organization, Regional Office for South-East Asia.

Saltman, R. B. (2004). Social health insurance in perspective: the challenge of sustaining stability. In R. Saltman, R. Busse and J. Figueras, eds., *Social Health Insurance Systems in Western Europe*. Maidenhead: Open University Press, pp. 3–20.

Saltman, R. B. (2008). Decentralization, re-centralization and future European health policy. *European Journal of Public Health*, 18(2), 104–106.

Saltman, R. B. & Bankauskaite, V. (2006). Conceptualizing decentralization in European health systems: a functional perspective. *Health Economics, Policy and Law*, 1(2), 127–147.

Saltman, R. B. & Figueras, J. (1997). *European Health Care Reform. Analysis of Current Strategies*. Copenhagen: World Health Organization.

Saltman, R. B. & Figueras, J. (1998). Analyzing the evidence on European health care reforms. *Health Affairs*, 17(2), 85–108.

Saltman, R. B. & Teperi, J. (2016). Health reform in Finland: current proposals and unresolved challenges. *Health Economics, Policy and Law*, 11(3), 303–319.

Saltman, R., Bankauskaite, V. & Vrangbaek, K., eds. (2007). *Decentralization in Health Care. Strategies and Outcomes*. London: Open University Press.

Saltman, R., Rico, A. & Boerma, W., eds. (2006). *Primary Care in the Driver's Seat? Organizational Reform in European Primary Care*. Maidenhead: Open University Press.

Saltman, R., Allin, S., Mossialos, E., Wismar, M. & Kutzin, J. (2012). Assessing health reform trends in Europe. In J. Figueras and M. McKee, eds., *Health Systems, Health, Wealth and Societal Well-Being*. Maidenhead: Open University Press, pp. 209–246.

Savedoff, W. D., de Ferranti, D., Smith, A. L. & Fan, V. (2012). Political and economic aspects of the transition to universal health coverage. *The Lancet*, 380, 924–932.

Schieber, G. J. & Poullier, J. P. (1989). Overview of international comparisons of health care expenditures. *Health Care Financing Review*, Supplement, 1–7.

Schmid, C. P. & Beck, K. (2016). Re-insurance in the Swiss health insurance market: fit, power, and balance. *Health Policy*, 120(7), 848–855.

Schoen, C., Doty, M. M., Robertson, R. H. & Collins, S. R. (2011). Affordable Care Act reforms could reduce the number of underinsured US adults by 70 percent. *Health Affairs*, 30(9), 1762–1771.

Schokkaert, E. & van de Voorde, C. (2011). User charges. In S. Glied and P. C. Smith, eds., *The Oxford Handbook of Health Economics*. Oxford: Oxford University Press, pp. 329–353.

Schut, F. T. & Varkevisser, M. (2017). Competition policy for health care provision in the Netherlands. *Health Policy*, 121(2), 126–133.

Scott-Samuel, A., Bambra, C., Collins, C., Hunter, D. J., McCartney, G. & Smith, K. (2014). The impact of Thatcherism on health and well-being in Britain. *International Journal of Health Services*, 44(1), 53–71.

Shi, L. & Singh, D. A. (2017). *Essentials of the U.S. Health Care System*, 4th ed. Burlington: Jones & Bartlett Learning.

Shortell, S., Gillies, R. & Anderson, D. (1994). The new world of managed care: creating organized delivery systems. *Health Affairs*, 13(5), 46–64.

Shortell, S. M., Gillies, R. R., Anderson, D. A., Erickson, K. M. & Mitchell, J. B. (2000). *Remaking Healthcare in America: The Evolution of Organized Delivery Systems*. San Francisco: Jossey-Bass.

Siciliani, L. & Hurst, J. (2005). Tackling excessive waiting times for elective surgery: a comparative analysis of policies in 12 OECD countries. *Health Policy*, 72(2), 201–215.

Siciliani, L., Borowitz, M. & Moran, V., eds. (2013). *Waiting Time Policies in the Health Sector: What Works?* Paris: OECD Publishing.

Simões, J., Augusto, G. F., Fronteira, I. & Hernández-Quevedo, C. (2017). Portugal: health system review. *Health Systems in Transition*, 19(2), 1–184.

Simonet, D. (2011). The new public management theory and the reform of European health care systems: an international comparative perspective. *International Journal of Public Administration*, 34(12), 815–826.

Simou, E. & Koutsogeorgou, E. (2014). Effects of the economic crisis on health and healthcare in Greece in the literature from 2009 to 2013: a systematic review. *Health Policy*, 115(2–3), 111–119.

Skocpol, T. (1993). Is the time finally ripe? Health insurance reforms in the 1990s. *Journal of Health Politics, Policy and Law*, 18(3), 531–550.

Skocpol, T. (1995). *Social Policy in the United States: Future Possibilities in Historical Perspective*. Princeton: Princeton University Press.

Sowada, C., Sagan, A. & Kowalska-Bobko, I. (2019). Poland: health system review. *Health Systems in Transition*, 21(1), pp. 1–235.

Starfield, B. (1998). *Primary Care: Balancing Health Needs, Services and Technology*. New York: Oxford University Press.

Starfield, B., Shi, L. & Macinko, J. (2005). Contribution of primary care to health systems and health. *The Milbank Quarterly*, 83(3), 472–502.

Starr, P. (1982). *The Social Transformation of American Medicine*. New York: BasicBooks.

Steffen, M. (2010). The French health care system: liberal universalism. *Journal of Health Politics, Policy and Law*, 35(3), 353–387.

268 REFERENCES

Steinmo, S. and Watts, J. (1995). It's the institutions, stupid! Why comprehensive national health insurance always fails in America. *Journal of Health Politics, Policy and Law,* 20(2), 329–372.

Steinmo, S., Thelen, K. & Longstreth, F., eds. (1992). *Structuring Politics.* New York: Cambridge University Press.

Stewart, E., Greer, S. L., Ercia, A. & Donnelly, P. D. (2020). Transforming health care: the policy and politics of service reconfiguration in the UK's four Health Systems. *Health Economics, Policy and Law,* 15(3), 289–307.

Stolper, K., Boonen, L., Schut, F. & Varkenvisser, M. (2019). Managed competition in the Netherlands: do insurers have incentives to steer on quality? *Health Policy,* 123(3), 293–299.

Stuckler, D., Feigl, A. B., Basu, S. & McKee, M. (2010). *The Political Economy of Universal Health Coverage.* Montreux, Switzerland: First Global Symposium on Health Systems Research.

Suter, E., Oelke, N., Adair, C., Waddell, C., Armitage, G. &Heubner, L. A. (2007). *Health Systems Integration. Definitions, Processes and Impact: A Research Synthesis.* Edmonton: Alberta Health Services.

Szigeti, S., Evetovits, T., Kutzin, J. & Gaál, P. (2019). Tax-funded social health insurance: an analysis of revenue sources, Hungary. *Bulletin of the World Health Organization,* 97(5), 335–348.

Tatar, M., Mollahaliloğlu, S., Şahin, B., Aydın, S., Maresso, A. & Hernández-Quevedo, C. (2011). Turkey: health system review. *Health Systems in Transition,* 13(6), 1–186.

Tediosi, F., Gabriele, S. & Longo, F. (2009). Governing decentralization in health care under tough budget constraint: what can we learn from the Italian experience? *Health Policy,* 90(2–3), 303–312.

Terris, M. (1978). The three world systems of medical care: trends and prospect. *American Journal of Public Health,* 68(11), 1125–1131.

Thaldorf, C. & Liberman, A. (2007). Integration of health care organizations. *The Health Care Manager,* 26(2), 116–127.

Thomson, S., Foubister, T. & Mossialos, E. (2009). *Financing Health Care in the European Union. Challenges and Policy Responses.* Copenhagen: European Observatory on Health Systems and Policies.

Thomson, S., Busse, R., Crivelli, L., van de Ven, W. & van de Voorde, C. (2013). Statutory health insurance competition in Europe: a four-country comparison. *Health Policy,* 109(3), 209–225.

Thomson, S., Figueras, J., Evetovits, T., et al. (2014). *Economic Crisis, Health Systems and Health in Europe: Impact and Implications for Policy.* Copenhagen: World Health Organization-Regional Office for Europe.

Tikkanen, R., Osborn, R., Mossialos, E., Djordjevic, A. & Wharton, G. (2020). *International Profiles of Health Care Systems*. New York: The Commonwealth Fund.

Titmuss, R. (1974). *Social Policy: An Introduction*. London: Allen & Unwin.

Toth, F. (2009). *Le politiche sanitarie. Modelli a confronto*. Rome-Bari: Laterza.

Toth, F. (2010a). Healthcare policies over the last 20 years: reforms and counter-reforms. *Health Policy*, 95(1), 82–89.

Toth, F. (2010b). Is there a Southern European healthcare model? *West European Politics*, 33(2), 325–343.

Toth, F. (2013). The choice of healthcare models: how much does politics matter? *International Political Science Review*, 34(2), 159–172.

Toth, F. (2014). How health care regionalization in Italy is widening the North-South gap. *Health Economics, Policy and Law*, 9(3), pp. 231–249

Toth, F. (2015a). Italy. In K. Fierlbeck and H. A. Palley, eds., *Comparative Health Care Federalism*. Farnham: Ashgate, pp. 63–77.

Toth, F. (2015b). Like surfers waiting for the big wave: health care politics in Italy. *Journal of Health Politics, Policy and Law*, 40(5), 1001–1021.

Toth, F. (2016a). Classification of healthcare systems: can we go further? *Health Policy*, 120(5), 535–543.

Toth, F. (2016b). The Italian NHS, the public/private sector mix and the disparities in access to healthcare. *Global Social Welfare*, 3(3), 171–178.

Toth, F. (2019). Prevalence and generosity of health insurance coverage: a comparison of EU member states. *Journal of Comparative Policy Analysis: Research and Practice*, 21(5), 518–534.

Toth, F. (2020a). Integration vs separation in the provision of health care: 24 OECD countries compared. *Health Economics, Policy and Law*, 15(2), 160–172.

Toth, F. (2020b). Going universal? The problem of the uninsured in Europe and in OECD countries. *International Journal of Health Planning and Management*, 35(5), 1193–1204.

Toth, F. (2020c). Health politics. In P. Harris, A. Bitonti, C. Fleisher and A. Skorkjær Binderkrantz, eds., *The Palgrave Encyclopedia of Interest Groups, Lobbying and Public Affairs*. Cham: Palgrave Macmillan. http://doi-org-443.webvpn.fjmu.edu.cn/10.1007/978-3-030-13895-0_81–1

Toth, F. (2021). How policy tools evolve in the healthcare sector. Five countries compared. *Policy Studies*, 42(3), 232–251.

Treisman, D. (2007). *The Architecture of Government. Rethinking Political Decentralization*. Cambridge: Cambridge University Press.

Tsebelis, G. (1995). Decision making in political systems: veto players in presidentialism, parliamentarism, multicameralism and multipartyism. *British Journal of Political Science*, 25(3), 289–325.

Tsebelis, G. (2002). *Veto Players: How Political Institutions Work*. Princeton: Princeton University Press.

Tuohy, C. (1999). *Accidental Logics*. New York: Oxford University Press.

Tuohy, C. (2018). *Remaking Policy. Scale, Pace, and Political Strategy in Health Care Reform*. Toronto: University of Toronto Press.

Tuohy, C. & Glied, S. (2011). The political economy of health care. In S. Glied and P. C. Smith eds., *The Oxford Handbook of Health Economics*. Oxford: Oxford University Press, pp. 58–77.

Turner, B. (2015). Unwinding the State subsidisation of private health insurance in Ireland. *Health Policy*, 119(10), 1349–1357.

US Census Bureau (2020). *Health Insurance Coverage in the United States: 2019*. Washington: US Government Printing Office.

Valentijn, P. P., Schepman, S. M., Opheij, W. & Bruijnzeels, M. A. (2013). Understanding integrated care: a comprehensive conceptual framework based on the integrative functions of primary care. *International Journal of Integrated Care*, 13, e010.

van de Ven, W. (1996). Market-oriented health care reforms: trends and future options. *Social Science & Medicine*, 43(5), 655–666.

van de Ven, W. P. & Schut, F. T. (2008). Universal mandatory health insurance in the Netherlands: a model for the United States? *Health Affairs*, 27(3), 771–781.

van der Zee, J. & Kroneman, M. (2007). Bismarck or Beveridge: a beauty contest between dinosaurs. *BMC Health Services Research*, 7(94).

Vedung, E. (1998). Policy instruments: typologies and theories. In M. L. Bemelmans, R. Rist and E. Vedung, eds., *Carrots, Sticks and Sermons. Policy Instruments and Their Evaluation*. New Brunswick: Transaction Publishers, pp. 21–58.

Viberg, N., Forsberg, B. C., Borowitz, M. & Molin, R. (2013). International comparisons of waiting times in health care – Limitations and prospects. *Health Policy*, 112(1–2), 53–61.

Victoor, A., Delnoij, D., Friele, R. & Rademakers, J. (2012). Determinants of patient choice of healthcare providers: a scoping review. *BMC health services research*, 12(1), 272.

Vilcu, I. & Mathauer, I. (2016). State budget transfers to Health Insurance Funds for universal health coverage: institutional design patterns and challenges of covering those outside the formal sector in Eastern European high-income countries. *International Journal for Equity in Health*, 15(7).

Vonk, R. & Schut, F. (2019). Can universal access be achieved in a voluntary private health insurance market? Dutch private insurers caught between competing logics. *Health Economics, Policy and Law*, 14(3), 315–336.

Vrangbæk, K. & Christiansen, T. (2005). Health policy in Denmark: leaving the decentralized welfare path? *Journal of Health Politics, Policy and Law*, 30(1–2), 29–52.

Vrangbaek, K., Robertson, R., Winblad, U., van de Bovenkamp, H. & Dixon, A. (2012). Choice policies in Northern European health systems. *Health Economics, Policy and Law*, 7(1), 47–71.

Wagstaff, A. (2010). Social health insurance reexamined. *Health Economics*, 19(5), 503–517.

Wagstaff, A. & van Doorslaer, E. (1992). Equity in the finance of health care: some international comparisons. *Journal of Health Economics*, 11(4), 361–387.

Waters, H. R., Hobart, J., Forrest, C. B., et al. (2008). Health insurance coverage in Central and Eastern Europe: trends and challenges. *Health Affairs*, 27(2), 478–486.

Weaver, K. & Rockman, B., eds. (1993). *Do Institutions Matter? Government Capabilities in the United States and Abroad*. Washington: The Brookings Institution.

Weber, M. (1922). *Wirtschaft und Gesellschaft*. Tübingen: Mohr.

Weissert, W. G. & Weissert, C. S. (2019). *Governing Health. The Politics of Health Policy*. Baltimore: Johns Hopkins University Press.

Wendt, C. (2009). Mapping European healthcare systems: a comparative analysis of financing, service provision and access to healthcare. *Journal of European Social Policy*, 19(5), 432–445.

Wendt, C., Frisina, L. & Rothgang, H. (2009). Healthcare system types: a conceptual framework for comparison. *Social Policy & Administration*, 43(1), 70–90.

WHO (2000). *The World Health Report 2000. Health Systems: Improving Performance*. Geneva: World Health Organization.

WHO (2008). *The World Health Report 2008: Primary Health Care, Now More Than Ever*. Geneva: World Health Organization.

WHO (2010). *Health Systems Financing: The Path to Universal Coverage*. Geneva: World Health Organization.

WHO (2013). *Research for Universal Health Coverage*. Geneva: World Health Organization.

WHO (2015). *Tracking Universal Health Coverage: First Global Monitoring Report*. Geneva: World Health Organization.

Wilensky, H. & Lebeaux, C. (1958). *Industrial Society and Social Welfare*. New York: Russell Sage Foundation.

Willems, D. (2001). Balancing rationalities: gatekeeping in health care. *Journal of Medical Ethics*, 27(1), 25–29.

Wilsford, D. (1991). *Doctors and the State*. Durham: Duke University Press.

Wilsford, D. (1994). Path dependency, or why history makes it difficult but not impossible to reform health care systems in a big way. *Journal of Public Policy*, 14(3), 251–283.

Wilsford, D. (1995). States facing interests: struggles over health care policy in advanced industrial democracies. *Journal of Health Politics, Policy and Law*, 20(3), 577–613.

Wörz, M. & Busse, R. (2005). Analysing the impact of health-care system change in the EU member states–Germany. *Health Economics*, 14(S1), 133–149.

Wouters, O., Cylus, J., Yang, W., Thomson, S. & McKee, M. (2016). Medical savings accounts: assessing their impact on efficiency, equity and financial protection in health care. *Health Economics, Policy and Law*, 11(3), 321–335.

Wren, M. A. & Connolly, S. (2019). A European late starter: lessons from the history of reform in Irish health care. *Health Economics, Policy and Law*, 14(3), 355–373.

Yin, J. D. C. & He, A. J. (2018). Health insurance reforms in Singapore and Hong Kong: how the two ageing Asian tigers respond to health financing challenges? *Health Policy*, 122(7), 693–697.

Yıldırım, H. H. & Yıldırım, T. (2011). Healthcare financing reform in Turkey: context and salient features. *Journal of European Social Policy*, 21(2), 178–193.

Zahariadis, N. (2003). *Ambiguity and Choice in Public Policy*. Washington, DC: Georgetown University Press.

Zweifel, P. (2011). Voluntary private health insurance. In S. Glied and P. C. Smith, eds., *The Oxford Handbook of Health Economics*. Oxford: Oxford University Press, pp. 285–307.

Zweifel, P. & Manning, W. G. (2000). Moral hazard and consumer incentives in health care. In A. J. Culyer and J. P. Newhouse, eds., *Handbook of Health Economics*. Amsterdam: Elsevier, pp. 409–459.

Index

Abbott, Tony, 205–206
Advanced clinical activities, 155
Alber, J., 211, 224–225
Alternative insurance coverage, 47–48
Amsterdam Declaration (1994), 195
Amyotrophic Lateral Sclerosis (ALS), 19
Arena analogy, 219
Attlee, Clement, 227
Australia
  complementary insurance in, 43–44
  correlation of financing model with
    integrated–separated system
    dichotomy in, 95
  decentralisation in, 191
  foreign-trained nurses, recruitment of,
    159
  foreign-trained physicians, recruitment
    of, 159
  freedom of choice in, 101–102
  gatekeeping in, 99
  general practitioner–specialist ratio in,
    162–164
  group practice in, 104
  historical evolution of healthcare system
    in, 216
  hospitals in, 130–131
  incentives and disincentives in, 45
  insurance companies in, 131
  insurance coverage in, 79
  insurance policies in, 131
  Local Hospital Networks (LHNs),
    130–131, 133, 188–189
  Medicare, 129–130
  moderately separated system in, 109
  open enrollment in, 40–41
  physicians, payment of, 170
  Primary Health Networks (PHNs), 133,
    188–189
  private health insurance in, 131
  pro-integration reforms in, 188–189,
    205–206
  risk-adjustment mechanisms in, 41
  separated system in, 94, 97

  in separated universalist family, 129–131,
    244
  supplementary insurance in, 43–44
  task shifting in, 178
  universalist model in, 226–227
  voluntary health insurance component
    in, 75
Austria
  calculation of contributions in, 116
  freedom of choice in, 101–102, 114
  gatekeeping in, 99–100
  healthcare expenditures in, 69
  highly separated system in, 109
  historical evolution of healthcare system
    in, 216
  insurance coverage in, 79
  number of practising physicians in, 154
  patients' rights in, 196
  physician–nurse ratio in, 177
  population coverage in, 117
  risk-adjustment mechanisms in, 114–115
  separated system in, 94, 97, 108
  in SHI family, 112–113
  sickness funds in, 115
  social health insurance (SHI) in, 16–17,
    46, 223–224
  solo practice in, 104
  subsidies in, 118
  types of funds in, 115
  uninsured persons in, 82–83
Aznar, José María, 206

Balkenende, Jan Peter, 202–203
Belgium
  calculation of contributions in, 116
  encouragement of general practice in,
    164
  freedom of choice in, 101–102, 114
  gatekeeping in, 99–100
  healthcare expenditures in, 69
  highly separated system in, 109
  historical evolution of healthcare system
    in, 216

273

274 INDEX

Belgium (cont.)
  hospital physicians in, 171
  insurance coverage in, 79
  multiple funds in, 114
  not-for-profit hospitals in, 148
  patients' rights in, 195–196
  per capita healthcare expenditures in, 71
  population coverage in, 117
  pro-integration reforms in, 188
  risk-adjustment mechanisms in, 114–115
  separated system in, 94, 97, 108
  in SHI family, 112–113
  social health insurance (SHI) in, 224
  solo practice in, 104
  subsidies in, 118, 211
  types of funds in, 115
  uninsured persons in, 82
Bevan, Aneurin, 234
Beveridge, William, 212–213
Beveridge model, 111, 212–213, 240, 243. *See also* NHS family
Bildt, Carl, 196, 198, 205
Bismarck, Otto von, 13, 224–226
Bismarckian model, 13–14, 37, 45–47, 111, 113, 211–212, 217, 240, 243. *See also* Social health insurance (SHI)
Blair, Tony, 197
Blank, R.H., 220–221
Bobbio, Norberto, 207
Bolger, Jim, 182, 194, 205
Brazil
  healthcare expenditures in, 68
  out-of-pocket healthcare expenditures in, 76
BRIC countries
  healthcare expenditures in, 68
  out-of-pocket healthcare expenditures in, 76
Bulgaria, insurance coverage in, 79–80, 84

Canada
  Canada Care Act (1984), 129
  Canada Health Act (1984), 129
  complementary insurance in, 43, 132
  correlation of financing model with integrated–separated system dichotomy in, 95
  decentralisation in, 131, 191–193
  encouragement of general practice in, 164

  foreign-trained physicians, recruitment of, 159
  freedom of choice in, 101–102
  gatekeeping in, 100
  general practitioner–specialist ratio in, 162–164
  group practice in, 104
  historical evolution of healthcare system in, 216
  hospital physicians in, 171
  insurance coverage in, 79
  insurance policies in, 25, 132
  interest groups, role of, 234
  Medicare, 24–25, 44, 129, 132
  moderately separated system in, 109
  per capita healthcare expenditures in, 71
  pro-integration reforms in, 189
  Regional Health Authorities (RHAs), 132–133, 189, 192–193
  separated system in, 24–25, 94, 97
  in separated universalist family, 129–133, 244
  supplementary insurance in, 44
  task shifting in, 178
  universalist model in, 24–25, 226
  voluntary health insurance component in, 75
Capitation fees
  active capitation, 172–173
  general practitioners (GP), 172–173
  passive capitation, 172–173
  physicians, 165–169
  specialists, 172–173
Case-based reimbursement, 148–150
"Cherry picking," 40
China
  healthcare expenditures in, 68
  medical savings accounts (MSAs) in, 27
  out-of-pocket healthcare expenditures in, 76
Clark, Helen, 194
Clinical integration, 89–90, 110. *See also* Integrated systems
Clinton, Bill, 223
Cocktail analogy, 65
Co-insurance, 48–49, 55
Communitarian culture, 221
Community rating, 9, 40, 61–62
Complementary insurance. *See also specific country*

INDEX 275

defined, 42–43
hybrid systems and, 43–44
Co-payments, 41, 48–49, 121–122
Cost sharing
co-insurance, 48–49, 55
co-payments, 41, 48–49, 121–122
in NHS family, 121–122
COVID-19 pandemic, 1
"Cream skimming," 40–41, 62
Critical junctures, 219
Croatia, insurance coverage in, 84
Czech Republic
calculation of contributions in, 116
decentralisation in, 192, 206
encouragement of general practice in, 164
for-profit hospitals in, 148
freedom of choice in, 101–102, 114
gatekeeping in, 99–100
general practitioners (GP), payment of,
171–172
healthcare expenditures in, 69
highly separated system in, 109
historical evolution of healthcare system
in, 216
insurance coverage in, 79, 84
multiple funds in, 114
number of practising nurses in, 173
physicians, payment of, 170
population coverage in, 117
pro-competition reforms in, 184, 205
publicly owned hospitals in, 147
risk-adjustment mechanisms in, 114–115
separated system in, 94, 97, 108
in SHI family, 112–113
solo practice in, 104
subsidies in, 118
types of funds in, 115
universalist model in, 226
women physicians in, 160

Decentralisation. See also specific country
generally, 189–191, 244
continuum with centralisation, 190–191
deconcentration, 190, 192
devolution, 190, 192
different meanings of, 189–190
"political color" and, 206
pro-centralisation reforms, 193–194
Deconcentration, 190, 192
Deductibles, 41–42

Dekker, Wisse, 202
Denmark
cost sharing in, 122
decentralisation in, 123–124
freedom of choice in, 102
freedom to choose providers in, 197
gatekeeping in, 99
general practitioners (GP), payment of,
172
general practitioners (GP) in, 121
group practice in, 104
healthcare expenditures in, 69
highly integrated system in, 108
historical evolution of healthcare system
in, 216
insurance coverage in, 79
integrated system in, 94
in NHS family, 119, 125
patients' rights in, 195–196
quasi-integrated system in, 96–97
specialists, payment of, 172
subsidies in, 211
universalist model in, 226
voluntary health insurance component
in, 75
waiting time guarantees in, 199
women physicians in, 160
Devolution, 190, 192
Diagnosis Related Groups (DGRs), 148–149,
151–152
Direct lobbying, 229–230
Direct market system. See also specific
country
generally, 241
advantages of, 7
contribution methods, 32–33
disadvantages of, 7
freedom of choice in, 7, 34–35
healthcare triangle and, 6
in historical evolution of healthcare
systems, 211
number and legal status of insurers in, 32
payer–beneficiary correspondence in, 7,
29–32
provider–user interaction, 6
state, role of, 6–7, 36, 208–209
voluntary health insurance and, 8
Doctors. See Physicians
"Double coverage," 43
Dual practice, 171

276 INDEX

Eastern Europe. *See also specific country*
  historical evolution of healthcare
    systems in, 216
  political reforms, effect on insurance
    coverage, 84–85
Egalitarian culture, 220–221
Employer-provided insurance, 11–12
Erdogan, Recep Tayyip, 205–206
Essential services, 77
Estonia, insurance coverage in, 84
European Union. *See also specific country*
  insurance coverage in, 79–80, 83–86
  uninsured persons in, 242
  universal coverage, fluctuation regarding,
    83–84
Evolution of healthcare systems. *See*
    Historical evolution of healthcare
    systems
Expenditures. *See* Healthcare expenditures
Extension of insurance coverage. *See also*
    specific country
  generally, 199–200, 244
  "political color" and, 207
Extra-billing, 170

Families
  generally, 4, 111, 243–244
  MRI family (*See* MRI family)
  NHS family (*See* NHS family)
  outliers, 4, 63, 112, 137, 244 (*See also*
    specific country)
  separated universalist family (*See*
    Separated universalist family)
  SHI family (*See* SHI family)
  universalist family (*See* NHS family)
Fee-for-service (FFS)
  general practitioners (GP), 171–172
  physicians, 165, 168
  specialists, 171–172
Financial Crisis, effect on insurance
    coverage, 84–86
Financing models. *See also specific country*
  generally, 4, 6
  comparison of, 28–34, 39
  conflation of, 213
  contribution methods, 6, 32–33
  direct market system (*See* Direct market
    system)
  evolution of, 37
  freedom of choice in, 6, 34–35

insurer–provider relationship in, 6, 35
mandatory residence insurance (*See*
  Mandatory residence insurance
  (MRI))
medical savings accounts (MSAs) (*See*
  Medical savings accounts (MSAs))
moving beyond standard classification,
  240–241
national "translation" of, 37–38
number and legal status of insurers in, 6,
  32
payer–beneficiary correspondence in, 6,
  29–32
progressive versus regressive nature of,
  33–34
social health insurance (SHI) (*See* Social
  health insurance (SHI))
state, role of, 6, 36
targeted programs (*See* Targeted
  programs)
universalist model (*See* Universalist
  model)
voluntary health insurance (*See*
  Voluntary health insurance (VHI))
Finland
  cost sharing in, 122
  decentralisation in, 123–124
  freedom of choice in, 102
  gatekeeping in, 99, 121
  general practitioners (GP), payment of,
    172
  general practitioners (GP) in, 121
  group practice in, 104–107
  healthcare expenditures in, 69
  healthcare financing in, 120
  highly integrated system in, 108
  historical evolution of healthcare system
    in, 216
  insurance coverage in, 79
  integrated system in, 94, 96, 107–108
  National Health Insurance, 120
  in NHS family, 119, 125
  number of practising nurses in, 173–175
  patients' rights in, 195–196
  physician–nurse ratio in, 177
  specialists, payment of, 172
  task shifting in, 178
  universalist model in, 226
  waiting time guarantees in, 199
  women physicians in, 160

INDEX 277

Fixed salaries
    general practitioners (GP), 171–172
    physicians, 168–169
    specialists, 171–172
Flora, P., 224–225
For-profit hospitals, 148
France
    agences régionales de la santé (regional
        health agencies), 192–193
    Caisse Nationale de l'Assurance Maladie
        (CNAM), 54, 56
    co-insurance in, 49, 55
    complementary insurance in, 43, 54–55
    Couverture Maladie Universelle (CMU),
        55–56, 202
    decentralisation in, 192–193, 206
    encouragement of general practice in,
        164
    extension of insurance coverage in, 200,
        202
    freedom of choice in, 101–102, 114
    gatekeeping in, 99–100, 187–188
    group practice in, 104
    healthcare expenditures in, 68–69
    healthcare reforms in, 55–56
    High Authority for Health, 187
    highly separated system in, 109
    historical evolution of healthcare system
        in, 216
    hybrid system in, 64
    incentives and disincentives in, 45
    institutions, role of, 235–236
    insurance companies in, 53–54
    insurance coverage in, 79
    insurance policies in, 64
    insurer–provider relationship in, 54
    out-of-pocket healthcare expenditures in,
        76
    patients' rights in, 195–196
    per capita healthcare expenditures in, 71
    physicians, payment of, 170
    population coverage in, 117
    pro-integration reforms in, 187–188,
        205–206
    segmentation in, 53–54
    separated system in, 94, 97
    in SHI family, 112–113
    sickness funds in, 54
    social health insurance (SHI) in, 46,
        53–56, 224

    subsidies in, 211
    targeted programs in, 117
    types of funds in, 115
    uninsured persons in, 82
    universalist model in, 228
Freedom of choice
    generally, 208
    in direct market system, 7, 34–35
    in financing models, 6, 34–35
    general practitioners (GP) and, 101
    hospitals and, 101, 103
    indemnity plans and, 103
    in integrated systems, 101
    limits on, 102
    in mandatory residence insurance, 35
    in medical savings accounts (MSAs), 35
    patients' rights, 196–198
    providers, selection of, 196–198
    as right, 102–103
    in separated systems, 91, 100–101
    SHI family and, 114
    in social health insurance (SHI), 14–15,
        35, 46
    specialists and, 101
    in universalist model, 23, 35
    in voluntary health insurance, 8, 34–35
    waiting lists and, 102–103

Gatekeeping. *See also specific country*
    advantages of, 98–99
    circumventing, 98–99
    defined, 97
    direct access versus, 99
    disadvantages of, 99
    general practitioners (GP) and, 97–98
    in integrated systems, 99
    interpretations of, 98
    "inverse referrals" and, 98–99
    in mandatory residence insurance, 42
    in NHS family, 121
    in private health insurance, 42
    in voluntary health insurance, 42
General practitioners (GP). *See also specific*
      country
    capitation fees, 172–173
    correlation of payment with specific
        financing model, 171–173
    correlation with specific financing
        model, 164
    encouragement of general practice, 164

278 INDEX

General practitioners (GP). (cont.)
    fee-for-service (FFS), 171–172
    fixed salaries, 171–172
    freedom of choice and, 101
    gatekeeping and, 97–98
    general practitioner–specialist ratio,
      162–165
    group practice, 103–107
    in NHS family, 121
    payment methods, 171–173
    primary care centres and, 104–107
    solo practice, 103–104
Germany
    Act to Strengthen Competition in SHI
      (2007), 203
    calculation of contributions in, 116
    Central Reallocation Pool, 57
    communitarian culture in, 221
    contribution methods in, 136
    contribution rates in, 57
    encouragement of general practice in,
      164
    extension of insurance coverage in, 200,
      203, 207
    freedom of choice in, 101–102, 114
    gatekeeping in, 99–100
    healthcare expenditures in, 68–69
    healthcare reforms in, 56–58
    Health Care Structure Act (1993), 56–57,
      184
    highly separated system in, 109
    historical evolution of healthcare system
      in, 216–217, 238
    hybrid system in, 57–58
    insurance companies in, 58
    insurance coverage in, 79
    insurance policies in, 56–57, 203
    insurance premiums in, 59, 136–137
    legal status of insurers in, 136
    mandatory healthcare expenditures in,
      73
    mandatory residence insurance in, 63,
      212
    in MRI family, 133–134, 244
    multiple funds in, 114
    number of practising physicians in, 154
    obligation for coverage in, 135
    opting out in, 48
    patients' rights in, 196
    population coverage in, 117

    private health insurance in, 135–136
    pro-competition reforms in, 184, 205
    pro-integration reforms in, 188, 205–206
    regulation of private health insurance in,
      135
    risk-adjustment mechanisms in, 41,
      114–115
    segmentation in, 56, 58–59
    separated system in, 94, 97, 108
    in SHI family, 112–113
    sickness funds in, 56–57
    social health insurance (SHI) in, 13–14,
      45–47, 56, 63, 212, 224
    solo practice in, 104
    state, role of, 136–137
    targeted programs in, 117
    types of funds in, 115
    uninsured persons in, 82–83
    universalist model in, 57, 228
Gillard, Julia, 205–206
Global budgeting, 149–150
Gonzalez, Felipe, 206, 227
Greece
    extension of insurance coverage in, 200
    Financial Crisis, effect of, 137–138
    for-profit hospitals in, 148
    freedom of choice in, 102
    gatekeeping in, 99–100
    general practitioners (GP), payment of,
      172–173
    general practitioner–specialist ratio in,
      162–164
    group practice in, 104–107
    healthcare financing in, 120
    healthcare reforms in, 85–86
    historical evolution of healthcare system
      in, 216, 238
    insurance coverage in, 79
    integrated system in, 96
    mandatory healthcare expenditures in,
      73–75
    mixed system in, 94
    moderately integrated system in,
      108–109
    National Health Service (ESY), 125,
      137–139
    National Organization for the Provision
      of Services (EOPYY), 137–138,
      185–186
    in NHS family, 119, 125

INDEX 279

number of practising nurses in, 173–175
number of practising physicians in, 154
as outlier, 63, 137–139, 244
out-of-pocket healthcare expenditures in,
76, 139
patients' rights in, 195–196
physician–nurse ratio in, 177
pro-integration reforms in, 185–186
sickness funds in, 185–186
social health insurance (SHI) in, 224
specialists, payment of, 172–173
universalist model in, 227
Gross domestic product (GDP), healthcare
expenditures as percentage of, 66–67
Group practice, 103–107
Group rating, 9
Guterres, António, 205

Healthcare expenditures. *See also specific*
country
generally, 4, 66
correlation with specific financing
model, 68–69
current healthcare expenditures, 66–71
gross domestic product (GDP), as
percentage of, 66–67
growth in, 71–72
insurance policies as component of, 75
insurance premiums as component of,
73, 75
mandatory component, 72–75
in NHS family, 69
out-of-pocket healthcare expenditures,
73, 75–76, 139–141
per capita healthcare expenditures, 70–71
in separated universalist family, 69
in SHI family, 69
by type of financing, 74
variations in, 68
voluntary health insurance component,
73, 75
Healthcare reforms. *See also specific country*
generally, 4–5, 179–181
decentralisation (*See* Decentralisation)
exchange of ideas, 180
extension of insurance coverage (*See*
Extension of insurance coverage)
in financing, 179–180
historical conditioning of, 179
major themes of, 180, 244–245

in NHS family, 180–181
patients' rights (*See* Patients' rights)
policy transfer, 180
"political color" and, 204–207, 209
pro-competition reforms (*See* Pro-
competition reforms)
pro-integration reforms (*See* Pro-
integration reforms)
radical reforms, 179, 218–219, 238
in SHI family, 179–181
Healthcare triangle
generally, 3–4
direct market system and, 6
voluntary health insurance and, 8
Health Maintenance Organisations (HMOs),
95, 109
Health politics
generally, 209–211, 245–246
decentralisation and, 206
extension of insurance coverage and, 207
healthcare reforms and, 204–207, 209
historical evolution of healthcare
systems (*See* Historical evolution of
healthcare systems)
ideas, role of (*See* Ideas, role of)
inertia in, 237
institutions, role of, 235–237, 239, 245
interest groups, role of (*See* Interest
groups, role of)
national culture and (*See* National culture)
patients' rights and, 206–207
pro-competition reforms and, 205
pro-integration reforms and, 205–206
veto points, 239
"windows of opportunity" and, 237–239
Highly integrated systems, 108
Highly separated systems, 109
High-profile interest groups, 230
Historical evolution of healthcare systems.
See also specific country
generally, 211
arena analogy, 219
critical junctures and, 219
direct market system in, 211
financing models, 37
first stage, 211, 213–216
ideas, role of (*See* Ideas, role of)
institutions, role of, 235–237, 239, 245
interest groups, role of (*See* Interest
groups, role of)

280 INDEX

Historical evolution of healthcare systems.
(cont.)
 mandatory residence insurance in,
  211–212
 medical savings accounts (MSAs) in, 211
 national culture and (See National
  culture)
 path dependence and, 218–219
 reasons for differences in, 217–220
 second stage, 212–216
 social health insurance (SHI) in, 211–216
 social health insurance (SHI) to
  universalist model path, 216
 specific paths, 216–217
 targeted programs in, 211
 third stage, 212–216
 universalist model in, 211–216
 voluntary health insurance in, 211,
  213–216
 voluntary health insurance to social
  health insurance (SHI) path, 216
 voluntary health insurance to
  universalist model path, 216
 "why" question, 217–220
 working class strength and, 218
Hospitals. See also specific country
 generally, 4, 145
 case-based reimbursement, 148–150
 for-profit hospitals, 148
 freedom of choice and, 101, 103
 global budgeting, 149–150
 not-for-profit hospitals, 148
 pay-for-performance, 149
 payment for procedures, 148, 150
 payment methods, 148–151
 payment per day, 148, 150
 physicians, payment of, 171
 private hospitals, 147–148
 publicly owned hospitals, 147–148
 supply of, 145–147
 total hospital beds, 145–147
 universalist model and, 147
Hungary
 decentralisation in, 192, 206
 encouragement of general practice in,
  164
 freedom of choice in, 102–103
 gatekeeping in, 99–100
 general practitioners (GP), payment of,
  171–172

 healthcare expenditures in, 68–69
 historical evolution of healthcare system
  in, 216
 insurance coverage in, 79, 84
 moderately separated system in, 109
 patients' rights in, 195–196
 physicians, payment of, 170
 population coverage in, 117
 publicly owned hospitals in, 147
 separated system in, 94, 97
 in SHI family, 112–113
 single fund in, 113
 social health insurance (SHI) in, 224
 solo practice in, 104
 subsidies in, 118
 uninsured persons in, 82–83
 universalist model in, 226
 women physicians in, 160
Hybrid systems. See also specific country
 generally, 4, 38–39
 all national healthcare systems as, 37–38,
  241–242
 cocktail analogy, 65
 co-insurance in, 48–49
 complementary insurance and, 43–44
 co-payments in, 48–49
 healthcare services, segmentation of,
  49–50
 multiple models used in, 65
 opting out in, 47–48
 population, segmentation of, 49–50
 prevalence of, 63–64
 primary insurance and, 43–44
 supplementary insurance and, 43–44

Ideas, role of
 generally, 222–223, 245
 social health insurance (SHI), correlation
  with conservative governments,
  223–226, 228, 238–239
 universalist model, correlation with
  leftist governments, 226–228,
  238–239
Identikit model, 2–3
Immergut, Ellen, 236–237
Indemnity plans, 103, 109
India
 healthcare expenditures in, 68
 out-of-pocket healthcare expenditures in,
  76

INDEX 281

Indirect lobbying, 230
Individualistic culture, 220–222
Insider interest groups, 229–230
Institutions, role of, 235–237, 239, 245
Insurance. *See specific topic*
Insurance companies. *See also specific country*
   generally, 8–9
   in mandatory residence insurance, 20–21
   preferred providers networks, 10, 102
   regulation of, 44–45
   in voluntary health insurance, 8–10
Insurance coverage. *See also specific country*
   generally, 4, 66
   breadth of, 76–77
   current situation, 76–78
   Eastern European reforms, effect of, 84–85
   extension of (*See* Extension of insurance coverage)
   Financial Crisis, effect of, 84–86
   in non-universal countries, 77–80
   population coverage, 76–77
   in quasi-universal countries, 79
   uninsured persons (*See* Uninsured persons)
   in universal countries, 77–79
   variation over time, 80
Insurance policies. *See also specific country*
   deductibles, 41–42
   healthcare expenditures, as component of, 75
   in mandatory residence insurance, 20–21
   opting out, 47–48
   in social health insurance (SHI), 13
   in voluntary health insurance, 8–10
Insurance premiums. *See also specific country*
   contribution methods and, 22–23
   "cream skimming" and, 40–41
   healthcare expenditures, as component of, 73, 75
   in mandatory residence insurance, 20–21
   in voluntary health insurance, 8–10, 75
Integrated systems. *See also specific country*
   generally, 4, 88–89, 242–243
   advantages of, 93–94
   characteristics of, 91
   clinical integration, 89–90, 110

   comparison with separated systems, 105–106
   continuum with separated systems, 92, 107–110
   correlation with specific financing model, 94–95
   differing definitions of integration, 89
   dimensions of, 92–93
   freedom of choice in, 101
   gatekeeping in, 99
   highly integrated systems, 108
   as ideal type, 90
   insurer–provider relationship in, 35, 93
   integrated universalist family (*See* NHS family)
   internal organisation analogy, 91
   moderately integrated systems, 108–109
   organisational integration, 89–90, 110
   primary–secondary care interaction in, 96
   pro-integration reforms (*See* Pro-integration reforms)
   quasi-integrated systems, 96–97
   separated systems distinguished, 92–93
   vertical integration, 93
Integrated universalist family. *See* NHS family
Integration index, 107
Interest groups, role of. *See also specific country*
   generally, 229, 239, 245
   direct lobbying, 229–230
   high-profile groups, 230
   insider groups, 229–230
   low-profile groups, 230
   outsider groups, 230
   physicians, 232–235
   types of, 229
Internal markets, 181–183
"Inverse referrals," 98–99
Ireland
   centralisation in, 122, 124, 193, 206
   cost sharing in, 122
   foreign-trained physicians, recruitment of, 159
   freedom of choice in, 102
   gatekeeping in, 99, 121
   general practitioners (GP), payment of, 172

282 INDEX

Ireland (cont.)
general practitioners (GP) in, 121
general practitioner–specialist ratio in, 162
group practice in, 104
Health Act (2004), 193
healthcare expenditures in, 68
Health Service Executive (HSE), 122, 193
highly integrated system in, 108
historical evolution of healthcare system in, 216
insurance coverage in, 79
integrated system in, 94
interest groups, role of, 234
in NHS family, 119, 128
number of practising physicians in, 152–154
patients' rights in, 196
quasi-integrated system in, 96–97
specialists, payment of, 172
task shifting in, 178
universalist model in, 226
voluntary health insurance component in, 75
waiting time guarantees in, 199
Israel
Clalit (Health Plan), 140–141
co-payments in, 49
correlation of financing model with integrated–separated system dichotomy in, 95
extension of insurance coverage in, 200–201
foreign-trained physicians, recruitment of, 159
freedom of choice in, 102
gatekeeping in, 99
general practitioners (GP), payment of, 172–173
group practice in, 104–107
historical evolution of healthcare system in, 216–217
insurance companies in, 140–141
insurance coverage in, 79
Kupat Holim (Health Plans), 140
Leumit (Health Plan), 140
Maccabi (Health Plan), 140–141
Meuhedet (Health Plan), 140
mixed system in, 94
moderately integrated system in, 108–109

in MRI family, 133–134
National Health Insurance Law (1994), 140, 201
number of practising nurses in, 173–175
number of practising physicians in, 154
as outlier, 63, 139–142, 244
out-of-pocket healthcare expenditures in, 140–141
patients' rights in, 195–196
private health insurance in, 140–141
separated system in, 97
specialists, payment of, 172–173
Italy
complementary insurance in, 43–44
cost sharing in, 122
decentralisation in, 124, 191, 206
dental care in, 8
direct market system in, 8
Essential Levels of Assistance, 50
foreign-trained physicians, recruitment of, 159
for-profit hospitals in, 148
freedom of choice in, 102
gatekeeping in, 99, 121
general practitioners (GP), payment of, 172
general practitioners (GP) in, 121
group practice in, 104
healthcare expenditures in, 69
highly integrated system in, 108
historical evolution of healthcare system in, 216
insurance coverage in, 79
integrated system in, 94
interest groups, role of, 234
in NHS family, 119, 125
patients' rights in, 196
per capita healthcare expenditures in, 71
physician–nurse ratio in, 177
pro-competition reforms in, 182–183, 205
quasi-integrated system in, 96–97
segmentation of healthcare services in, 50
Servizio Sanitario Nazionale (National Health Service), 125
social health insurance (SHI) in, 224
specialists, payment of, 172
supplementary insurance in, 43–44
universalist model in, 226
waiting time guarantees in, 199

INDEX 283

Japan
    calculation of contributions in, 116
    communitarian culture in, 221
    freedom of choice in, 101–102, 114
    gatekeeping in, 99–100
    healthcare expenditures in, 68–69
    highly separated system in, 109
    historical evolution of healthcare system
        in, 216
    insurance coverage in, 79
    mandatory healthcare expenditures in, 73
    multiple funds in, 114
    number of practising physicians in, 154
    physician–nurse ratio in, 177
    population coverage in, 117
    separated system in, 94, 97, 108
    in SHI family, 112–113
    social health insurance (SHI) in, 224
    solo practice in, 104
    subsidies in, 118
    total hospital beds in, 145
    women physicians in, 160–162
Johnson, Lyndon, 19, 223
Jospin, Lionel, 187–188, 205–206
Juppé, Alain, 187–188, 205–206

Kohl, Helmut, 184, 205
Korea, Republic of. *See* South Korea

Latvia, insurance coverage in, 84
Lijphart, Arendt, 236
Lithuania, insurance coverage in, 84
Lloyd George, David, 224
Lobbying, 230
Low-profile interest groups, 230
Lubbers, Ruud, 205

Maioni, A., 223
Managed care, 19–20, 22–23
Mandatory residence insurance (MRI).
        See also specific country
    generally, 240–241
    advantages of, 21
    "cherry picking," 40
    complementary insurance (*See*
        Complementary insurance)
    contribution methods, 32–33
    co-payments, 41
    correlation with integrated–separated
        system dichotomy, 94–95

"cream skimming," 40
deductibles, 41–42
disadvantages of, 21
"double coverage," 43
freedom of choice in, 35
gatekeeping, 42
in historical evolution of healthcare
    systems, 211–212
incentives and disincentives, 45
insurance companies in, 20–21
insurance policies in, 20–21
insurance premiums in, 20–21
insurer–provider relationship in, 21, 35
moral hazard and, 40
MRI family (*See* MRI family)
as multi-payer system, 20
number and legal status of insurers in, 32
open enrollment, 40–41
opportunistic behavior in, 40
overconsumption, discouraging, 41–42
payer–beneficiary correspondence in, 21,
    29–32
policy sale restrictions, 44–45
prevalence of, 63
primary insurance (*See* Primary
    insurance)
regressive nature of, 33–34
regulation of, 44–45
renewal restrictions, 45
risk-adjustment mechanisms in, 41
state, role of, 21, 36, 208–209
supplementary insurance (*See*
    Supplementary insurance)
Marmor, Ted, 143
Medical profession. *See* Nurses; Physicians
Medical savings accounts (MSAs). *See also*
        specific country
    generally, 240–241
    advantages of, 26
    contribution methods, 32–33
    contributions to, 25
    freedom of choice in, 35
    funds in, 26
    in historical evolution of healthcare
        systems, 211
    insurer–provider relationship in, 35
    moral hazard and, 26
    number and legal status of insurers in, 32
    payer–beneficiary correspondence in,
        29–32

284 INDEX

Medical savings accounts (MSAs). (cont.)
state, role of, 26, 36, 208–209
as variant, 26–27
voluntary versus mandatory, 26
Merkel, Angela, 203, 205–207
Mestizo systems, 3
Mexico, uninsured persons in, 80
Moderately integrated systems, 108–109
Moderately separated systems, 109
Moral hazard
medical savings accounts (MSAs) and, 26
voluntary health insurance and, 9–10, 40
MRI. *See* Mandatory residence insurance
(MRI)
MRI family. *See also specific country*
generally, 111–112, 133–134, 244
contribution methods in, 136
differences in, 135–137
legal status of insurers in, 136
obligation for coverage in, 135
as recent model, 134
regulation of private health insurance in,
135
similarities in, 135
state, role of, 136–137
MSAs. *See* Medical savings accounts (MSAs)
Multi-payer systems, 20

National culture
generally, 220
communitarian culture, 221
egalitarian culture, 220–221
individualistic culture, 220–222
National Health Service (NHS) family. *See*
NHS family
National "translation" of financing models,
37–38
Navarro, V., 223
Netanyahu, Benjamin, 201
Netherlands
basic package for essential care (ZVW), 51
complementary care, 51
complementary insurance in, 43, 53
contribution methods in, 136
Dekker Report, 52, 202–203
exceptional medical expenses, 51
extension of insurance coverage in, 200,
202–203
freedom of choice in, 101–102
gatekeeping in, 99

group practice in, 104
healthcare reforms in, 52
historical evolution of healthcare system
in, 216–217
hybrid system in, 64
"in-kind" insurance, 53
insurance companies in, 43, 52
insurance coverage in, 79
insurance policies in, 203
insurance premiums in, 53–57, 136–137
legal status of insurers in, 136
long-term care insurance in, 51–52
mandatory residence insurance in, 51–53,
63
Medical Treatment Contract Act (1994),
195
moderately separated system in, 109
in MRI family, 133–134, 244
not-for-profit hospitals in, 148
number of practising physicians in,
152–154
obligation for coverage in, 135
open enrollment in, 40–41, 52–57
out-of-pocket healthcare expenditures in,
76
patients' rights in, 195
physicians, payment of, 170
primacy insurance in, 43
pro-competition reforms in, 183–184,
205
regulation of private health insurance in,
52–53, 135
"restitution" insurance, 53
risk-adjustment mechanisms in, 41
segmentation in, 51
separated system in, 94, 97
social health insurance (SHI) in, 51, 224
state, role of, 136–137
uninsured persons in, 82
universalist model in, 63
voluntary health insurance in, 51, 53
waiting time guarantees in, 199
women physicians in, 160
New Public Management, 181, 183, 205
New Zealand
centralisation in, 122, 124, 193–194
cost sharing in, 122
decentralisation in, 193–194
District Health Boards (DHBs), 122, 194
egalitarian culture in, 221

foreign-trained nurses, recruitment of, 159

foreign-trained physicians, recruitment of, 159

freedom of choice in, 102–103

gatekeeping in, 99, 121

general practitioners (GP), payment of, 172

general practitioners (GP) in, 121

group practice in, 104

Health Funding Authority (HFA), 194

highly integrated system in, 108

historical evolution of healthcare system in, 216, 238

hybrid system in, 64

insurance coverage in, 79

integrated system in, 94

in NHS family, 119

pro-competition reforms in, 182, 205

Public Health Commission, 182

quasi-integrated system in, 96–97

Regional Health Authorities, 194

specialists, payment of, 172

task shifting in, 178

universalist model in, 134, 212–213, 226–227

waiting time guarantees in, 199

NHS family. *See also specific country*
generally, 111, 119, 240, 243–244

centralisation versus decentralisation in, 122–125

cost sharing in, 121–122

gatekeeping in, 121

general practitioners (GP) in, 121

healthcare expenditures in, 69

healthcare financing in, 119–121

healthcare reforms in, 180–181

Nordic versus Southern European countries, 125–127

pro-competition reforms in, 181

provision of services in, 121–122

social health insurance (SHI) and, 119–121

total hospital beds in, 147

Norway
centralisation in, 193, 206

cost sharing in, 122

foreign-trained physicians, recruitment of, 159

freedom of choice in, 101–102

freedom to choose providers in, 197

gatekeeping in, 99, 121

general practitioners (GP), payment of, 172

general practitioners (GP) in, 121

group practice in, 104

healthcare expenditures in, 69

historical evolution of healthcare system in, 216

insurance coverage in, 79

integrated system in, 94

mandatory healthcare expenditures in, 73

moderately integrated system in, 108–109

in NHS family, 119, 125

number of practising nurses in, 173–175

number of practising physicians in, 154

patients' rights in, 195–196

quasi-integrated system in, 96–97

semi-decentralised system in, 123–124

social health insurance (SHI) in, 224

specialists, payment of, 172

universalist model in, 226

voluntary health insurance component in, 75

women physicians in, 160

Not-for-profit hospitals, 148

Nurses
generally, 4, 145, 173

diachronic analysis, 175

foreign-trained nurses, recruitment of, 159

number of practising nurses, 173–175

physician–nurse ratio, 175–177

task shifting, 177–178

Obama, Barack, 12–13, 44–45, 61–62, 200, 204, 207, 223, 231–232

OECD. *See* Organisation for Economic Co-operation and Development (OECD)

Okma, Kieke, 143

Open enrollment, 40–41, 52–57

Opportunistic behavior, 40

Opting out, 47–48

Organisational integration, 89–90, 110. *See also* Integrated systems

Organisation for Economic Co-operation and Development (OECD). *See also specific country*

286 INDEX

Organisation for Economic Co-operation and Development (OECD). (cont.)
freedom of choice, move toward, 101
healthcare expenditures in, 68
Health Statistics, 3
insurance coverage in, 79–80, 83–87
mandatory healthcare expenditures in, 73
per capita healthcare expenditures in, 71
on recruitment of foreign-trained physicians, 157
total hospital beds in, 145
uninsured persons in, 242
universal coverage, move toward, 83–84
Outliers, 4, 63, 112, 137, 244. *See also specific country*
Out-of-pocket healthcare expenditures, 73, 75–76, 139–141
Outsider interest groups, 230
Overconsumption, discouraging, 41–42

Papandreou, Andreas, 227
Partisanship. *See* Ideas, role of
Path dependence, 218–219
Patients' rights. *See also specific country*
generally, 194–196, 244
charters, 195–196
"core-package," 194–195
freedom to choose providers, 196–198
"political color" and, 206–207
special laws, 195–196
"split legislation," 196
waiting time guarantees, 198–199
Pay-for-performance
hospitals, 149
physicians, 170
Payment for procedures, 148, 150
Payment per day, 148, 150
Pearson, Lester, 226
Per capita healthcare expenditures, 70–71
Persson, Göran, 198–199
Physicians
generally, 4, 145
capitation fees, 165–169
correlation with specific financing model, 234–235
diachronic analysis of, 154
dual practice, 171
extra-billing, 170
fee-for-service (FFS), 165, 168

fixed salaries, 168–169
foreign-trained physicians, recruitment of, 157–159
general practitioners (GP) (*See* General practitioners (GP))
interest groups, 232–235
mixed remuneration systems, 169–170
number of practising physicians, 152–156
pay-for-performance, 170
payment methods, 165–171
physician–nurse ratio, 175–177
private practice, 171
shortage of, 156–157
specialists (*See* Specialists)
synchronic analysis of, 154–155
task shifting, 177–178
women physicians, 160–162
Poland
encouragement of general practice in, 164
foreign-trained nurses, recruitment of, 159
foreign-trained physicians, recruitment of, 159
for-profit hospitals in, 148
freedom of choice in, 102
gatekeeping in, 100
general practitioner–specialist ratio in, 162
group practice in, 104
healthcare expenditures in, 68–69
historical evolution of healthcare system in, 216
insurance coverage in, 79–80, 84
mixed system in, 109, 111
Narodowy Fundusz Zdrowia (National Health Fund), 185
number of practising nurses in, 173–175
number of practising physicians in, 154
patients' rights in, 195–196
population coverage in, 117
pro-integration reforms in, 185, 205–206
publicly owned hospitals in, 147
separated system in, 94, 97
in SHI family, 112–113
sickness funds in, 185
single fund in, 113
social health insurance (SHI) in, 224
subsidies in, 118
uninsured persons in, 82–83

INDEX 287

universalist model in, 226
women physicians in, 160
Policies. *See* Insurance policies
Political parties
conservative governments, correlation
with social health insurance (SHI),
223–226, 228, 238–239
leftist governments, correlation with
universalist model, 226–228,
238–239
Political perspectives. *See* Health politics
Population coverage
generally, 76–77
in SHI family, 116–117
Portugal
centralisation in, 122, 124
cost sharing in, 122
decentralisation in, 192, 206
freedom of choice in, 102–103
gatekeeping in, 99, 121
general practitioners (GP), payment of,
172
general practitioners (GP) in, 121
general practitioner–specialist ratio in,
162
group practice in, 104–107
healthcare expenditures in, 69
healthcare financing in, 120
highly integrated system in, 108
historical evolution of healthcare system
in, 216, 238
insurance coverage in, 79
integrated system in, 94, 96, 107–108
mandatory healthcare expenditures in,
73–75
in NHS family, 119, 125
number of practising physicians in, 154
out-of-pocket healthcare expenditures in,
76
patients' rights in, 196
physician–nurse ratio in, 177
pro-competition reforms in, 183, 205
Serviço Nacional de Saúde (National
Health Service), 122, 125
social health insurance (SHI) in, 223–224
specialists, payment of, 172
"subsystems" in, 120
waiting time guarantees in, 199
women physicians in, 160
Preferred providers networks, 10, 102

Premiums. *See* Insurance premiums
Pressure groups. *See* Interest groups, role of
Primary care
defined, 95
integrated systems, primary–secondary
care interaction in, 96
separated systems, primary–secondary
care interaction in, 96
Primary care centres, 104–107
Primary insurance. *See also specific country*
defined, 42
hybrid systems and, 43–44
Private health insurance. *See also specific
country*
mandatory residence insurance (*See*
Mandatory residence insurance
(MRI))
voluntary health insurance (*See*
Voluntary health insurance (VHI))
Private hospitals, 147–148
Private practice, 171
Private–public provider dichotomy, 88
Pro-competition reforms. *See also specific
country*
generally, 181, 244
insurers, competition between, 183–184
internal markets, 181–183
in national Health Service (NHS) family,
181
New Public Management and, 181, 183,
205
"political color" and, 205
purchaser–provider split and, 181–183
in SHI family, 181
Progressive nature of financing models, 34
Pro-integration reforms. *See also specific
country*
generally, 184, 244
"political color" and, 205–206
provision of services, integration of,
186–189
in separated universalist family, 188–189
in SHI family, 184–186, 188
sickness funds, integration of, 184–186
Provider payment methods
capitation fees, 165–169
case-based reimbursement, 148–150
extra-billing, 170
fee-for-service (FFS), 165, 168
fixed salaries, 168–169

288 INDEX

Provider payment methods (cont.)
    global budgeting, 149–150
    hospitals, 148–151
    mixed remuneration systems, 169–170
    pay-for-performance, 149, 170
    payment for procedures, 148, 150
    payment per day, 148, 150
    physicians, 165–171
Provision of services
    integration of, 186–189
    in NHS family, 121–122
Publicly owned hospitals, 147–148
Public–private provider dichotomy, 88

Quasi-integrated systems, 96–97

Reforms. *See* Healthcare reforms
Regressive nature of financing models, 34
Regulation
    mandatory residence insurance, 44–45
    private health insurance, 52–53, 61–62, 135
    voluntary health insurance, 44–45
Residual programs. *See* Targeted programs
Risk-adjustment mechanisms
    in mandatory residence insurance, 41
    in SHI family, 114–115
Risk pooling, 9
Romania, insurance coverage in, 79–80, 84
Roosevelt, Franklin D., 223
Russia
    healthcare expenditures in, 68
    out-of-pocket healthcare expenditures in, 76

Savage, Michael Joseph, 227
Schröder, Gerhard, 188, 205–206
Secondary care
    defined, 95–96
    integrated systems, primary–secondary care interaction in, 96
    separated systems, primary–secondary care interaction in, 96
Segmentation. *See also specific country*
    of healthcare services, 49–51, 53–54
    of population, 49–50, 53–54, 56, 58–60
Semashko model, 216
Separated systems. *See also specific country*
    generally, 4, 88–89, 242–243
    advantages of, 93–94

characteristics of, 90
comparison with integrated systems, 105–106
continuum with integrated systems, 92, 107–110
contracts in, 91
correlation with specific financing model, 94–95
dimensions of, 92–93
direct access in, 99
freedom of choice in, 91, 100–101
highly separated systems, 109
as ideal type, 90
insurer–provider relationship in, 35, 93
integrated systems distinguished, 92–93
moderately separated systems, 109
primary–secondary care interaction in, 96
separated universalist family (*See* Separated universalist family)
Separated universalist family. *See also specific country*
    generally, 64, 111–112, 129–130, 244
    correlation with integrated–separated system dichotomy, 94–95, 109–110
    healthcare expenditures in, 69
    pro-integration reforms in, 188–189
SHI. *See* Social health insurance (SHI)
SHI family. *See also specific country*
    generally, 64, 111–113, 240, 243–244
    calculation of contributions, 115–116
    corporate funds in, 115
    differences in, 118–119
    freedom of choice and, 114
    healthcare expenditures in, 69
    healthcare reforms in, 179–181
    occupational funds in, 115
    population coverage in, 116–117
    pro-competition reforms in, 181
    pro-integration reforms in, 184–186, 188
    risk-adjustment mechanisms in, 114–115
    similarities in, 118–119
    single versus multiple funds, 113–114
    subsidies and, 117–118
    targeted programs and, 117
    territorial funds in, 115
    total hospital beds in, 147
Sickness funds. *See also specific country*
    assignment to, 46
    integration of, 184–186

INDEX 289

number of, 32, 46–47
in social health insurance (SHI), 13–14
Singapore
individualistic culture in, 221
medical savings accounts (MSAs) in,
27–28
Medifund, 28
Medisave, 27–28
MediShield Life, 28
Single-payer systems, 23
Slovakia, insurance coverage in, 84
Slovenia, insurance coverage in, 84
Social health insurance (SHI). *See also*
specific country
advantages of, 14–15
assignment to sickness funds, 46
conservative governments, correlation
with, 223–226, 228, 238–239
contribution methods, 32–33, 47
correlation with integrated–separated
system dichotomy, 94–95
disadvantages of, 15
freedom of choice in, 14–15, 35, 46
in historical evolution of healthcare
systems, 211–216
insurance policies in, 13
insurer–provider relationship in, 35
mandatory versus voluntary
contributions, 13
as neither progressive nor regressive,
33–34
NHS family and, 119–121
non-profit nature of insurers, 15
number of sickness funds, 32, 46–47
as occupational system, 14–15
opting out, 48
payer–beneficiary correspondence in, 15,
29–32
prevalence of, 63
SHI family (*See* SHI family)
sickness funds, 13–14
state, role of, 36
variants of, 45–47
Socialist International, 223
Solo practice, 103–104
South Africa, medical savings accounts
(MSAs) in, 27
South Korea
calculation of contributions in, 116
freedom of choice in, 101–102

gatekeeping in, 99–100
highly separated system in, 109
historical evolution of healthcare system
in, 216
insurance coverage in, 79
mandatory healthcare expenditures in,
73–75
Medical Aid Program, 117
not-for-profit hospitals in, 148
number of practising nurses in, 173
number of practising physicians in, 154
out-of-pocket healthcare expenditures in,
76
population coverage in, 117
pro-integration reforms in, 185, 205–206
separated system in, 94, 97, 108
in SHI family, 112–113
sickness funds in, 185
single fund in, 113
social health insurance (SHI) in, 223–224
solo practice in, 104
targeted programs in, 117
total hospital beds in, 147
women physicians in, 160–162
Spain
cost sharing in, 122
decentralisation in, 124, 191, 206
dental care in, 8
direct market system in, 8
freedom of choice in, 102
freedom to choose providers in, 197
gatekeeping in, 99, 121
general practitioners (GP), payment of, 172
general practitioners (GP) in, 121
group practice in, 104–107
healthcare expenditures in, 69
healthcare financing in, 120–121
highly integrated system in, 108
historical evolution of healthcare system
in, 216, 238
Instituto Social de las Fuerzas Armadas
(ISFAS), 127
insurance companies in, 48, 127
insurance coverage in, 79
integrated system in, 94, 96, 107–108
mutual funds in, 127–128
Mutualidad General de Funcionarios
Civiles del Estado (MUFACE), 127
Mutualidad General Judicial (MUGEJU),
127

290 INDEX

Spain (cont.)
  in NHS family, 119, 125, 127–128
  opting out in, 48
  patients' rights in, 195–196
  per capita healthcare expenditures in, 71
  physician–nurse ratio in, 177
  pro-competition reforms in, 183
  Sistema Nacional de Salud (National
    Health Service), 125
  social health insurance (SHI) in, 224
  specialists, payment of, 172
  universalist model in, 227
  waiting time guarantees in, 199
  women physicians in, 160
Specialists
  capitation fees, 172–173
  correlation of payment with specific
    financing model, 171–173
  correlation with specific financing
    model, 164
  fee-for-service (FFS), 171–172
  fixed salaries, 171–172
  freedom of choice and, 101
  general practitioner–specialist ratio,
    162–165
  payment methods, 171–173
State, role of
  generally, 208
  in direct market system, 6–7, 36, 208–209
  in financing models, 6, 36
  in mandatory residence insurance, 21, 36,
    208–209
  in medical savings accounts (MSAs), 26,
    36, 208–209
  in MRI family, 136–137
  in social health insurance (SHI), 36
  in targeted programs, 18–19, 36
  in universalist model, 24, 36, 208–209
  in voluntary health insurance, 10, 36,
    208–209
Steinmo, S., 235–236
Substitutive insurance. See Primary
  insurance
Supplementary insurance. See also specific
  country
  defined, 43
  hybrid systems and, 43–44
Sweden
  co-payments in, 49
  cost sharing in, 122

decentralisation in, 123–124
egalitarian culture in, 221
freedom of choice in, 101–102
freedom to choose providers in, 196–197
gatekeeping in, 99–100
general practitioners (GP), payment of,
  172
general practitioners (GP) in, 121
group practice in, 104–107
healthcare expenditures in, 69
historical evolution of healthcare system
  in, 216
institutions, role of, 235–236
insurance coverage in, 79
integrated system in, 94, 96
mandatory healthcare expenditures in, 73
moderately integrated system in,
  108–109
in NHS family, 119, 125
number of practising physicians in, 154
patients' rights in, 196
pro-competition reforms in, 183, 205
specialists, payment of, 172
subsidies in, 211
total hospital beds in, 145
universalist model in, 226
voluntary health insurance component
  in, 75
waiting time guarantees in, 198–199
"0-7-90-90" formula, 198–199
Switzerland
  contribution methods in, 136
  correlation of financing model with
    integrated–separated system
    dichotomy in, 95
  deductibles in, 42
  encouragement of general practice in,
    164
  extension of insurance coverage in,
    200–202
  foreign-trained nurses, recruitment of,
    159
  foreign-trained physicians, recruitment
    of, 159
  freedom of choice in, 102–103
  gatekeeping in, 99–100
  healthcare expenditures in, 68
  Health Insurance Law (1994), 202
  Health Maintenance Organisations
    (HMOs) in, 95

INDEX 291

highly separated system in, 109
historical evolution of healthcare system
in, 216–217
incentives and disincentives in, 45
institutions, role of, 235–236
insurance companies in, 22–23
insurance coverage in, 79
insurance premiums in, 22–23, 136–137
legal status of insurers in, 136
mandatory residence insurance in, 22–23,
63
in MRI family, 133–134, 244
number of practising nurses in, 173–175
obligation for coverage in, 135
open enrollment in, 40–41
out-of-pocket healthcare expenditures in,
76
physician–nurse ratio in, 177
policy sale restrictions in, 45
primary insurance in, 43
regulation of private health insurance in,
135
risk-adjustment mechanisms in, 41
separated system in, 94, 97
solo practice in, 104
state, role of, 136–137

Taaffe, Eduard, 224
Targeted programs. See also specific country
generally, 240–241
advantages of, 18–19
contribution methods, 32–33
disadvantages of, 18–19
financing of, 17–18
in historical evolution of healthcare
systems, 211
insurer–provider relationship in, 19, 35
number and legal status of insurers in, 32
payer–beneficiary correspondence in,
17–18, 29–32
SHI family and, 117
state, role of, 18–19, 36
Task shifting, 177–178
Thatcher, Margaret, 181–182, 184, 205
Treaty of Versailles (1919), 224
Truman, Harry, 223
Tsebelis, George, 236
Turkey
calculation of contributions in, 116
extension of insurance coverage in, 200

foreign-trained nurses, recruitment of,
159
foreign-trained physicians, recruitment
of, 159
for-profit hospitals in, 148
freedom of choice in, 101–102
gatekeeping in, 99–100
General Health Insurance Scheme
(GHIS), 185
general practitioners (GP), payment of,
171–172
"green card," 200
group practice in, 104–107
healthcare expenditures in, 68–69
highly separated system in, 109
historical evolution of healthcare system
in, 216
insurance coverage in, 79
number of practising nurses in, 173–175
number of practising physicians in,
152–154
patients' rights in, 195–196
per capita healthcare expenditures in, 71
physician–nurse ratio in, 177
population coverage in, 117
pro-integration reforms in, 185, 205–206
publicly owned hospitals in, 147
separated system in, 94, 97
in SHI family, 112–113
sickness funds in, 185
single fund in, 113
social health insurance (SHI) in, 224
subsidies in, 116–118
targeted programs in, 200
total hospital beds in, 147
uninsured persons in, 82–83
women physicians in, 160–162

Uninsured persons. See also specific country
generally, 78, 242
categories of, 82–83
mandatory coverage but not all paying
into, 82
mandatory coverage not applying to all, 82
minimal healthcare services provided to,
83
no mandatory health insurance, 81–82
United Kingdom
British Medical Association (BMA),
233–234

292 INDEX

United Kingdom (cont.)
  Care Quality Commission, 198
  centralisation versus decentralisation in, 123–124
  cost sharing in, 122
  decentralisation in, 191–192, 206
  District Health Authorities (DHAs), 181–182
  egalitarian culture in, 221
  encouragement of general practice in, 164
  foreign-trained nurses, recruitment of, 159
  freedom of choice in, 102
  freedom to choose providers in, 197–198
  gatekeeping in, 99, 121
  general practitioners (GP), payment of, 172
  general practitioners (GP) in, 121
  group practice in, 104
  Health and Social Care (HSC), 123
  Healthcare Commission, 197–198
  highly integrated system in, 108
  historical evolution of healthcare system in, 216, 238
  insurance coverage in, 79
  integrated system in, 25, 94
  interest groups, role of, 233–234
  National Health Service (NHS), 2, 24–25, 125, 171, 191–192, 195, 197, 212–213, 221, 233–234 (*See also* NHS family)
  NHS and Community Care Act (1990), 181
  NHS England, 123
  in NHS family, 119
  NHS Scotland, 123
  NHS Wales, 123
  number of practising nurses in, 173
  Patients' Charter (1991), 195
  patients' rights in, 195
  physicians, payment of, 170–171
  pro-competition reforms in, 181–182, 205
  quasi-integrated system in, 96–97
  social health insurance (SHI) in, 224
  specialists, payment of, 172
  subsidies in, 211
  task shifting in, 178
  universalist model in, 25, 212–213, 226–227
  waiting time guarantees in, 199

United States
  Affordable Care Act (2010), 61–62, 204
  AFL–CIO, 231
  American Association of Retired Persons (AARP), 231
  American College of Physicians, 231
  American Hospital Association, 231
  American Medical Association (AMA), 231–232
  America's Health Insurance Plane (AHIP), 231
  Chamber of Commerce, 231
  Children's Health Insurance Program (CHIP), 20, 60
  community rating in, 61–62
  correlation of financing model with integrated–separated system dichotomy in, 95
  "cream skimming" in, 62
  decentralisation in, 191
  deductibles in, 42
  employer-provided insurance in, 11–12
  encouragement of general practice in, 164
  extension of insurance coverage in, 200, 204, 207
  Federal Employees Health Benefits (FEHB), 60
  foreign-trained nurses, recruitment of, 159
  fragmentation in, 143
  freedom of choice in, 102–103
  gatekeeping in, 99–100
  general practitioners (GP), payment of, 171–172
  general practitioner–specialist ratio in, 162–164
  group practice in, 104
  healthcare expenditures in, 68
  healthcare reforms in, 12–13, 61–62, 231–232
  health insurance marketplaces, 12
  Health Maintenance Organisations (HMOs) in, 95, 109
  historical evolution of healthcare system in, 217
  incentives and disincentives in, 45
  indemnity plans in, 103, 109
  Indian Health Services, 60
  individualistic culture in, 220–222

institutions, role of, 235–236
insurance companies in, 44–45, 61–62, 231
insurance coverage in, 79
insurance policies in, 11–13, 61, 103
insurance premiums in, 44–45
interest groups, role of, 231–232
lack of social democratic party in, 223
managed care in, 19–20
mandatory healthcare expenditures in, 73
Medicaid, 20, 60
medical savings accounts (MSAs) in, 27
Medicare, 19–20, 60, 143
moderately separated system in, 109
national culture in, 220–222
number of practising physicians in, 154
as outlier, 63, 142–144, 244
out-of-pocket healthcare expenditures in, 76
"patchwork" of healthcare programs in, 59–60, 143–144
per capita healthcare expenditures in, 71, 75
PhRMA, 231
physician–nurse ratio in, 177
physicians, payment of, 170
policy sale restrictions in, 44–45
primary insurance in, 43
private health insurance in, 60
regulation of private health insurance in, 61–62
renewal restrictions in, 45
segmentation in, 60
separated system in, 94, 97
targeted programs in, 19–20, 60, 142–143
task shifting in, 178
Tricare, 60
uninsured persons in, 75, 80–82, 143, 242
Veterans Health Administration (VHA), 60, 109, 143
voluntary health insurance in, 11–13, 75, 142–143
women physicians in, 160–162
working class strength in, 218
Universalist family. See NHS family
Universalist model. See also specific country
contribution methods, 32–33
equality of benefits in, 23
executive power and, 245–246

extension of insurance coverage (See Extension of insurance coverage)
freedom of choice in, 23, 35
in historical evolution of healthcare systems, 211–216
hospitals and, 147
insurer–provider relationship in, 35
integrated systems, 23–24 (See also Integrated systems)
integrated universalist family (See NHS family)
leftist governments, correlation with, 226–228, 238–239
number and legal status of insurers in, 32
opting out, 48
payer–beneficiary correspondence in, 24, 29–32
prevalence of, 63
progressive nature of, 34
redistributive objective of, 23
separated systems, 23–24 (See also Separated systems)
separated universalist family (See Separated universalist family)
as single-payer system, 23
state, role of, 24, 36, 208–209
taxation and, 23

Variants
generally, 4
medical savings accounts (MSAs) as, 26–27
of social health insurance (SHI), 45–47
Vertical integration, 93
Veto points, 239
VHI. See Voluntary health insurance (VHI)
Voluntary health insurance (VHI). See also specific country
generally, 240
advantages of, 9
"cherry picking," 40
complementary insurance (See Complementary insurance)
contribution methods, 32–33
co-payments, 41
correlation with integrated–separated system dichotomy, 94–95
"cream skimming," 40
deductibles, 41–42
direct market system and, 8

294 INDEX

Voluntary health insurance (VHI). (cont.)
disadvantages of, 9–10
"double coverage," 43
employer-provided insurance, 11–12
freedom of choice in, 8, 34–35
gatekeeping, 42
healthcare expenditures, as component
of, 73, 75
healthcare triangle and, 8
in historical evolution of healthcare
systems, 211, 213–216
incentives and disincentives, 45
insurance companies in, 8–10
insurance policies in, 8–10
insurance premiums in, 8–10, 75
insurer–provider relationship in, 10, 35
moral hazard and, 9–10, 40
number and legal status of insurers in,
8–9, 32
open enrollment in, 40–41
opportunistic behavior in, 40
overconsumption, discouraging, 41–42

payer–beneficiary correspondence in, 10,
29–32
policy sale restrictions, 44–45
primary insurance (*See* Primary
insurance)
regressive nature of, 33–34
regulation of, 44–45
renewal restrictions, 45
state, role of, 10, 36, 208–209
supplementary insurance (*See*
Supplementary insurance)

Waiting lists, 102–103
Watts, J., 235–236
Whitlam, Gough, 227
"Windows of opportunity," 237–239
Wisford, David, 234
Women physicians, 160–162
Working class strength, historical
evolution of healthcare systems and,
218
World Health Organization (WHO), 76

Printed in the United States
by Baker & Taylor Publisher Services